THE
CAESARS

Allan Massie

THE
CAESARS

SECKER & WARBURG
LONDON

For Robert and Elizabeth Langlands

First published in England 1983 by
Martin Secker & Warburg Limited
54 Poland Street, London W1V 3DF

Copyright © Allan Massie 1983

British Library Cataloguing in Publication Data
Massie, Allan
The Caesars.
1. Roman emperors – Biography
I. Title
937'.06'0922   DG274

ISBN 0-436-27347-0

Photoset by Rowland Phototypesetting Limited
Bury St Edmunds, Suffolk
Printed in Great Britain by
R. J. Acford Limited, Chichester, Sussex

CONTENTS

The Julio-Claudians

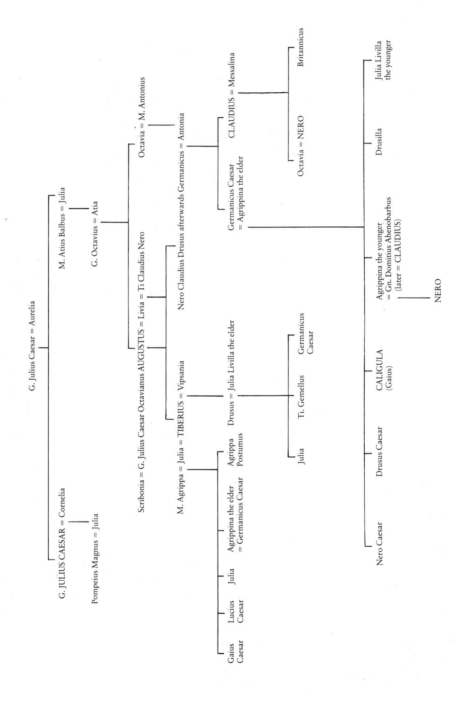

INTRODUCTION

FOR A LONG time *The Twelve Caesars* by Suetonius has been among my favourite books; those who have enjoyed a similar relationship with that most entertaining of biographers may find it presumptuous of me to have attempted a companion volume, and some may regard the effort as unnecessary. Yet, at least in my earliest readings of Suetonius, that is just what I would have liked to have had myself; and that is the first excuse for this book.

Later, living in Rome, walking frequently over the Palatine Hill, reading much history of the city and the Empire, I found myself wondering what manner of men these emperors were, what was the nature of their power and how it affected them. I doubt if it is possible to spend much time in that gallery on the Capitol where the busts of the emperors are displayed without reflecting on such matters. This book is my attempt to answer such questions.

There are of course no final answers to historical questions. However much we know we cannot know enough for that. Yet one of the fascinations of ancient history is the limited and self-contained nature of the evidence. It would of course be absurd to claim that we now know all about Ancient Rome that survives to be known; further discoveries will still be made. Nevertheless it is the case that we have to make up our minds about Roman history and the characters of the chief actors on the basis of a few books, and a quantity of inscriptions and edicts which can only amount to a small fragment of what once existed.

Take Suetonius himself as an example. We know the titles of seventeen books that he wrote. Yet, apart from fragments of his *Illustrious Writers*, only *The Twelve Caesars* survives. When we consider how many of the familiar and vivid anecdotes of Roman history come from this one book, we can gauge something of what we have lost; we can also consider how dull and inadequate our knowledge would have been if this too had perished.

The principal authorities for the first century of empire are Suetonius and Tacitus. Neither was exactly contemporary with the events he recounted, though both lived through the time of the Flavian emperors, Suetonius being born in AD 70 and Tacitus in 55. Both had particular means of knowledge, Tacitus as a senator and the son-in-law of the great general Agricola, Suetonius as Director of the Imperial Libraries; yet, when it came to writing of the Julio-Claudians, they were historians, most of whose sources have been lost, treating of events before their own birth. It is easy for the imagination to conflate Ancient history, but it should be remembered that, since Julius Caesar, the earliest of his biographical studies, was born one hundred and seventy years before Suetonius himself, Suetonius was as distant from him in time as a historian, born in 1920, who writes today of Charles James Fox and Pitt the Younger; while even Tacitus, in writing of Tiberius, was like the same historian writing of Gladstone.

More contemporary material survives for Julius and Augustus than for later emperors. We have Sallust's account of the Cataline conspiracy, Cicero's voluminous letters and speeches, Caesar's own memoirs of the Gallic and Civil Wars, and Augustus' own lapidary record, the *Res Gestae*, as well as fragments of his other writings. In addition, there is much incidental evidence and the flavour of the age to be had from the poets Virgil, Horace and Lucan, and Livy recounted the years that preceded the Civil War.

Augustus, Tiberius and Claudius all wrote autobiographies, which have not survived but which were used by Greek and Roman historians, among them Plutarch and Dio Cassius as well as Suetonius and Tacitus. For Tiberius a valuable corrective to Tacitus' hostile portrait can be got from Velleius Paterculus. Other contemporary evidence is provided by the essays of Seneca, Nero's tutor, and the *Letters* and *Natural History* of the elder Pliny. Josephus' account of the Jewish War, though it involves special pleading as do all histories written by men who have played a leading part in the story they tell, offers a remarkable picture of imperial Rome as seen by a man educated outside the Graeco-Roman culture.

Nevertheless, if all the other evidence is gathered up, it weighs lightly in the balance when the works of Suetonius and Tacitus are placed in the other scale. It is not too much to say that our picture of the Roman Empire is essentially theirs. Had Suetonius' *The Twelve Caesars* and Tacitus' *Histories* and *Annals* been lost, we would still, from coins and inscriptions and the work of later historians, have known much of the later Republic and of the first century of empire; but this knowledge would have lacked the vivid personality and the appeal to the imagination which Suetonius and Tacitus present. It would have been much drier history, and Tiberius, Caligula, Claudius and Nero would never have occupied the place they have held in the mind of Europe since the Middle Ages; while the Year of the Four Emperors would have been as little known as some of those convulsive years in the third and fourth centuries, and Domitian as uncelebrated as the numerous tyrants before and after Diocletian. That the first century of empire is, despite Gibbon's masterly concentration on Rome's decline, still the best-known period of empire, the only one which has entered in any degree into the popular imagination, is due to the writing of Suetonius and Tacitus. And I have therefore naturally drawn most on them.

I owe a profound debt to the work of many modern historians, too numerous to list here. It would however be churlish not to mention Sir Ronald Syme, whose incomparable works *The Roman Revolution* and *Tacitus* must be among the most illuminating historical writing of recent times. I have drawn deeply on other academic historians, and valued the collections of documents made by A. H. M. Jones, V. Ehrenburg and M. P. Charlesworth; I also have found much of use and interest in the *Journal of Roman Studies* and in Graham Webster's study of the Roman army.

This is a work of popular history; as such, it owes a deep debt to Professor Michael Grant, the greatest popularizer of Antiquity this century, and to Robert Graves, whose *Claudius* novels and racy and idiosyncratic translation of Suetonius first aroused my interest in the subject. I should like to mention also, as an act of personal *pietas*, John Buchan, whose *Augustus* is the best biography known to me of any figure of the Ancient World. In the same spirit I might call attention to Norman Douglas's essay on Tiberius published in *Siren Land*.

A word finally on the translations given in the text. These are mostly free renderings of my own. I have gratefully, like several generations of schoolboys, employed the cribs provided by the Loeb Classical Library, and for Suetonius, Robert Graves and Michael Grant; for Tacitus, Michael Grant again for the *Annals*, and the old translation by A. J. Church and W. J. Broadribb for the *Histories*.

This is a work written out of, and for, enjoyment of the period and characters. I hope it will prove entertaining and illuminating, and that it gives some insight into the incomparable achievements of Ancient Rome, and into the working of that remarkable institution, the Roman Empire.

Allegorical representation of Julius Caesar as subsequent centuries saw
him, emerging from Chaos to restore order: master of Rome, who made
Rome master of the world

The Crisis of the Republic

CAESAR, KAISER, TSAR: the words resound through European history, symbols of absolute power. Yet they have their origin in a Roman family name meaning, perhaps, 'hairy'; a name among many others, of no special importance. It was the genius of one member of the family, Gaius Julius Caesar,* born in 100 BC, that separated the name from a mass of others, and, making it a word of authority and power, converted it into what it was to be for two thousand years: the mark of empire.

Great men, epoch-formers, arise in troubled times and turbulent societies. Only then can history be bent, even in a small degree, to the individual will; a Switzerland produces no Napoleons. To understand how Julius Caesar came to dominate Rome and the Mediterranean world, and so bequeath his name as an imperial word, it is first necessary to consider the Roman Republic at the time of his birth, that Republic which he first threatened, then destroyed, but proved unable to reform or replace.

Rome was a city-state which, some six hundred years after its foundation in 753 BC, had come to rule the Mediterranean world. In this achievement disorder and tension were bred, for the conquest of empire created political problems with which the machinery of the Roman state had not been devised to cope. By the end of the Third War with Carthage in 146 BC, a war which saw the final defeat of their only great rival power in the Western Mediterranean, the question whether the Romans could reform their polity to answer the demands of empire was already urgent. It

---

* A note on Roman names may be useful to some readers. The first name was the personal one, Gaius. The second indicated *gens* or clan; the third the particular branch of that clan. Thus there were more Julians than Caesars, for the Caesars were only one branch of the Julian *gens*. Intimates might have addressed Julius as Gaius, and he spoke of himself as Gaius Caesar, though it is as Julius that he is known to posterity.

took a century to come to a solution, and, whatever the peculiar strengths and durability of imperial Rome, it is reasonable to regard the emergence of the Augustan Empire as evidence of the failure of the Roman political class.

The origins of Rome's constitution are lost in legend. After the expulsion of the kings, traditionally dated 510 BC, the Roman nobility, fearful of the tyranny of a single person, elaborated a constitution designed to prevent any danger of the return of monarchy. Power was vested in the Assembly of the People who, meeting in the Forum, or market-place, elected magistrates. (The restricted modern meaning of the word 'magistrate' is confusing and should be forgotten; ancient magistrates combined judicial, administrative and priestly duties.) The two chief magistrates were called consuls. They commanded the army and carried out the principal ceremonial and sacrificial functions. They shared power equally (even sometimes to the extent of commanding the army on alternate days), and the fact that their tenure of office lasted only for one year made it impossible for one of them to come to dominate the State. If one consul died in office, another was elected. Recognizing that absolute authority might occasionally, in a crisis, be desirable, the Romans made provision for the office of dictator; but a dictator's power, which superseded that of the consuls, was limited in time; and the appointment was exceptional. Lesser magistrates were also appointed by means of election, and eventually there was to be a ladder which the aspirant politician would be required to ascend: quaestor, aedile, praetor, consul. Quaestors' duties were principally financial; aediles looked after public works and organized public games; praetors acted mainly as judges; consuls as judges, generals and celebrants. Since the gradations of honour constituted a pyramid rather than a ladder – there were many more quaestors than praetors and of course only two consuls – many candidates for office got no further than the first step.

In form Rome was a democracy, for power stemmed from the Assembly of the People. They not only elected the magistrates but had to approve any law that was proposed. Originally the Assembly of the People meant exactly that; it was composed of all adult male citizens. In time, as citizenship was extended beyond Rome itself, and as the city grew in size, it was no longer possible for all citizens to come together. The Assembly became, as it were, a token body; the location of power therein, once a fact, became a fiction. Yet it was a fiction that was to be honoured right up to the early days of empire, and even beyond.

In reality however even Republican Rome was an oligarchy. Office, and therefore power, were confined to a few families. In the hundred years before 133 BC (the date usually accepted as marking the beginning of the constitutional crisis which was only to be resolved by the establishment of the Augustan Empire after the Battle of Actium in 31 BC) one hundred and fifty-nine out of two hundred consulships went to only twenty-six families, and a hundred of them to only ten. In the early days of the Republic a sharp division had existed between the patricians (the original aristocracy) and the plebeians (the common people). By the second century BC most legal distinctions had been removed; plebeians could stand for any magistracy;

though the one specially established to protect their interests, the tribunate (a magistracy outside the pyramid of honour), was still restricted to plebeian families. These tribunes had the right to propose laws to the Assembly like any other magistrates. They had no administrative responsibilities, but their chief importance lay in the provision which allowed a single tribune (and there were ten of them) to interpose a veto on any legislation. The tribunes therefore had an unmatched potential either to initiate reform or to render government well-nigh impossible.

All magistrates except tribunes automatically became members of the Senate. This was originally an advisory and deliberative body, there to give the magistrates of the year the benefit of its experienced counsel. It had no power, but possessed immense authority which derived from its composition, from the fact that its members had all held office. It did not pass laws itself, but magistrates would normally bring proposed measures before the Senate for consideration and debate. Inevitably, over the centuries, its authority increased. It was the repository of political wisdom; it dealt with foreign ambassadors; its pronouncements carried weight. So the balance between the Assembly and the Senate shifted. As the Assembly became less and less what it purported to be, the authentic voice of the whole citizenry, so the Senate grew in importance. By the second century BC a senatorial edict (*senatus consultus*) had come to possess the force of law; pronouncements were made in the name of the Senate and the Roman People (SPQR).

The Senate was dominated by those families which had provided a consul. These were known as *nobiles* (nobles). Such a family might be either patrician or plebeian; Mark Antony was an example of a plebeian noble. It was however very difficult to break into the charmed circle in one generation. Anyone who succeeded in doing so was sufficiently rare and remarkable to be designated a *novus homo* (new man). Cicero was one of the few to manage it; another was the great military hero Marius.

The expansion of Rome as an imperial power imposed strains on the constitution which in time were to break the Republic from a number of causes. First, the acquisition of empire brought provinces to be governed. This was done by the appointment of magistrates called proconsuls or propraetors (depending on the status of the province). Geographical considerations meant that such offices could not be held for one year only – as was still the rule in Rome itself – and eventually five years became the customary term of office. Command of a province offered the ambitious a chance to grow rich, and to exercise patronage and so build up an extensive clientship. A governor would frequently require to have a military force at his disposal; and since no line divided the civil from the military power this command allowed a proconsul to secure a quasi-independent power base. For this reason the importance of office in Rome came to lie principally in the chance it offered of a rich provincial command.

Second, the nature of the Roman army had changed. The old Republican force had been composed of citizens, small farmers and artisans serving part-time. It was such an army, essentially a militia, that had conquered Italy and withstood Hannibal in the second war with Carthage (218–202 BC). But the far greater tasks that empire imposed altered its character. Citizen soldiers were replaced by professionals – and these looked first to their commander, not to the Republic. They served Marius or Sulla, Pompey or Caesar, Antony or Octavian, rather than Rome. It was to their general that they looked for reward; he it was whom they expected to provide them with land and pensions when their term of service had expired. So arose the Great Men, the Dynasts,* who burst the bonds of the conventional State and escaped from its control. And from the birth of Caesar to his nephew's victory at Actium, which saw the end of the Civil Wars and the establishment of Caesar Augustus as ruler of Rome, the Mediterranean world was torn by their struggles.

That was not all. The rapid expansion of the Roman world, and the enemies it faced on its new frontiers, led to the creation of extraordinary commands. First, the dangers of a German invasion of Italy between 105 BC and 101 had resulted in Gaius Marius holding five successive consulships. It was unprecedented; it was necessary; it was direly inauspicious for the Republic. Then the long war in the East against Mithridates, King of Pontus, enabled L. Cornelius Sulla to build up an army with which he eventually returned to Italy, defeated Marius and his adherents in a bloody civil war, seized command of the State and set himself up as dictator for the purpose of instituting constitutional reform. A few years later, Sulla's lieutenant, Gnaeus. Pompeius Magnus (Pompey), even before his first consulship, was granted the first of a series of sweeping commands: to clear the sea of pirates; to suppress rebellion in Asia Minor; to reorganize Rome's corn supply. All such emergency measures threatened the traditional structure of the Republic. What might a dynast less benevolent than Sulla, more certain of his aim than Marius or Pompey, do with such power? What might be the outcome if the power were seized by a dynast indifferent to Republican tradition? 'The extreme medicine of the constitution,' in Burke's phrase, 'threatened to become its daily bread.'

Not only the constitution was strained by empire. The influx of wealth it brought had disturbed the traditional society and economy of Italy. Everywhere small farmers, the backbone of the community, were being dispossessed of properties they could no longer profitably farm. Instead came great capitalist slave-worked ranches, called *latifundia*. The deprived peasantry swarmed to the city. They found no work there; how could there be work for all of them in a slave economy? Accordingly they subsisted, dole-fed, unreliable, inflammable, an under-class ready to form a mob. By Caesar's time some three hundred and twenty thousand citizens were receiving free corn.

The gravity of the agrarian problem was long realized; ambitious politicians recognized it also as a means by which they might acquire popularity and power. The crisis of the constitution was first precipitated by Tiberius Gracchus and his brother Gaius, tribunes respectively in 133 and 123. Their programme of land reform was enthusiastically backed by the dispossessed, and the Gracchi used their

---

* The word 'Dynast' in English has come to have associations of heredity which it lacked in ancient times. Then, being derived from the Greek, *dynamis* (power), it simply meant a powerful man, hence a ruler, a big shot.

support to foment a crisis which the oligarchy recognized as revolutionary. The Gracchi were met with violence, and both brothers were murdered. Control was re-established; but they were nonetheless to have their heirs.

Thus, agrarian reform and the cancellation of debt remained at the heart of the programme offered by the radical politicians who succeeded the Gracchi. Because they ostentatiously took the part of the people against the aristocracy (even though they were themselves aristocrats, like the Reform Whigs of early nineteenth-century Britain) they were known as *Populares*. Their opponents, defenders of the *status quo*, were called *Optimates*, since they stood for the rule of the 'best' families. To solve the developing political and social crisis, the Popular party sought to shift power back from the Senate, where they were weak, to the Assembly, which they could dominate. The sincerity of some at least need not be questioned, for the problems that engaged their attention were real enough; but there was always an element of radical chic about the *Populares*; they easily descended to that flattery of the mob and expression of extravagant promises which are characteristic of the demagogue.

They were essentially an opposition group, and when they at last managed to seize power, in 87 BC, having won the support of the aged hero Marius who felt that his great services to the State had been insufficiently rewarded by the ruling oligarchy, they found practical measures of reform beyond them. It was in reality impossible to govern effectively through the Assembly, where the veto of a single tribune could inhibit action. Instead they embarked on a reign of terror; they were a rival establishment, who, having at last achieved power, were only anxious to ensure that they could retain it and enjoy the spoils. The eighties were a desperate decade, as power alternated between the *Populares* on the one hand, and Sulla, the other Dynast, who had emerged as the champion of the established order. The prize was control of the city and therefore of the Republic; the penalty for failure, proscription. Counter-terror succeeded terror.

Sulla triumphed, cut down his opponents and was made dictator with a commission to reconstitute the State. Such a commission was itself testimony to the inadequacy of the Republic; Sulla had in effect been granted temporary monarchy in order to make monarchy impossible. The paradox hardly escaped contemporaries; but they had no answer to its implications. Yet in fact Sulla himself was at a loss. He did no more than refurbish the Senate, claiming that this gave it renewed legitimacy, before retiring into private life to die, reputedly of the effects of debauchery, the following year (78). He had solved nothing; his measures were no more than a palliative. Yet Sulla's actions had one long-term effect: he had shown how power might be concentrated in a single person; Caesar was later to say that his abdication showed the dictator didn't know his ABC.

Parade of the Dynasts

The last years of the Republic were dominated by five men whose characters and careers, conveniently for us, expose both the nature of the crisis and the difficulty of its resolution. They were Cato, Crassus, Cicero, Pompey and Caesar. Alliances between them were shifting; enmity was often bitter. Yet all were bound together within a narrow circle of kinship, interest and history; bound, and yet also divided by fear, ambition, greed. Cato was the simplest and most principled of them, Crassus the richest and least interesting, Cicero the most sympathetic, Pompey most enigmatic and Caesar the most brilliant, and final victor, whom Cicero alone survived. Between them they box the compass of the Roman political world.

M. Porcius Cato was the sternest defender of senatorial government, which meant in effect the rule of the leading Optimate families. He was a curiosity, a biological sport, being a throwback to the type of the early days of the Republic. He was very conscious of this and modelled himself on a famous ancestor, Cato the Censor. He tried to live in the antique manner, which he was accustomed to praise: he prized simplicity of dress and manner, hated the Greeks (foreign decadents), deplored all foreign habits and imports, drank heavily and was extremely rude. He was naturally fiercely opposed to innovation of any kind, and distrusted and hated Caesar, Pompey and Crassus; but Caesar most of all. A little crazy perhaps, his utter refusal to compromise and his presumed integrity (he was always loud in praise of his own virtue) won him influence. He was indeed the complete diehard conservative with nothing creative to offer. Circumstances prevented him from advancing beyond the praetorship, but his importance, being moral, could not be measured by the offices he held. He was a man of authority rather than power.

Cato did not lack political acumen, a sense of realities. He recognized the danger to the Republic of granting extraordinary commands, and consistently opposed any such proposals; certainly he would have been quite prepared to curtail empire in order to preserve Republican virtue. This recognition that the two were incompatible was clear-sighted enough; but few were prepared to accept the logic of Cato's anti-imperialist stance. Consequently, though he always provided a rallying-point for disgruntled conservatives, Cato's power was limited to obstruction. He saw where Rome was tending; he even saw how its apparent destiny might be avoided. But he could not advance a programme of sufficiently persuasive cogency to win the sort of support that might have enabled him to save the Republic at the expense of further conquest. Caesar disliked him intensely, which was not surprising. When, after Cato's suicide, Cicero produced a eulogy, Caesar replied with an 'anti-Cato'; it was abusive in the extreme.

Marcus Licinius Crassus, consul for the first time (with Pompey as his colleague) in 70, could hardly have offered a sharper contrast to Cato. The richest man in Rome, he was as much at home in the new imperialist age as Cato was uncomfortable. As such he became the spokesman for the *equites*, the upper middle class who controlled Roman finance (nobles were supposed to abstain from commerce).

Crassus was a figure of very little interest in himself; in a sense he was simply his wealth – that was all you needed to know about him. He thrived on building, money-lending, army supply contracts, all the wheeling and dealing of a corrupt expansionist age. He became indispensable to ambitious but impoverished politicians; he could buy an election and finance a candidate's campaign by, for instance, guaranteeing his debts. He did so for Caesar, who in 61 owed twenty-five million *denarii*; and if he hadn't come to an agreement with Crassus, his political career could hardly have advanced.

Crassus however was not content with influence. He hankered after military glory too – every Roman noble was a soldier. He had indeed suppressed the dangerous slave rebellion led by Spartacus, having been granted a special proconsulship to do so. Later, jealous of Pompey's and Caesar's achievements and renown, he led an army against the Parthian Empire, only to be defeated and killed at Carrhae in the Arabian desert. Crassus' political career was a record only of selfishness; he stood for nothing more than the aggrandizement of his own position. This made him the Dynast *par excellence*; but it was only an exaggeration of the stance taken by Caesar and Pompey.

Marcus Tullius Cicero, intellectual and supreme orator, was that rarity among Roman statesmen, the self-made man, the outsider. He came from the municipality of Arpinum, seventy miles from the city; and had made his way by his talents. As the greatest advocate of the day, he found himself in constant demand (the Romans were extremely litigious, and prosecution of one's political enemies was a common gambit). Cicero's reward was the consulship, in 63, when he received the backing of rich Optimate families nervous of the popularist tendencies of the other candidates, who were on that occasion supported by Crassus. This consulship was marked by the suppression of a revolutionary conspiracy led by a discredited nobleman, L. Sergius Catiline, whom Cicero had defeated in the elections. Asserting that Catiline and his followers were plotting to overthrow the Republic, Cicero acted promptly and efficiently. In his own view he had saved the State, and he had medals struck applauding his actions. Unfortunately for his own future, he was carried away by his success and had some of the captured conspirators put to death as enemies of the State, without the formality of a trial. It was an offence extraordinary in a lawyer and upholder of constitutional legality, and one which was to cost him dear. Caesar, meanwhile, who had family connections with some of the Catilinarians (and perhaps other connections also), opposed the death penalty for the conspirators, and was to ensure that Cicero's actions cost him dear. Cicero's consulship left him infatuated with an aristocracy that showed little gratitude and treated him badly. However, unlike Cato and Crassus, Cicero had thought deeply about the crisis of the State and had a remedy to propose. He called it *concordia ordinum* – the concord of the classes. He invited the *boni*, who might be translated as 'men of good will and good standing', to come together and work in harmony. It was an idealistic programme, not necessarily impractical, though dangerously vague. Presumably Cicero envisaged it as a preliminary to some structural reform, for he could hardly have imagined that this sort of change of heart could be enough by itself to rescue the Republic. That would surely have required an administrative reform sufficiently thorough to attach the army to the system rather than to its commanders – nothing less could prevent one of the Dynasts from seizing power and subverting the Republic. In old age, after Caesar's murder, Cicero would be reduced to seeking a weapon which in turn could abolish government by the sword. The young man he hit on, Caesar's nephew Octavian, was indeed to do just that and bring an end to the anarchy of civil strife; but he did it for himself, not for Cicero.

Cicero was defeated by the logic of power; but he was also betrayed by the limits of his own imagination. Despite his own roots, in Italian provincial stock, he still thought in terms simply of the city of Rome. He could not see that government by the city was an anachronism – any more than he realized Roman democracy was made a sham by the fact that only a minority of the citizens (and those the least worthy and stable) could find the opportunity to take part in political life. In due course, Octavian was to call on the stability and health of Italy to dominate the fevered city of Rome, just as Napoleon was to summon up the whole of provincial France against the dictatorship of Paris. Cicero however could not lift his horizon above the limits of the Forum, just as he failed to see that the Empire could not be ruled by a city-state that had found no means of bridling its military commanders.

For twenty years or more Gnaeus Pompeius Magnus was the man to be bridled. Pompey puzzled his contemporaries, and puzzles historians even now. What did he want? Perhaps he did not know himself. . . His career had been wholly extraordinary, for he had by-passed the normal route to political authority. A protegé of Sulla, and a man of remarkable administrative competence, he had been given independent commands to suppress insurrection in Spain and Italy in his twenties, before he was eligible to stand for any magistracy. He had become consul in 70 by means of another special enactment, granting him dispensation from the law by which Sulla had attempted to regulate a man's progress to that supreme office. Yet another special law – the *Lex Gabinia* – gave him for three years *imperium infinitum* (supreme command) by sea throughout the Mediterranean, and authority on land equal to that of all provincial governors, together with vast supplies of ships, men and money, that he might rid the sea of the pirates who infested it. Another extraordinary command followed almost at once – to end the long struggle against Mithridates, King of Pontus, Rome's most tenacious enemy, and thus extend Rome's frontiers to the Euphrates and the bounds of the Parthian Empire. He then thoroughly reorganized government in the East, almost doubling Rome's revenue from that part of the world and bringing Asia Minor peace, security and the prospect of prosperity.

By such achievements Pompey won for himself a reputation and authority unequalled in the Roman world. But what would he do next? That was the question which alarmed Rome as he returned triumphant from the East. He had not played the political game; he had simply ignored it, and in so doing had become immeasurably great. There was no way in which he could be fitted into the board-game of Roman politics. At the same time Rome's immediate military and security problems had been solved; no new extraordinary command beckoned to Pompey. What was he to do? What was to be done with him?

He had no clear notion himself, but he did know that he wanted respect. Romans talked much of their *dignitas*; their self-esteem, based on achievement and recognized by their fellows. The Mediterranean has not changed so greatly that the same requirement cannot be found there today. A modern Italian, particularly one from the South, will have an intense regard for his *bella figura*; a Sicilian seeks to be regarded as an *uomo rispettato*. Pompey demanded this: his dignity required that his settlement in the East be accepted by the Senate, and that his veterans be rewarded with land. Myopically, the Senate denied him both satisfactions. Pompey, in dudgeon, a state of mind into which he was wont to lapse whenever the way ahead was not apparent, began to cast around for some means of satisfying his wounded *dignitas*. Curiously apathetic, without imagination, he brooded over the State, a massive Sphinx, whose riddle none could decipher, whose presence none could forget.

Throughout the sixties and fifties his shadow obscured other lights; but thereafter there was Caesar.

Julius Caesar

JULIUS CAESAR

GAIUS JULIUS CAESAR could boast of an unequalled heredity; the Julians claimed descent from the goddess Venus and from the old royal house of Alba Longa. Yet despite this he was no more acceptable to the senatorial majority than Pompey was, for his more recent inheritance was dubious. His aunt had been married to Gaius Marius, and this brought him within the orbit of the *Populares*. His first wife also belonged to that party, being Cornelia, daughter of L. Cornelius Cinna, Marius' chief associate in the leadership of the *Populares*. It was Cinna who had shown one way in which order might be restored in the State, by securing his own election to the consulship in three successive years; already it was apparent that such continuity of office might be a means of providing authority under the guise of respect for Republican institutions.

Caesar's youth was dangerous. As a well-born member of the defeated party he nearly lost his life in the Sullan proscriptions; indeed he was only saved by the pleas of distinguished kinfolk. Sulla himself wished to get rid of him: 'in that young man there are many Mariuses' were his reported words. But Caesar showed character in the crisis: when he was ordered to divorce his wife – presumably his compliance would have been interpreted as evidence that he was not seditiously minded – he refused.

Unlike Pompey, Caesar developed slowly. In their early years they had little in common beyond their attractiveness to women. (Pompey was said to be so beautiful that every woman wanted to bite him; while the number of Caesar's affairs was notorious. Pompey indeed divorced his wife Mucia because of her adultery with Caesar, though that didn't stop him from later marrying Caesar's daughter Julia.) But, for twenty years, the zenith of Pompey's glory, Caesar's career was that of a daring but conventional noble struggling to make his way up the foothills of Roman politics. Like every noble, he saw military service, and like most he showed courage, being decorated with the *corona civica* (civic crown) for saving the life of a fellow-citizen at the capture of Mytilene on the Black Sea in 80. Like most he

15

attracted scandal; in his case the charge that while on a diplomatic mission to King Nicomedes of Bithynia (in the course of the same campaign) he had allowed the king to take him to his bed. Caesar always denied the story, but it stuck to him throughout his life; even his soldiers made up songs about it. Such accusations of sexual vice were the common currency of Roman insult, as they are to this day. Augustus in turn was to be accused of being Caesar's catamite, and someone once said in the Senate that Caesar was 'every woman's husband and every man's wife'. The second part of the slander was absurd, for there was no sequel to the alleged affair with Nicomedes.

Only two incidents marked out Caesar as different from the run of nobles. The first happened in 75. Sailing off Rhodes, he was captured by pirates. (Pompey had not yet done his work.) While waiting for his ransom to arrive, he consorted with them in friendly fashion, playing games and taking part in athletic contests. All the time however he assured them (or so he later said) that when he was free he would come back and string them up. They seem to have thought it a good joke, for when the ransom had been paid, they released him. He was as good as his word, however. Although a private citizen, only twenty-five, without any special authority, he commandeered a fleet, sailed back, seized his erstwhile captors and crucified them.

That showed character. The second incident, politically more important and evidence of the courage that distinguished him throughout his life, was the already mentioned opposition to the execution of the Catilinarian conspirators. It was a rash act, for there were many ready to assert that Caesar himself had been privy to the plot. Yet it also showed political good sense and principle. Caesar had already concluded that the wounds to the Roman body politic could not be healed by more blood-letting. Clemency was to be a feature of his career; reconciliation the goal. As he said very much later, 'History proves that by practising cruelty you earn nothing but hatred. Nobody has ever achieved a lasting victory by such means except Sulla, and Sulla is a man I do not propose to imitate.'

Moreover Caesar was attached to the Catilinarians by family and party ties. To abandon them completely would have been to deny his Popular inheritance. To condone what they had done was of course impossible, but he did manage to speak out for them. The affair, evidence of his nerve and ability to walk a tightrope, did him no harm with the people, whose favour he had already gained by the lavish Games he had provided when aedile in 65. These games left him even more deeply in debt than usual – one reason why many thought he might have been involved with Catiline, a notorious bankrupt himself whose revolution threatened to make Roman banking-houses shiver with apprehension. Caesar however was indifferent to the scale of his debts. Money would come somehow; it always had. It was more important to build up political credit with the people. To court them he established himself in the Subura, an unfashionable quarter lying between the Esquiline and Viminal hills, now traversed by the winding Via dei Serpenti.

Through family influence, Caesar had become *pontifex maximus* (high priest). Roman religion was severely practical, and it was characteristic that the nobility

Cicero's attack in the Senate on Catiline – the isolated figure in the
foreground. A neo-classical wall-painting by Cesare Maccari

had always kept its management in their own hands, thus preventing the development of a potentially troublesome priestly caste. Caesar himself was a sceptic –
owning no goddess but Fortune – but there was no reason why he shouldn't
perform the office of priest satisfactorily. Moreover the position – virtually that of
head of the State religion – was honourable; it reflected well on his *dignitas*, which
Caesar valued as highly as Pompey did his. The following year, indeed (62), while
he was praetor, he divorced his second wife for becoming involved in a scandal,
when a debauched young aristocrat, Publius Clodius, penetrated the Festival of the
Bona Dea in female disguise. 'Caesar's wife must be above suspicion,' said the
praetor – not that this prevented him from collaborating with Clodius in years to
come when the roaring boy (the brother of that scandalous Clodia whom Catullus
loved and hated) turned politician and became first gang-leader and then tribune.

In 61 Caesar got his first overseas command, proconsul in the province of Further

Spain where he carried out a victorious campaign against the Lusitanians. It won him a triumph – which however he never celebrated. The reason was simple, the consequences profound. Caesar was aiming for the consulship in 59, which meant that he had to fight the 60 elections. He could not campaign as a military commander; he could not receive the triumph as a civilian. He was required to choose.

He was made aware at this moment of the depth of the continuing Optimate hostility towards him, a hostility deeply rooted in distrust. He did not hesitate long: he had to be consul. Without that, he was nothing; his career would founder; his ambitions, inchoate and unfocused but certainly urgent, could never be satisfied; his creditors might even catch up with him.

Opposition was certain to be fierce; and Caesar looked around for support. It was not hard to find. There, ready – for a consideration – to sustain him, were the two aggrieved dynasts, Crassus and Pompey, both slighted in their *dignitas* by the staid Optimates, those men of family who wished only to keep the game of make-believe politics in motion. Both dynasts had reason to respond to Caesar's appeal. Crassus, whose perfect cynicism was exemplified by his off-the-cuff remark that anyone who sought power should be rich enough to maintain an army out of income, had been losing ground since his consulship back in 70. No great achievements had marked his last decade, and he was still smarting from the defeats Cicero had inflicted on him. As for Pompey, who could say 'I have only to stamp my foot on the soil of Italy for cavalry and infantry to rise from the ground' – Pompey, who had done the State service equalled by no other man – he too now felt the ground slipping away, his glory dimming, his star obscured by myriads of pygmy aristocrats.

True, they distrusted and resented each other; but in that distrust and resentment the cool diplomatic Caesar might discern opportunity. It was his task to reconcile them, for his fertile imagination saw that the three, working in harness, could dominate the State. Fortunately his own relations with both were good. Without help from Crassus he could never have taken up his post in Spain, for the millionaire had then satisfied Caesar's creditors. As for Pompey, Caesar had gained his gratitude by voting for the *Lex Gabinia*; besides which Pompey now needed a consul he could trust to try to satisfy his veterans' requirements, and so allow the Great Man to preserve his *dignitas*.

Their alliance, soon known as the Triumvirate, represented a coming together of interests. Its formation marked a new turn of the spiral that was eventually to lead to war and the destruction of the Republic. Three men, backed by the threat of armed force, by money, by the Roman mob (organized on their behalf by the vicious Clodius), now imposed their will on the State. For the moment the reluctant Republic found itself incapable of offering resistance to the usurpers. Meanwhile Caesar's consulship would give the three of them the opportunity to repair past damage, to provide for their future interests, to satisfy their greed for power and self-esteem. Its like had hardly been seen before.

The business of Caesar's consulship must be seen in this light; it was first a matter of self-gratification. Yet, because Caesar was aware of the source of his own political influence, because he paid his political, if not his money, debts and because he was not lacking in that liberal generosity which great aristocrats can occasionally display, his legislation also revived elements in the old Popular programme; certainly sufficiently so to alarm the Optimate senators, for whom Caesar still represented red revolution, Catiline's attack on the social order.

First Caesar brought in an Agrarian Bill to satisfy the land-hunger of Pompey's old soldiers. With that scrupulous and formal correctness of which he was always a master, he brought it first before the Senate for their consideration. Foolishly they rejected it. So, thwarted, he took the bill to the Assembly. There his fellow-consul M. Calpurnius Bibulus, a stuffy conservative whose vision perhaps extended the length of his nose, tried to obstruct its passage. His efforts failed. Next, Caesar got one of the tribunes, his client P. Vatinius, to carry a Bill which confirmed everything Pompey had done in the East. Caesar's debt to Pompey was thus repaid; the compact between them, already sealed by Pompey's marriage to Caesar's daughter Julia, was fully honoured. The dynast's *dignitas* shone; everything the Senate had denied him Caesar had won. Then Crassus in his turn was satisfied with a measure which remitted one-third of their contract to the Asian tax-collectors, an enormous windfall profit; Caesar knew that you can always buy the rich with cash.

This consulship was the watershed of Caesar's career: everything flowed from it. It established him as one of the great men of Rome. It also won him the undying hatred of the Optimates, despite good legislation like the *Lex Julia de Repetundis*, which defined and controlled the powers of provincial governors. Such measures might have convinced the unbiased that Caesar, unlike his Popular predecessors, had not come to power merely to spoil the State; but the unbiased were hard to find. His enemies saw only that he had put through his measures with very doubtful legality. That was not his fault; indeed his course was forced on him if he wished to achieve anything substantial, for his hostile colleague Bibulus not only refused to co-operate in any way, but carried his opposition to absurd lengths. He tried to prevent the passage of any public business by declaring all omens to be inauspicious, and then proclaiming all remaining days of the year to be public holidays on which no business could be lawfully transacted; having done so he retired to his house. Caesar, unabashed, simply ignored him and pressed ahead. The joke went round that that year's consuls were Julius and Caesar.

The consulship was the means of providing for Caesar's own future, too. Anticipating his election, his Optimate enemies had already tried to shackle him. Back in 60, when he was only consul-elect, they had passed a measure establishing as a proconsular province for 58 'the woods and forests of Italy' instead of the overseas command which was usual. Caesar however was not a man to be so easily bound. His henchman, Vatinius again, carried a bill in the Assembly granting him Cisalpine Gaul and Illyricum for five years, with command of three legions and the right to appoint his own officers and to found colonies – two provisions which gave enormous opportunity for patronage. Then the Governor-elect of Transalpine Gaul suddenly died. Pompey proposed in the Senate that his province also should be added to Caesar's command. Unnerved, and fearful of the Dynasts' solidarity, the Senate yielded. Caesar had secured his future. Not only did he have a huge command, but, being in office, he was immune from prosecution for any alleged irregularities of his consulship for at least five years; much might happen in that time.

Gaul made Caesar great; it gave him the opportunity to become Pompey's equal. Even at the moment of his appointment it was not difficult to recognize the opportunities it offered him; and the dangers for the Republic. Cicero was later to reflect that the command 'led to the murder of the ancestral constitution'. Cato, even while the matter was being debated, opposed the addition of Transalpine Gaul to Caesar's command: 'The Senate,' he said, 'was itself placing the tyrant in the citadel.' Others realized how Caesar hungered for Gaul. The historian Sallust, a contemporary, observed that 'Caesar passionately desired a great command, an army and an unprecedented war which would give his ability the chance to display himself.' The word Sallust used, here translated as 'ability', was *virtus*. It cannot be exactly rendered, for the concept is dead in modern English. It may be taken to mean, in Macbeth's phrase, 'all that may become a man'. Sallust also said, 'Caesar was reckoned a great man on the score of the favours he did and of his generosity'; things impossible without previous achievement. And besides this, Gaul made Caesar extremely rich; plunder and extortion transformed the chronic debtor into a millionaire. Yet the strange thing is that Gaul hardly altered Caesar himself; latent qualities became apparent, that was all. Furthermore, the fear he aroused even in pre-Gallic days showed how his enemies recognized what he was capable of doing.

Three features of the command made it ideal. First, Cisalpine Gaul and Illyricum, the provinces first granted, made him a patron on a huge scale. Cisalpine Gaul consisted of what we now call north Italy – Lombardy, Piedmont, the Veneto and the Marches, extending as far south as Ravenna. Illyricum stretched down the Balkan coast. In these peaceful provinces, ready to absorb Italian influence, Caesar could establish colonial settlements and tend to the interests of civilized provincials – and he treated all townships on the north side of the Po as colonies of Roman citizens. Their gratitude was enormous and lasting. It was from this region that he drew his reinforcements for the Gallic Wars and so created the devoted army that stood by him in the civil war that followed. This sort of patron-client relationship was vital in Roman politics, as it is today in the political life of the United States, or was in eighteenth-century Britain. Caesar, courteous, quick, approachable, quite without side yet possessed of aristocratic charisma, was a master at the game of connection-politics.

Second, the province was near enough to Rome for Caesar to keep his finger on the pulse of political life in the city. Winters were usually spent in Cisalpine Gaul near the Italian frontier – a proconsul was forbidden to leave his province during his term of office. Wherever he was indeed, Caesar kept a special office at his headquarters, devoted to political correspondence. (It was his habit to dictate to three secretaries simultaneously.) His agents visited him regularly. In the words of his German biographer Gelzer, 'he never lost himself in activity on the periphery of Empire; what mattered was always its effect on Rome'. It would of course have been more difficult to measure this effect from a more distant province.

Finally, the addition, of Transalpine Gaul, then merely a strip of territory along the Mediterranean coast and round to the Pyrenees, gave him the chance of winning military glory equal to Pompey's and adding to the Roman Empire. Probably if this province had not been granted him, he would have prosecuted a Balkan war, anticipating the efforts of Tiberius in Pannonia, even perhaps, like Trajan, a century and a half later, pushing Rome's frontier to where the Danube runs into the Black Sea. As it was he had Gaul; the Rhine took the place of the Danube; and he dazzled the Roman imagination by crossing the Channel to the fabled mist-girt island of Britain.

What he achieved in Gaul might have been thought a matter for dreams; but Caesar was no dreamer. His Gallic triumph fed his *dignitas*; at the same time it made his Roman enemies tremble. In two years the greater part of the country up to the Rhine was overrun, Caesar employing the strategy, used in the creation of so many empires, of favouring and promoting the interests of certain tribes, which were then willing to serve as allies or clients of the Roman people. Even his enemies back in the city could not withstand the effect of what he achieved. In an upsurge of national pride a thanksgiving of fifteen days was ordained. Such rejoicings however were premature. Gallic resistance had not yet been broken; Caesar's conquest was superficial. Sporadic risings broke out, aided by the Germans and the Celtic tribes of south-east Britain. Caesar's response was atrocious. In 55 two tribes, the Usipetes and Tencteri, were wiped out, even the women and children being massacred. For Caesar this genocide was deliberate and necessary policy. But it prompted Cato, back in Rome, to propose that Caesar be handed over to the Germans as a war criminal. No doubt Cato's moral indignation was quickened by his political enmity; yet it is astonishing that the Romans, accustomed to ruthlessness – hadn't Cato's own celebrated ancestor ended every speech in the Senate for months with the demand that Carthage should be destroyed? – should have found something shocking in Caesar's actions. Certainly the man who made a point of showing clemency towards his fellow-citizens showed none to barbarians. 'No man ever made war so horrible as Caesar did in Gaul,' wrote Field-Marshal Lord Montgomery; and Caesar had no philosophy of progress to offer specious justification for his atrocities.

The greatest rising against the Romans was led by the Gallic hero, Vercingetorix, in 52. He raised all central Gaul in what was to be the last effort to preserve liberty. The crisis didn't find Caesar wanting; all his life he was sharpened by danger. Now, in his most brilliant and audacious campaign, he forced Vercingetorix into the

A reconstruction of Caesar's siegeworks at Alesia

hill-town of Alesia, threw up lines of investment, fought off a huge relieving army and compelled surrender. Within a few months Gaul was secured as a Roman province. The Rhine had become the limit of Empire. As for Vercingetorix himself, he was preserved to make a show at Caesar's triumph six years later. Then, having furnished a show for the Roman mob, he was hustled off to the dank cell of the Mamertine prison for execution.

Caesar's methods were horrible, but the magnitude of his achievement cannot be overestimated. Mediterranean civilization was carried into northern Europe and there established. Caesar's conquest of Gaul made mediaeval Christendom possible; it made France; it made modern Europe. It was the most important single action between the defeat of Carthage and Constantine's adoption of Christianity as the official religion of the Roman Empire.

Yet of course what he achieved in Gaul meant something different to him. For Caesar, Gaul had been a means of acquiring muscle in Roman politics. It had also been a delight: as a soldier, Caesar, formerly the foppish debt-ridden dandy among politicians, the notable orator, unscrupulous demagogue and ornament of Roman society, had found himself. The camp provided him with his true metier. Opinions vary as to where he ranks among great commanders. Field-Marshal Lord Wavell found him 'an impressive soldier in offence and defence, and a writer of dull and lengthy military reports'. For Montgomery, he was 'to say the least, an erratic strategist'; 'he showed no originality as a tactician'; 'he was often rash and hasty – but overall his reliance on mobility paid off'. Acutely, Montgomery remarked that 'as great a factor as any other in bringing Caesar success was his own personality and character. His presence with the troops seems to have filled them with the same certainty of victory that he had.' Undoubtedly the legionaries adored him – he quelled one incipient mutiny by addressing them as 'citizens' instead of 'soldiers'. They loved him for his panache, his capacity to surprise, his willingness to live rough and march along with them on foot, to take the lead in dangerous enterprises like swimming a swollen river. Yet – and this was inauspicious – he didn't inspire the same unquestioning devotion among his lieutenants, who of course regarded themselves as his social equals and had anyway their own political connections to maintain and obligations to discharge; some of them also resented his manifest superiority. The most able of them, T. Labienus, in fact deserted him at the beginning of the Civil War, and though at that time others stuck to him, his eventual murderers included men who had worked with him or whom he had befriended.

In his ability to win the love of his soldiers, and his inability to compel a similar loyalty from his generals, he resembles Napoleon; and of course the two had much in common. They were the two great comets of European history, the two men of unquestionably transcendent powers of intellect and will. As generals, both relied principally on speed, élan and the promotion of morale rather than on tactical or strategic originality. Both could exercise enormous charm: but the devotion they aroused faded into distrust and resentment the closer men came to them.

In all Caesar spent ten years in the provinces: ten years in which he had almost no private life, and in which the constitutional crisis intensified back in Rome. There, the Triumvirate which had been established in 60 soon came under attack – as soon indeed as the initial shock of its formation had weakened. In 58 Caesar and Crassus between them had contrived to have the gang-leader Clodius elected tribune. (He had to have himself adopted as a plebeian in order to be eligible; for a few hours he became the son of a man half his age; a farce that tells us something of the hidebound Roman respect for legality.) Clodius had first pursued his personal enemy Cicero, a persecution which the Triumvirs did nothing to discourage. Cicero had after all been offered the chance of joining them, in 60 – Caesar had offered him second place in Gaul; he had turned them down; he should be made to feel the consequences. Now, Clodius drove him into alarmed exile by sponsoring a bill which would outlaw anyone who had condemned a Roman citizen to death without trial. He then turned on Cato, who was despatched to Cyprus on a mission. That got rid of him; he could exert little influence from there. But thereafter Clodius proved difficult to control; his waywardness threatened Caesar's interests, for he even had the audacity to snap at Pompey's heels. So irritating did this prove that the Great Man even withdrew from public life for a few months and delegated the task of dealing with the obstreperous tribune to a rival gang-leader, T. Annius Milo. The incident showed how fragile was the link that bound the Triumvirs; Pompey was sure that Crassus had encouraged Clodius. For the same reason he soon began to listen more favourably to Cicero's pleas that he be permitted to return. In August 57 he was allowed to do so, and at once showed his gratitude by proposing that Pompey be given proconsular authority to reorganize Rome's corn supply. It was symptomatic of the State's decadence that Cicero, the proponent of constitutional government, should find himself urging one of those extraordinary commands which were a mark of that government's failure. In his search for the *concordia ordinum* he was reduced to an attempt to detach Pompey from Caesar and Crassus. Nothing could so clearly demonstrate how the formation of the Triumvirate had restricted the ordinary politician's freedom of action.

There was a chance though that Cicero would succeed; interest, not affection, was what had drawn the Triumvirs together, and Pompey now so distrusted Crassus that he even alleged the millionaire had engaged in a plot against his life. Caesar was alarmed, the more so because an Optimate senator, L. Domitius Ahenobarbus, one of his most determined enemies, was a candidate for the consulship in 55 and had announced that, if elected, he would demand Caesar's recall. Caesar acted. He called Crassus to Ravenna, and together they then moved to Luca to confer with Pompey. No summit conference was ever more baleful. Some hundred and twenty senators, clients of the Dynasts, followed Pompey to the meeting-place, their colleagues waited in Rome, apprehensive.

Caesar's charm and diplomacy prevailed over the others' distrust, and peace was patched up. The biographer Plutarch called Luca 'a conspiracy to share the sovereignty and destroy the constitution'; and it was Caesar who had made this possible. The Triumvirate carved up power among themselves. Crassus and Pompey would be consuls in 55 – so much for Ahenobarbus. To ensure this, it was arranged that the elections would be postponed till after the autumn when the campaigning season in Gaul was over; Caesar would then despatch troops to Rome to cast their votes as instructed. Once elected, the consuls would pass a bill prolonging Caesar's Gallic command for another five years. That would give him time to settle affairs in Gaul. After that, in 49, he would stand for his second consulship. Another law would be passed, enabling him to stand in his absence and so avoid any interval in which he would be a civilian out of office who could be prosecuted for the alleged misdeeds of his first consulship. (That Caesar feared this likely prosecution is proved by the pains he took to avert it.) As for the other two, they would receive important proconsulships in 54, Pompey taking Spain (in addition to his corn supply commission) and Crassus Syria, a post which offered him the chance of the military glory he had long craved. Meanwhile Caesar and Crassus promised Pompey that they would restrain Clodius, while Pompey assured the other two that he would gag Cicero.

Everything was thus amicably settled; Caesar could feel satisfied with the results of his conference. If the three held together, the conservative party in the Senate would be helpless. Caesar, Crassus and Pompey would severally command the armies of Rome, and provincial wealth, sufficient to buy any election, would flow into their coffers.

It didn't work out like that. 'Events,' as Bismarck said, 'are stronger than the plans of men.' Events and temperaments. The Triumvirate was a triangle of forces held in tense equipoise, its members all the while fearing and distrusting each other. Fate, which Caesar's foresight could not anticipate, which even his will could not manage, was destined to break the triangle. First, Pompey's wife, Caesar's daughter Julia, died. Both were fond of her; while she lived she created sympathy between them. Then, it struck through Crassus, pursuing his dreams of glory in the Syrian desert, in a war against the Parthian Empire which was intended to do for him what the war against Mithridates had done for Pompey and the conquest of Gaul for Caesar. He found himself marooned in the desert sands at Carrhae, surrounded by the Parthian cavalry. The legions were annihilated and Crassus himself killed, his severed head thrown before the Parthian monarch. Caesar and Pompey were left gazing at each other across a widening gulf of distrust. And Pompey was in Rome, since his corn commission allowed him exemption from the rule that proconsuls must reside in their provinces, while Caesar was still confined to Gaul.

So the Republic moved towards catastrophe. In Rome itself disorder and corruption made it impossible to hold elections in 53. The gang warfare between Clodius and Milo intensified; when Clodius was murdered in an affray his followers burned down the Senate House. The choice seemed to be anarchy or dictatorship. Men turned to Pompey as the only man with the authority to save the Republic. But was he ready to do so? Characteristically, he hesitated. On the one hand he listened to such proposals, which flattered him; on the other, unwilling to break with Caesar, mindful also of how the Optimates had tarnished his *dignitas*, he arranged that all ten tribunes should sponsor that bill promised at Luca which would allow Caesar to stand for his next consulship in his absence. That reassured his colleague; but then the Senate proposed a bill, introduced by Caesar's old enemy Bibulus and supported, reluctantly, even by Cato, that Pompey should be made consul without a colleague. Caesar could not fail to see that they were trying to drive a wedge between him and Pompey and subsequent legislation suggested that Pompey was more anxious to secure his own position than mindful of his colleague's interests.

Caesar, with the sure touch of a popular politician, appealed to the general public. His enemies wished him recalled? Very well, he would show what he had achieved for Rome. He published his account of the Gallic War: and the publication was at the same time witness to his glory, defence of the necessity of his actions and a warning to his enemies. They should learn what manner of man they were dealing with; meanwhile too the public should be convinced that no one had excelled Caesar in what he had won in the name of the Roman people.

Still his enemies pursued him. M. Marcellus, consul in 51, proposed that Caesar should be superseded on the grounds that the war in Gaul was over; he had proved this out of his own mouth. Marcellus suggested that the Law of the Ten Tribunes was invalid. He advised that the question of Caesar's successor be debated in the Senate, on 1 March 50. Tension rose. Caesar's agent, the tribune G. Scribonius Curio (a bankrupt nobleman – Caesar attracted them, as a honey-pot does flies), vetoed the proposal: first round to Caesar. Meanwhile Pompey himself remained in that state of heavy-lidded ambiguity that was his wont in a crisis; nobody could surely guess how he would commit himself; probably his own will was still uncertain.

Caesar and his Optimate opponents were now both animated by fear. His enemies were convinced that another Caesarean consulship, with the Dynast fresh from his Gallic victory and backed by a devoted army, meant ruin for the free State; nothing in the crisis is more remarkable than this certainty on their part. But he for his part was equally sure that they meant to destroy him. He was fighting for power; but he was also fighting for his life.

Yet even a Caesar has little control over his destiny. Events in far-off Syria, threatened by a Parthian invasion after Crassus' disaster, sharpened the crisis in the West. The Senate voted that both Caesar and Pompey should surrender a legion to reinforce the army in Syria. Pompey outmanoeuvred his rival-colleague by nominating one which he had lent Caesar two years before: Caesar's strength was thus doubly reduced. In fact, neither legion left Italy, better news having arrived from the East; but both were lost to Caesar.

Still Caesar seemed to shrink from the prospect of civil war; the memory of the old wars between Marius and Sulla was terrible. He proposed that both he and Pompey should disarm and give up their commands. On 1 December 50, Caesar's man Curio forced the Senate to vote on this proposal. Such was the longing for peace that it was carried by three hundred and seventy votes to a mere twenty-two. But the diehards who opposed it would not believe that Caesar could be trusted. Any such proposal emanating from him must be a trick, calculated to work to his advantage. They may have been correct; Caesar had now shown himself in conciliatory mood and thus won a propaganda victory, all the while perhaps certain that he would not be called upon to carry out his proposal. At any rate, despite the Senate's vote, the Optimates now found a tribune to veto Curio's bill. The next day Marcellus asked Pompey to assume command of all forces in Italy and save the Republic. He accepted. Civil war lay in his decision; it was a measure of the decadence of the Republic that its most ardent supporters could only hope to check one Dynast by entrusting supreme power to another. It is a measure too of the hatred and fear which Caesar aroused.

This was the crisis of Caesar's life; and for a few days this man of supreme boldness shrank from it. It could not be wondered at. For more than ten years his career had been supported on the suspension bridge which he had, laboriously as any spider, constructed between himself and Pompey; now it was all but swept away. At Luca he had thought to have secured his future; now he found his plans and certainties merely chimerical. Desperately, he still proposed compromise. He despatched his officer, Mark Antony, tribune in 49, to Rome, where he compelled the Senate, on 1 January, to read a letter from Caesar in which he renewed his offer to carry out Curio's proposal if Pompey was willing to do the same. The enterprise had no chance of success – why should it, when those who had first prevented its enaction now felt themselves stronger than they had been then? No vote was even taken; instead it was declared that Caesar would be deemed a public enemy if he did not disarm within two months. Antony vetoed this proposal in turn, but this time the defenders of legality disregarded the tribunician veto. Antony and a fellow-tribune who had supported him were advised to leave the city. They fled to Caesar. On the seventh of the month Pompey was granted the authority of a dictator.

The moment of decision had arrived. Peaceful manoeuvre was no longer possible; Caesar must either yield or commit his fortunes to the chance of war. True, that need not be fought to the limit; he could just conceivably still hope to use his military strength, fortified by his proven willingness to fight, in order to obtain a better bargaining position. Yet, once he embarked on action, he had made the gambler's throw that could not be recalled; he was separated from the legality of conventional politics in which, however uneasily, he had dwelt all his life. Italy was divided from Cisalpine Gaul by a little stream called the Rubicon; to cross that was to make war on the Republic. 'We may still draw back,' he said to his staff officers, as they gazed at Italy in a winter dawn, 'but once we cross that little bridge, we shall have to fight it out.'

A sombre moment, in cold morning mist. To submit meant disgrace and a powerless future – danger too. It had been rumoured in Rome for months that the trial Caesar feared would take place, in a court ringed by armed men. But to cross the Rubicon laid Caesar and all his officers and legions open to the charge of treason. Every man who followed Caesar put himself at risk.

Caesar had built his career on boldness; Fortune was his only goddess and he believed in her as Napoleon trusted his own star. 'Let the dice fly high,' he said (speaking in Greek and quoting the dramatist Menander). As he stood and the light grew, and his officers shifted their feet, partly from nerves, partly to keep warm, a figure of rare beauty and size was discerned sitting on the bank of the stream. The figure, which some took to be the god Faunus (the Greek Pan), began to play a reed pipe, strange and unearthly music in that uncertain dawn. Shepherds gathered round to listen, and some of Caesar's men broke from their ranks to do the same. The apparition seized a trumpet from one of the bandsmen, raised it to his lips and blowing the call to advance, marched into the river and over to the other side. Caesar cried out that it was a sign from the gods; let them follow to avenge themselves on their treacherous enemies.

The die was cast, as word of the omen and of Caesar's decision spread. Throughout the morning the legions crossed the Rubicon into Italy, and marched against the Republic.

Once on the other side, Caesar welcomed the tribunes who had fled from Rome, drew up the troops for review and made a speech reciting the indignities inflicted on him; he tore open his tunic and exposed his breast, showing his men that he threw himself on their mercy. He promised rewards; and though he offered danger, it was, he said, in a just cause. They cheered him, and looked south to where the Apennines broke the winter sky. The war was on.

It was a war Caesar would have avoided, but a war he had started himself. He bears the first responsibility; the dice had fallen from his hand, on the prompting perhaps of Curio who, according to the poet Lucan, advised him that delay was always harmful to men who were ready for action; for which counsel Dante was to place Curio in the ninth chasm of Hell. Sir Ronald Syme saw that 'Caesar was the aggressor; he was fighting for no nobler cause than to frustrate the efforts of his enemies to bring his public career to a premature and dishonourable end.' No nobler cause, but none dearer to a Roman noble, who could not conceive life without a public career, or life wherein his *dignitas* was degraded. Caesar had no difficulty in exculpating himself. Standing eighteen months later on the field of Pharsalus, he looked down on the bodies of his slain enemies and said: 'they wanted it this way. I, Gaius Caesar, would have been condemned in spite of all my achievements if I had not sought help from my armies. . .' And he claimed that he had offered many concessions in an attempt to avert the war.

Only, no one had believed in his concessions; they were suspect, tainted fruit. His enemies believed that his second consulship in 48 – and he never conceded his right to that – would give him the opportunity to order the State according to his will. He would make himself a tyrant; Cicero recorded that Caesar had often quoted Euripedes' lines:

> Is crime consonant with nobility?
> Then noblest is the crime of tyranny –
> In all things else obey the laws of heaven.

They could not risk it.

Yet they had put themselves technically in the wrong by over-riding Mark Antony's tribunician veto; that too had been an unconstitutional act. In fact responsibility for the war stretched beyond those immediately involved. In a sense it extended to the whole body of the Senate over a period of at least fifty years. 'The civil war,' wrote Caesar's biographer Gelzer, 'was the result of the failure of the Republic and its ruling oligarchy to cope with the social and political problems of the empire which they had conquered.' The consequences of that failure were now clear, and the Optimates' decision to force Caesar to choose between dishonour and civil war was itself the last fling of a gambler. It is hard to believe that the war could have saved the Republic, even if they had won.

The group centred on Cato and Marcellus were ready for the war that might wipe out the hated Caesar. Italy and most of the senators (as the vote of 1 December suggested) viewed it with dismay and apprehension. Cicero, travelling from Brindisi to Rome that December had found no one who did not prefer a concession to Caesar to war. That longing, though, was disregarded. Caesar in turn might make the theme of his account of the civil war 'quanto studio pacem petissem' – 'with how great zeal I had sought peace'; but concession and compromise were crunched to dust in the autonomous machinery of war.

In the end any attempt to fix personal responsibility for the war rests on the one man who could have prevented it without personal risk: Pompey. The great supine Dynast had allowed himself to be led, unwilling, almost blindfold, to the head of the Optimate coalition, to associate with those who had always feared and distrusted him, even viewed him with a certain contempt as one ill at ease in politics. They had accepted him, however, because Caesar roused still deeper fear and distrust; they needed Pompey and his reputation – 'I have only to stamp my foot on the soil of Italy for cavalry and infantry to rise from the ground'; they needed his influence in the East; they needed his military and administrative skill. So they flattered him: he was the man to save the Republic. But Pompey could have refused; he could have stood by his agreement with Caesar; and if he had done so, the Optimates could hardly have raised an army.

Why didn't he? Caesar's explanation was simple: 'Pompey had become estranged from me because he wished no one to equal him in *dignitas*.' The Great Man was jealous. It was not surprising; when he and Caesar had first been associated, Pompey was everything, Caesar merely ambitious, skilful and unscrupulous; now Caesar's glory equalled his. Pompey had not advanced since the sixties; what would the next decade bring? He felt Caesar would eclipse him. At the same time the oligarchy, who had always suspected him, now invited him to save the Republic. What appeal could more certainly satisfy his *dignitas*? Pompey was again the indispensable man. Even so, he had hesitated long. He knew the risks. . .

Caesar's advance into Italy was rapid. He darted down the Adriatic coast, seized the passes to Etruria and over-ran Picenum, Pompey's home territory. The consuls and Senate, aghast, left Rome; Pompey meanwhile concentrated on building up an army in Apulia. Caesar's speed had overcome the difficulties of a winter campaign and on 21 February he compelled the surrender of a senatorial army in Corfinium, commanded by his old enemy L. Domitius Ahenobarbus. Caesar exercised that clemency which was to be his consistent policy throughout the war; most of the troops came over to him, and their leaders were permitted to depart. A week later Cicero wrote that Caesar's clemency was winning public opinion.

Inevitably that concerned Caesar; he was after all first a politician. He knew that military victory would not be enough in itself; he had no wish to appear a revolutionary; he must strive to attract politically respectable adherents. As it was, the debtors, bankrupts, broken men, political failures, all those who had nothing to hope for from the *status quo*, flocked to him. He must appeal to others more substantial; policy, as well as his own nature, commended clemency. He wanted to blur the lines of division, not sharpen them.

Hence the importance he attached to Cicero. He sent one of his staff, Cornelius Balbus, to him immediately after Corfinium, to tell him of his wish for peace. Balbus even reported that Caesar would be prepared to live under Pompey's rule, if he could be assured of his personal safety. Cicero wasn't convinced. He wrote to his friend Atticus of 'Caesar's treacherous clemency' – but Pompey, he added, was treacherous also, for he was preparing to abandon Italy and withdraw across the Adriatic to Greece. Caesar was now revealed as the man who spared his enemies, Pompey as one who deserted his friends. And these friends would somehow or other have to make their peace with the victor. All the same, for Cicero, Caesar's victory still threatened 'massacre, confiscation, recall of exiles, a clean sweep of debts, every worst man raised to a position of honour, and the sort of rule that not only a Roman citizen but even a Persian could not endure'. In short, Caesar's victory threatened first social revolution, then tyranny. Cicero, torn by anxiety, carried away by his gift for words, might exaggerate; but his fear was shared by others. The prospect of absolute power in the hands of Caesar and his disreputable followers was terrible for the *boni* to contemplate.

Meanwhile Caesar still pursued Cicero with his friendship. He knew what influence he had: he was the one man whose integrity was generally recognized. (Well, there was Cato also, but Caesar could never hope to win him; nor did he wish to.) He now assured Cicero that his aim was 'repose for Italy, peace for the provinces, security for the empire'. They met, by appointment, at Formia, on the Naples road. Caesar urged him to attend the Senate, which he himself had summoned; his example would govern the rest. Cicero's reply was testing. He asked for assurance of freedom of speech. He could not agree to blame Pompey; he could not approve of attacks on the Pompeian armies in Spain and Greece. Would he be permitted to put forward such arguments? Caesar remained polite; he smiled; he spoke with respect of Cicero's reputation and abilities; he praised his talents and character. But he added that of course he could not permit him to speak in that way. That was it: Cicero indicated that in that case he would be unable to attend. Caesar was genuinely sorry, for more than political reasons; he really respected Cicero. But when they met afterwards, he confined the conversation to philosophy and literature (in which he was genuinely interested; as well as his memoirs he wrote a book on literary style).

He had failed with Cicero; but he still called the Senate, and spoke to the few senators who attended, in a manner clear and simple. It was an opportunity to put his case on record. He had asked, he said, for nothing extraordinary in the way of honours. He had waited the legal period of ten years for a second consulship; he had been promised that he would be allowed to stand for office in his absence; and that promise had been broken. Caesar spoke of his own moderation, of the concessions he had proposed, of the injustice of his recall and of the violent suppression of the legal authority of the tribunes. He had proposed peace, he had asked for interviews, he had been refused everything. If the Senate now feared to commit itself to his side, then he was willing to carry on the government in his own name, but he asked them to send deputies to Pompey to treat for an arrangement.

Nothing could have been more moderate. It was all in vain however. Perhaps his forbearance was interpreted as weakness; perhaps even those senators who were still in Rome believed Pompey would win and so feared to be associated with Caesar (though their presence there was in fact association); most probably they did not trust his intentions. He had after all failed to convince Cicero. And these senators were the moderates who feared the victory of either side. As Cicero wrote to Atticus, 'Pompey means to strangle Rome and Italy with famine and then waste and burn the country and seize property. Caesar may do the same thing. The prospect is appalling. . . I dread this terrible war, the like of which has never been seen. They will say, "Sulla did such and such. Why shouldn't I do likewise?" Sulla, Marius, Cinna, all had a constitutional cause; yet how cruel was their victory. I shrink from war. . .'

The terrible war was at last inevitable. Caesar had made his moderate bid, unsuccessfully. Opinion still favoured Pompey, even after the summer of 49 when Caesar destroyed the Pompeian legions in Spain. After all, Pompey had been Rome's supreme general for twenty-five years; Caesar had beaten only barbarians. Moreover, Pompey's army contained the noblest blood of Rome, and his strategic position seemed superior. Cicero explained it thus: 'Pompey will not lay down arms because he has lost Spain. He agrees with Themistocles that those who are masters of the sea will win in the end. He neglected Spain. He has given all his attention to building up a fleet. When the time comes he will return to Italy with this overwhelming fleet. . .'

'When the time comes. . .' It was not in Caesar's nature to await such time. He too assumed the office of dictator; then, to prove his point, his second consulship as planned; and crossed the Adriatic in the spring of 48. Pompey's position might seem superior to armchair strategists; Caesar knew better. He had three advantages.

First, his possession of Italy allowed him to act on interior lines. The Pompeian forces were scattered around the Mediterranean basin. Despite Pompey's new fleet, they could not assemble quickly; co-operation was beyond them. Caesar planned to pick them off one by one, Second, his veteran troops were hardened fighters, devoted to their general. They had conquered Gaul, relished victory, trusted Caesar. By contrast, Pompey's were either raw recruits or old soldiers who had been softened by civil ease. Few of them had recent experience of campaigning – nor indeed had Pompey; it was thirteen years since his eastern triumphs. Lassitude had grown on him. He had always been cautious; now he was slow and over-deliberate. He hardly compared to Caesar.

Finally there was no dissension in Caesar's army; his supremacy was unquestioned. Things were different with his enemies. Pompey knew well that many of the Optimates had never liked or trusted him. They would be quick to look for a chance to get rid of him when he had served his turn.

For these reasons the issue did not remain long in doubt. Though Pompey managed to break out from Dyrrachum, where Caesar had confined him since April, the respite was brief. Caesar chased him into Thessaly. Battle was joined on 9 August on the plain of Pharsalus and the Optimate army cut to pieces. Pompey himself fled to Egypt, where in September he was murdered – it was not in the Egyptian nature to have any time for a loser.

Caesar had pursued him there. What he would have done with Pompey can only be matter for conjecture; probably exile would have been the Great Man's fate. As it was, Caesar was able to show his nobility by expressing dismay at the murder and arranging the transport of the body back to Italy to be buried with splendour on his Alban estates, where the tomb can still be seen, in the public garden of Albano.

Though there were still Optimate armies in Africa, and though Pompey's sons were looking for a chance to renew the contest, Caesar delayed some months in Egypt. The country was nominally an independent kingdom, ruled by the Ptolemies, descendants of one of Alexander the Great's generals. It was a country of enormous wealth, the granary of the Mediterranean; and the advantages of bringing it under closer Roman control were sufficiently obvious to make it seem to Caesar that delay in ending the civil war could be justified. Besides, there was another attraction in Egypt, the sixteen-year-old Queen Cleopatra. No woman had ever exercised much influence over Caesar; his three marriages had all been tepid, calculated affairs, while his closest relationship, that with Servilia, mother of Marcus Brutus, had combined political usefulness – she had many connections – with a sense of warm comradeship. The list of his mistresses is long – it included other queens, as well as the wives of his fellow-Triumvirs – but they had been creatures of pleasure, no more. Now, as Rome wondered at his delay in Egypt, gossip happily fastened on Cleopatra as the reason. Certainly it was Caesar who established her on the throne

Cleopatra, on a silver coin of Ascalon. The portrait indicates intelligence and strength of character rather than beauty

32

instead of her half-brother – and, in the course of doing so, he found his life momentarily in danger as a result of a street-riot in Alexandria. Later too she followed him to Rome and was established in a house on the Aventine. She bore a son, alleging Caesar as the father – Mark Antony indeed later said that Caesar had admitted paternity – and the boy was challengingly named Caesarion. Others denied that Caesar was the father; most people, though, thought they knew what had kept him in Egypt. The great Victorian historian J. A. Froude knew better: 'to suppose that such a person as Caesar, with the concerns of the world upon his hands, would have allowed his public action to be governed by a connection with a loose girl of sixteen, is to make too large a demand on human credulity; nor is it likely that, in a situation of so much danger and difficulty as that in which he found himself, he would have added to his embarrassments by indulging in an intrigue at all'. So the eloquent moralist; but credulity was more elastic in the Ancient World than in nineteenth-century England, and Cicero found his stretched not at all.

Caesar returned to Rome in October 47, only to be off for North Africa within two months. There he caught up with Cato and an Optimate army at Thapsus, where his victory led to Cato's suicide. By July 46 he was back in Rome. He was now named as dictator for ten years, and was at the same time in his third consulship. A fourth followed in 45, in which year he also defeated the last army of his enemies, ironically commanded by his old lieutenant Labienus, at Munda in Spain. The Civil Wars were over, for the moment; and Caesar was supreme. Extravagant decrees were passed in his honour: he was to be made dictator for life and elected to a fifth consulship for 44.

He had entered on the last phase of his career, and the fundamental questions remained unsettled. What would Caesar do with his power? Would he reconstitute the State? Would he restore the Republic? Or would he supplant it?

The State indeed lay at his mercy. The abject Senate – or what was left of it – fell over itself in its obsequious zeal to grant him extravagant and unprecedented honours, of which, privately, many senators were ashamed. No man before Caesar had been made dictator for life. What did it not imply? No wonder that Cicero in talking to his friends now bitterly referred in jest to Caesar as *rex* (king). In the East, too, Caesar had been called a god; a monument at Ephesus paid tribute to 'Gaius Julius Caesar, son of Gaius, high priest, imperator and consul for the second time, descended from Ares and Aphrodite, god made manifest and common saviour of mankind. . .' Romans might dismiss such language as Greek hyperbole; but in Rome itself the fifth month of the year was renamed July in Caesar's honour (the Roman year started in March), and in the ancient priesthood of the Luperci a new college of the Luperci Julii was formed.

As if this were not enough, Caesar himself was acting in an ever more extraordinary manner, setting himself above and apart from other nobles. In private conversation and at dinner-parties he was still the affable Caesar of old; but when, in December 45, two tribunes, Marullus and Flavus, opposed the granting of further honours to him, and even removed garlands from his statues, they were rudely made aware that the time for such Republican illusions of the nature and power of their office was past. The man who had started the Civil War ostensibly in defence of a violated tribunate was now seen to violate that office himself. The resentment this occasioned was made visible by the votes cast, in defiance of his instructions, for the deposed tribunes in the elections held for the offices to be filled in 42. And in the elections moreover, Caesar now commended candidates in a manner that made their election certain.

In minor or ceremonial matters too his behaviour gave cause for concern. On festive occasions for instance he had taken to wearing long red boots different from the normal footwear of patrician senators. This might have been taken for a revival of his youthful dandyism – the young Caesar had been notorious for his eccentricities of dress – if he hadn't insisted that the boots belonged to the dress of the ancient Alban kings, and so befitted him as their descendant. No wonder the rumours grew ever louder that Caesar planned to make himself king. Not only could they not be silenced by his assurance 'I am not king, but Caesar'; but not all were put about by his enemies to discredit him.

The rumours were brought into the open by the curious events during the ancient Festival of the Lupercal on 15 February 44, the day on which Caesar's title *dictator perpetuus* was confirmed. Shakespeare, whose account is drawn from the biographer Plutarch, has Mark Antony, in his funeral oration just a month later, recount that:

> You all do know that on the Lupercal
> I thrice presented him the kingly crown
> Which he three times refused. . . Was this ambition?

But the events were open to another interpretation, which Shakespeare allots to Casca:

> I saw Mark Antony offer him a crown; yet 'twas not a crown neither, 'twas one of these coronets, and, as I told you, he put it by once; yet for all that to my thinking, he would fain have had it. Then he offered it to him again; but, to my thinking, he was very loth to lay his fingers off it. And then he offered it a third time; he put it the third time by; and still as he refused it the rabblement shouted and clapped their chopped hands and threw up their sweaty night-caps, and uttered such a deal of stinking breath because Caesar had refused the crown, that it had almost choked Caesar. . .

There were many to Casca's way of thinking that hard February. The scene can only have been bizarre, for the Lupercal was a festival that linked Rome to its earliest legendary history. Disguised as wolves, the priests of the Luperci danced round the Capitol, re-enacting a ceremony of mythic-historical import. That day, in the midst of the dancers, Caesar sat god-like, in a purple toga and adorned with a golden wreath, on a gilded chair. Then, out of the dancers, Antony leapt up, dressed in wolfskins, offering this crown; three times it was offered and three times put aside, while the crowd howled and Rome waited.

Who had devised the charade and for what purpose? Perhaps it was a genuine attempt to make Caesar king. If so, then the public offer was designed to test the crowd's feeling, and they can only have been disappointing. On the other hand it may have been staged to enable Caesar to prove that he Caesar had no intention of calling himself king; a charade to scotch the rumours. If so, it failed; rumours and fears persisted.

Meanwhile Caesar pushed on with preparations for a Parthian war which would expunge the memory of Crassus' defeat and secure the eastern frontier of the Empire. (A prophecy was discovered meanwhile to suggest that only a king could conquer the Parthians.) Nothing shows more clearly the intractable nature of the constitutional crisis than Caesar's decision to set out for the East, on 18 March, on a campaign expected to last three years; for nothing had been settled at Rome. It is as if Caesar was dismissing the possibility of reforming the constitution; as if, baffled by the problem, he was turning aside to seek oblivion and recreation in action. No doubt he expected his authority would prevail at Rome even in his absence, so long as he held the office of dictator and was at the head of the army. But what if he died? (And he was, after all, fifty-six.) He had done nothing to provide for Rome's future. He had come, seen, conquered and was departing; brilliant as a comet, and ineffective. His career had revealed the infirmity of the old system, but he had put nothing substantial in its place, and his decision to set off on a war which was hardly urgent suggests that he had nothing to put there in any case. The oligarchy had been, for the moment at least, destroyed; while Caesar lived, Rome was in effect a military monarchy; but there was nothing durable in this. The authority of Caesar's will and the power of his army dominated the State, that was all. All his other reforms had been no more than tinkering; it was no doubt useful to have reformed the calendar, but it was of marginal importance compared to the necessity of reforming the constitution.

Cicero, in a speech in the Senate that spring, said:

War has laid low our institutions. . . Men will read with amazement of empires and provinces, of the Rhine, the ocean and the Nile, of countless battles, astonishing victories, of innumerable monuments and triumphs; but unless this State is re-established in institutions which you bestow on us, your name will certainly travel widely over the world, but it will have no resting-place; posterity will argue about you as we have argued about you. Some will praise you to the skies, others will find something lacking, and that the most important element of all. . .

Prophetic words, truly describing Caesar's failure. Others, as Cicero forecast, have read Caesar's vague fantasies as firm intentions, thwarted by the murder:

Marcus Brutus, on a coin
commemorating Caesar's murder.
The striking of such a coin
emphasizes how the Liberators saw
their deed as an act of civic duty

It was to be a new kind of Empire. Something had been drawn from the dreams of
Alexander, but for the most part it was the creation of his own profound and
audacious mind. There were to be wide local liberties. He proposed to decentral-
ize, to establish local government in Italy as the beginning of a world-wide system
of free municipalities. Rome was to be only the greatest among many great and
autonomous cities. There was to be a universal Roman nation, not a city with a
host of servile provinces, and citizenship in it should be open to all who were
worthy. The decadence of the Roman plebs would be redeemed by the virility of
the new peoples. . .

So, in a flush of romantic enthusiasm, wrote John Buchan, reading vast and
profound schemes into such acts as Caesar's gift of the franchise to the municipalities of Cisalpine Gaul and the admission of provincials to a Senate that now
numbered nine hundred members; seeing, that is, a broad plan in a Roman
politician's reward to his clients.

Perhaps it was in fact so; but if this was Caesar's idea, he imparted it to no one. He
was concerned rather with the securing of his own power. If the admission of Gauls
to the Senate would bolster his support, he would admit them. If the title of king
would help, he would take it. If it proved too offensive, he would abstain . . . Caesar
had always been practical.

But, in these last months, the disease of power had begun to attack him; he was
losing that intuitive responsiveness to the effect of his actions on others. Among
Caesar's attributes had been his sensitivity, his ability to put himself in the other

man's place. That was now deserting him, as arrogance – fully displayed by Shakespeare in his version of Caesar's response to his wife Calpurnia's forebodings – took over. Consciousness of one's own nobility, generosity and clemency carries its own danger; and it now blinded Caesar to the implications of what he had done. He had bestowed life and safety on his enemies, even admitted them to his favour. Nothing showed so clearly his conscious superiority; nothing so certainly fostered their resentment.

A conspiracy was formed. It involved at least sixty men; yet its secret was guarded from Caesar and his agents; that suggests the existence of a still much wider ring of sympathizers. Its leaders were G. Cassius Longinus and M. Junius Brutus, brothers-in-law, of whom Brutus claimed descent from that legendary Republican hero who had expelled Rome's earlier tyrants, the house of Tarquin. The characters of both are known to everybody through Shakespeare's play. Both owed their lives to Caesar's clemency, for both had fought against him; both, as part of his programme of reconciliation, had achieved office. Cassius was one of that year's praetors; he now called Caesar his 'old and merciful master'. Brutus had a closer connection with the dictator. His mother Servilia was Caesar's best-loved mistress, a lover turned friend and political confederate; it was even asserted that Caesar was Brutus' father – and indeed he addressed him affectionately as 'my son'. But other family allegiances drew Brutus in a different direction; Cato had been Servilia's half-brother and in 45 Brutus married Cato's daughter Porcia (Portia). Moreover, Brutus was a young prig, a philosopher inclined to the Stoic doctrines, a natural admirer of the impossible Cato, and just the sort of fellow given to consciously virtuous self-dramatization.

As a group the conspirators were animated by resentment and thwarted ambition:

> . . . we petty men
> Walk under his huge legs, and peep about
> To find ourselves dishonourable graves. . .

But they were also moved by their conception of Liberty (as a young mint-official in 59 Brutus had issued coins bearing his ancestor's image and the inscription *Libertas*). For them Caesar was a tyrant. Cicero, not party to the conspiracy himself, yet subsequently expressed their feelings in his second speech against Antony:

What does it matter whether I wished it done or approved the deed? Is there anyone, except Antony and those who were glad to have Caesar reign over us, who did not wish for his death or who disapproved of what was done? All were responsible, for all the *boni* joined in killing Caesar. Some didn't know of the plot, some lacked courage, others the opportunity. None lacked the will. . .

Caesar was smothering the Republic which was every Roman noble's possession. The *boni*, alert to what they were losing, were nonetheless blind to the problems of empire. They did not understand how narrow was their own conception of liberty. That does not mean that nothing could have grown from their action; no wider sense, after all, animated men like Pym and Hampden, themselves admirers of Brutus and Cassius, in their opposition to Charles I; but parliamentary democracy ultimately owes its being to their resistance.

The conspirators struck on the Ides of March, just three days before the proposed departure for the East. After the deed, all sorts of happenings were reported which seemed to have foreshadowed it. Caesar, at supper the night before, had been asked what was the best sort of death, and, lifting his cup of wine and water, had replied 'a sudden one'. He had dismissed his Spanish bodyguard as if careless of his fate. The augur Spurinna had advised him to beware the Ides of March. Calpurnia's dreams had led her to beg him not to attend the Senate. He himself had dreamed that he was shaking hands with Jupiter.

The Senate was meeting in the Theatre of Pompey, just behind the Campo dei Fiori, the usual house being closed for repairs after a fire. Caesar went there unarmed. On the way he met Spurinna and mockingly observed that the Ides of March had come. 'Aye, Caesar, but not gone.' Someone handed him a note, listing those who were plotting against his life; but he merely added it to the sheaf of petitions he was carrying in his left hand. Or so legend has it, stressing the noble carelessness of the doomed man. He entered the Assembly Room and the conspir-

The death of Caesar, as depicted in a neo-classical painting by J.-L. Gérome

Julius Caesar

ators clustered round him, some of them mouthing requests. Casca struck the first blow from behind. The others closed in with daggers in their hands; he looked up and saw no friendly hand, nothing but daggers. Brutus was among them. Caesar saw him and exclaimed in Greek, 'you too, my son'. He offered no more resistance, but pulled his toga over his head, and fell to the ground. His body lay at the foot of Pompey's statue; it was less than four years since Egyptian boatmen had brought him Pompey's head. The conspirators ran through the streets, waving bloody daggers and proclaiming liberty; the city was appalled.

Caesar was dead, but not his work. He had, it was true, established nothing that would last. Rome would experience another thirteen years of civil war before a settlement came in sight – a harsher, more savage war, marked by the massacres Caesar's clemency had spared his enemies. But what Caesar had destroyed was never repaired. The old oligarchic constitution lay in ruins. He himself had said that 'the Republic was a mere name, without form or substance'; and no daggers could restore that substance.

And Caesar would have an heir, his great-nephew, who was also his adopted son; the young man Octavius.

AUGUSTUS

ON THE BANK of the Tiber, at the edge of the Campus Martius (the Field of Mars) stands the monument to the Augustan Age, known as the Ara Pacis, the Altar of Peace. Unveiled by Augustus himself in 13 BC, it represents his gift to the Roman world. A carved frieze round the altar shows Augustus and his family on their way to sacrifice in the Field of Mars; it is a scene of piety and decorum. Another carving represents Italy as Mother Earth, surrounded by symbols of abundance and happiness. Then there is Aeneas, the father of the Roman people, their link with the immemorial Trojan past, sacrificing a pregnant sow on the site of Alba Longa, the mother city of Rome.

The Ara Pacis is the supreme statement of the Augustan Age made stone, the visible equivalent of the promise of renewal after strife and discord, which Virgil had held out in his *Fourth Eclogue* and had fully celebrated in the *Aeneid*. No study of Augustus can do justice to him that does not begin with the realization that a Golden Age was being consciously created:

> Augustus Caesar, divi genus, aurea condet
> Saecula qui rursus Latio regnata per arva
> Saturno quondam. . .

('Caesar Augustus, son of a god, who shall establish the age of gold in Latium over fields that once were Saturn's realm. . .' Virgil, *Aeneid*.)

Of course in all this there was a strong element of party propaganda. Augustus, like Napoleon, or, in debased form, Hitler and Mussolini, assiduously cultivated his own legend. Celebration of the Augustan peace cannot be quite divorced in the modern mind from the bombast of the 'Fascist Era' or the 'Thousand-Year Reich', just as 'the immense majesty of the Roman Peace' is offset by the barbarian version, recorded by Tacitus: 'they make a desert and call it peace'. Yet there was a difference in quality amounting to a difference in kind. It was not only that

(*Opposite*) Augustus: a statue found in Livia's villa near Rome. Dating from 20–17 BC, it shows Augustus in middle age. Detail on his breastplate depicts the return to Rome in 20 of the standards lost by Crassus at Carrhae in 59

Ara Pacis, Rome: a reconstruction, from original remains and copies, of the
altar consecrated by Augustus himself in 13 BC

Augustus had poets of the genius of Virgil and Horace to sing his achievements, but
that these achievements were genuinely worthy of praise. There might be arguments
as to their exact nature, but one thing was certain: Augustus had brought the
Roman world out of the darkness of the atrocious Civil Wars into the golden
sunlight of its high noon. That there were losses too was a fact to be bitterly felt by
succeeding generations: but these had not experienced the Civil Wars.

The murder of Caesar solved nothing. The self-styled Liberators had removed the
dictator, but they had neglected to prepare a coup. They seem to have assumed that,
with Caesar absent, the Republic would stand forth in pristine purity. Nothing of
the sort occurred. Caesar's faction remained in control; his lieutenant, Mark
Antony, was still, and of course legally, consul.

All the same Antony found it wise to come to an accommodation with the
Liberators. A compromise was attained. On Cicero's proposal in the Senate,
Caesar's murderers were to be granted an amnesty, while Caesar's will and acts
were to be accepted as valid, and his funeral celebrated. Illogical, but necessary. The
conspirators had no choice; nor had Antony; for the number of the conspirators

(*Above*) Detail of the processional frieze which decorated the longer sides of the Altar of Peace and showed Augustus offering libation, followed by priests, members of his family and a long file of senators

(*Below*) One of four panels depicting allegorical scenes of Empire, on the shorter ends of the Ara Pacis. This panel represents goddesses of Air, Earth and Water, surrounded by scenes of fertility, repose and beauty

proved the strength of their party. On the other hand, Antony had quickly recruited an influential noble, P. Dolabella, as fellow-consul and, more important, had troops at his disposal. (These were provided by Marcus Aemilius Lepidus, who had been appointed Governor of Narbonese Gaul and Nearer Spain, and had legions, waiting to march, who happened to be stationed just outside the city.) Power therefore still rested with the faction of the murdered dictator, but the strength of the opposition made them necessarily hesitant to use it. Things were accordingly patched up for the moment. Brutus and Cassius dined on the Capitol with Antony and Lepidus; it must have been a macabre occasion, Cassius bitterly regretting his failure to persuade Brutus that the jackal Antony should die with the wolf Caesar.

That was the prologue. Antony then published Caesar's will. The gift to the People of his gardens beyond the Tiber and of three hundred sesterces a man inflamed the crowd. Antony, permitted to deliver the funeral eulogy, fanned the fire. Within a month rioting mobs persuaded Brutus and Cassius that Rome was unsafe; they fled, leaving Antony in charge. He proceeded to consolidate his position by binding others to him. Lepidus, important for his legions and aristocratic connections, took Caesar's place as *pontifex maximus*. Two of the Liberators were allowed to proceed to their provinces, Decimus Brutus to Cisalpine Gaul and G. Trebonius to Asia; both had been Caesarean appointments in the first place. Antony was working to divide the opposition. He passed an agrarian bill to secure land for Caesar's veterans, and at the same time appeased the Senate by the empty gesture of proposing the permanent abolition of the dictatorship. In the first weeks after the murder he displayed a political acuity that contradicted his reputation as a swashbuckling and high-living soldier.

But Antony was not Caesar's heir. That was the factor he had left out of account. He could not certainly carry the whole of Caesar's faction with him. True, he had inherited something of his aura with the legions. He was clearly, for the moment, chief man in the party. And he was consul, with, therefore, the opportunity to secure his power for some years to come. He was already planning to have Transalpine and Cisalpine Gaul transferred to him for five years, while retaining control of Macedonia and its legions – his original portion when proconsulships had been allocated by the dictator. The significance of Gaul was clear: it had made Caesar; its proximity allowed constant influence in Roman politics; and the provinces were rich, producing forty million sesterces in taxation a year. Anthony's manoeuvres inevitably aroused suspicion. Was he aiming at Caesar's place? Yet he was not Caesar's legal heir.

That position, honourable and perilous, belonged to one who was hardly more than a boy, the dictator's great-nephew, Gaius Octavius Thurinus. On his father's side the young man's family was respectable but hardly distinguished. They came from the small town of Velletri on the flank of the Alban Hills, where they had been municipal magistrates for generations. G. Octavius' father was the first member of the family to enter the Roman Senate. Mark Antony indeed claimed that the boy's great-grandfather had been a freedman and rope-maker, and his son a money-changer. Not so; these were mere libels. The family was of equestrian rank, the grandfather a solid banker. On his mother's side the boy belonged to a very similar family from the nearby township of Aricia, hanging on the very edge of the Alban Hills over the great golden sweep of the Campagna. His maternal grandfather had, however, made a brilliant marriage, to Julia, Caesar's sister. Hence the family's elevation.

It is tempting to dwell longer on this heredity; the young man's roots were entrenched in the Italy of olive groves and vineyards. He was to display the characteristics of the Italian countryman: sobriety, common sense, the strongly developed sense of family; all such qualities were, and are, quintessentially Italian. To think of him as Italian is an aid to comprehension, and it was indeed on Italy and on his reading of its desires that he was to base his career.

The boy took the dictator's fancy, which of course gave rise to slanders. Antony alleged that Caesar had compelled him to become his catamite as the price of adoption. The consul's brother, Lucius Antonius, further claimed that the boy had also prostituted himself to Aulus Hirtius (consul in 43) for three thousand gold pieces, and sneered at an effeminacy so pronounced that he used to soften the hairs on his legs by singeing them with red-hot walnut shells. Certainly the boy was soft and delicate in appearance: but the appearance belied his nature. Suetonius says that he had gained Caesar's favour rather by the determination he had shown in joining him on campaign in Spain when still recovering from a serious illness. In fact it is not difficult to account for the adoption. Caesar had no legitimate son; Octavius was clearly a youth of character and brains. No other explanation is necessary.

In March 44 Octavius was studying at Apollonia on the Dalmatian coast, perfecting his knowledge of Greek literature and acquiring a mastery of rhetoric. He would soon be joining his uncle for the Parthian war. The assassination changed everything. He learned the news in a letter from his mother brought by one of her freedmen: 'the time has come when you must play the man, decide and act, for no one can tell the things that may come forth. . .' Though he did not yet know of his adoption and inheritance (for the will had not been read when his mother wrote) he sailed at once for Italy, taking with him three friends, two of whom, M. Vipsanius Agrippa and G. Clinius Maecenas, were to be life-long allies and confidants.

His mother and stepfather (Philippus, a timid old Pompeian) urged him to decline the inheritance. He was only nineteen; let it devolve on some other Caesarean; he, Octavius, would still be a rich man. This advice was wise enough. As Caesar's heir the young man could not fail to be a target for those forces which had destroyed Julius; they could not allow anyone to inherit the charisma which emanated from the name. At the same time, the other leaders of Caesar's faction were not likely to welcome this boy who had nothing to offer but his inheritance, an inheritance that might yet eclipse them. They were bound to resent him. Antony was to address him in contemptuous words, 'you, boy, who owe everything to a name. . .'*

As the boy advanced to Rome in the spring of 44 to claim his inheritance (though carefully discounting the suggestion that he had any political ambitions) he was made aware of the power and authority that lay in that name. Angry soldiers crowded round him; municipalities paid him honour; veterans clamoured that he lead them to revenge. He reached Rome at the end of April and found Antony hostile and suspicious and unwilling to hand over Caesar's treasure. Accordingly Octavian began to pay off Caesar's legacies from his own resources, and took care to let everyone know that this was what he was doing.

The political situation was amazingly confused. All trust had broken down, all association was dissolved. Men manoeuvred desperately for position, for a foothold in the glissade towards extinction. It was as if the Roman world was wilfully tearing itself apart. In the shifting chaos the murder had unloosed, all groupings were provisional, all alliances could be disowned in an instant. Nevertheless five different groups may be discerned.

First, there was Antony and that part of the Caesarean faction which he had inherited. He had the advantage of office and of control of some of the legions. To secure his position, he had attempted the transfer of the Gallic provinces, only to discover that Decimus Brutus prudently refused to cede Cisalpine Gaul. Accordingly by late summer Antony was besieging him in Mutina (Modena).

Then the chief Liberators, Brutus and Cassius, had, it was learned, gone to Macedonia and Syria respectively, even though they had been assigned the unimportant provinces of Crete and Cyrene. They might not yet be ready for war, but all the indications were that what they had started by murder they would attempt to perfect by military action. They lurked in the background all through 44 and into 43, the hope of the traditionalists, the ultimate enemy of the Caesareans.

Another enemy in exile was Sextus Pompeius, son of the great Dynast. His opposition to the Caesareans was even deeper rooted than that of the Liberators. He received support from surviving members of the old Optimate grouping who had never made even a temporary truce with Caesar. Pompey was based in Sicily, a stronghold of strategic importance. Yet the natural alliance between him and the Liberators was never quite to be effected.

Back in Rome, Cicero was still pursuing his old dreams. Now he was trying to persuade the Senate to summon up its nerve, restore the true Republic and outlaw Antony, whom he had marked down as an adventurer, a would-be dictator, the enemy of all the *boni*, and the true heir of Catiline. In August he delivered the speech

---

* At this time he was called Gaius Octavius Thurinus. On adoption he became Gaius Julius Caesar Octavianus. People then called him either Caesar or Caesar Octavianus. To refer to him as Caesar is unnecessarily confusing, though Shakespeare calls him that in *Antony and Cleopatra*; to use the name Caesar Octavianus is pedantic. The traditional English form, Octavian, is preferable. In 27 the Senate granted him the honorific name 'Augustus'. I shall therefore call him Octavian till 27, Augustus thereafter.

known as the First Philippic, one of a number named after their resemblance to the orations in which the Greek orator Demosthenes had attacked Philip of Macedon, the enemy of the free constitution of Athens. In the later Philippics Cicero was to assail Antony in terrible terms, oratory of genius from which Antony's reputation never wholly recovered. Cicero however recognized the weakness of his position. In the absence of Brutus and Cassius he needed a sword. All the obvious champions of the Republic were out of Italy. What of the young man Octavian?

Octavian himself had raised an army, on his own responsibility and illegally. (But what was legality when the State had collapsed?) All the same he desired respectability – he had no wish to appear an adventurer and thus alienate the men of property. Cicero could satisfy his needs. The young man knew that Julius had respected Cicero, and he now greeted the old statesman as 'father'. He sought his advice, and swore that he would not act save by his counsel. He wanted also to act through the Senate, because by doing so he would be seen to have gained the support of 'the best men'. His problem was acute; he had yoked in harness an ill-suited pair of horses. On the one hand the origin of his power rested with Caesar's veterans, who wished to avenge the murder; on the other hand a section of the Roman aristocracy and bourgeoisie was turning to Octavian as their saviour from Antony. In the party Octavian was building up, it was hard to reconcile these two elements.

Cicero's position was simpler. He wanted to use the young man and then discard him: 'laudandum adulescentem, ornandum, tollendum', he wrote: 'the young man should be praised, decorated and got rid of'. Still, he could not help being flattered by the attentions Octavian paid him (he had never been able to resist flattery), and he may even have been deceived by Octavian's protestations of loyalty to the Republic. At any rate the old man's hatred of Antony had become so intense that he was prepared to take any risk to destroy him. Here however he failed to take Octavian's measure. Octavian himself was not out to destroy Antony but rather to impress him. At this stage he had to show Antony that he was to be reckoned with, strong enough to be treated as an equal. Only thus could Caesar's faction be re-united; only in this way could Julius be avenged, and his own position secured.

Cicero's epigram therefore recoiled on his own head. He, not Octavian, was to be flattered first, and then disposed of. All the to-ing and fro-ing, the bluff and counter-bluff, the exchange of menaces, the tortuous manoeuvring between the summer of 44 and October 43 tended towards this reunion of the Caesareans and the burial of the Free State. And yet when Cicero spoke of Octavian to the Senate, and said 'I know intimately the young man's every feeling. There is nothing dearer to him than the Free State, nothing is more prized by him than your good opinion, the opinion of virtuous men, nothing more pleasing than glory'; he was not only setting out to delude the Senate, and in the process perhaps deluding himself: he was paradoxically speaking the truth. The young man desired all these things – but on his own terms and in his own way.

Impossible not to admire the cool nerve Octavian showed in these tormented months. By the end of 44 he had apparently severed relations with Antony; he had even made overtures to the Caesar-killer Decimus Brutus; he had got himself an army, and was established as the hope of the Senate. In January 43 Cicero had challenged Antony in the Fourth Philippic and urged the Senate to name him as a public enemy – his consulship had now of course expired. Then in the Fifth Philippic he had called on them to turn to Octavian: 'what God has given this god-like youth to the Roman People?' The Senate succumbed. Octavian was given the rank of senator; more important, he was joined with that year's consuls, Hirtius and Pansa, in command of the army that was to march against Antony, and he was granted the *imperium* of a pro-praetor. He had got what he needed; an official status.

Yet he could not fail to be aware that his new allies were hardly committed to him; Antony indeed assured him of this in a correspondence he had opened. Moreover, news came from the East that Brutus and Cassius had also got themselves an army; eyes of true friends of the Republic were again turning in their direction. Time was hardly on Octavian's side. Nevertheless he did not waver. The first essential was to obtain mastery in Italy, and to do that he had to use the senatorial party in order to persuade Antony that he must be treated with respect. This was the purpose and outcome of the confused scrambling campaign that is given the name of Mutina. It began with Antony's renewed attempt to dislodge Decimus Brutus. It ended with Antony in flight across the Alpes Maritimes, with the consuls Hirtius and Pansa dead, and with the Senate believing itself triumphant and accordingly ready to discard Octavian.

This last was easier resolved than done. The young man refused to hand over the legions he had acquired. Instead he opened negotiations with Antony. Keeping these concealed he proposed terms to the Senate: he wanted the vacant consulship. His request was turned down in July. His men clamoured that he lead them to Rome. Resistance collapsed. Three legions, encamped outside the city, declared for him. He marched unopposed down the Flaminian Way, entering the city by the Porta del Popolo. Trembling senators advanced to greet him, Cicero among them; 'Ah, the last of my friends,' said Octavian.

On 19 August he was elected to the vacant consulship along with an obscure cousin called Quintus Pedius. Twelve vultures flew overhead as he took the auspices for the first time; a happy omen, for everyone knew that Romulus, the founder of the city, had been greeted in the same way. Even this could not disguise what had happened: Rome had fallen again to a military coup d'état. This was clear as the young man began to pay his debts. He rewarded his troops as he had promised. The law necessary to confirm his adoption by Caesar was at last passed. The amnesty offered the Liberators in March 44 was rescinded, and a special court was set up to outlaw them. Cicero left Rome, a broken man, never to return; he, and the Senate, had been duped by the boy Octavian.

It was only sixteen months since Octavian had arrived in Rome, a youth of nineteen with no military or political experience, dependent on the goodwill of Caesar's veterans for his importance, even perhaps his survival. Now he met with Antony and Lepidus on a small island in a river near Bologna. They were come together, like Pompey, Caesar and Crassus before them, to re-order the State. The Second Triumvirate was born. Yet there were two differences between the groupings. The First Triumvirate had been a private compact between politicians, designed to exercise an unofficial domination over the free State; it had been informal, even secret. The new combination was an institution to be ratified by form of law; it was imposed upon – though it did not replace – the institutions of the Republic. (Consuls etc. continued to be elected throughout the ten years of its duration.*) Second, it was born out of war – the three were war-lords as much as politicians, and they had come together for the purpose of prosecuting war. Brutus and Cassius had built up an army in Greece; Pompey's son Sextus held Sicily and the western Mediterranean Sea. There was more fighting to be done, and the first business of the Triumvirate was to make Italy ready for war.

Caesar's faction had already won one civil war; they were now compelled to fight another. They had seen Julius triumph, and they had seen him destroyed by those he had spared. They were in no mood, even had they been so temperamentally inclined, to repeat his experiment of clemency. The new round of war would open with a return to the savage methods of the struggle between Sulla and Marius: proscriptions.

There was strong reason for ruthlessness, compelling to desperate men. War was impossible without confiscation of property; such confiscations required the exercise of dictatorial power. The proscriptions were an exercise in persuasion; terror used as an instrument of policy. The lists of the proscribed were well publicized. Opportunity was given for escape. Clearly the war-lords were more anxious for the property of their victims than for their lives. Exceptions to this generalization existed of course, of which Cicero was the most prominent. The old man, so often accused of vacillation, had crowned his career with a campaign of the utmost commitment. His attacks on Antony had been violent, unforgivable; they ring down the centuries, colouring Antony's record for all time. Antony was determined he should die. Octavian, whom he had befriended, made no effort to save him; that epigram had revealed how shallow was Cicero's commitment to him.

The proscriptions remain the blackest stain on Octavian's record; they seemed worse in him than in Antony, for there was a cold calculation about the young man's actions lacking in his senior. A hundred and thirty senators fell out of three hundred proscribed. Three thousand members of the equestrian order and of leading men from the Italian municipalities had been named; there is no record of the number actually slain. Land was seized from eighteen prosperous Italian cities; a revolutionary exchange of property.

---

* Though in fact nominated, even years in advance, by the Triumvirs.

The only defence for the proscriptions is 'reason of State'; identifying themselves with the State, the Triumvirs took such action as they deemed necessary to furnish the material for successful war. Bearing in mind how Caesar had been murdered by men to whom he had shown clemency, they knew also what fate would befall them should they meet with defeat.

Having thus secured their power and finances in Italy, Antony and Octavian led twenty-eight legions against the Liberators, Brutus and Cassius, in Greece. In two battles at Philippi the Republican cause was irretrievably destroyed. Caesar's revenge was complete. The glory in these battles went to Antony rather than to Octavian, who was a sick man during most of the campaign. In any case he was no military genius, a fact which makes his career all the more remarkable.

After Philippi they divided the interests of the Empire unequally. Antony retained the proconsulship of Transalpine Gaul, and took over the Narbonne province. (Cisalpine Gaul became part of Italy.) Octavian took Africa and Spain and also, in theory, Sicily and Sardinia, which were however actually held by the condottiere Sextus Pompey. Of the eleven legions they kept under arms Antony took six, Octavian five. Antony's military position was superior, however, for there were over twenty other legions at his disposal in Gaul, a far stronger force than Octavian had in Spain.

They also divided the tasks confronting the new government. These may be categorized as follows. First, they had to demobilize the bloated military establishment and satisfy the disbanded soldiers with land and gratitudes. That meant restoring the revenues of the State. Then they had to crush the remaining disaffection, in particular that of Sextus Pompey to whom the broken Republican remnants were rallying. They had also to re-establish Roman power and prestige, which were badly shaken in the East, and defend the vulnerable frontier there. Antony undertook this last task, which offered glory – his mind was already turning to Caesar's postponed war against Parthia which would avenge Crassus and bring back the Eagles he had lost at Carrhae. Octavian was left with the difficult and certainly unpopular job of tackling the Italian land problem.

It might seem that Antony, clearly the senior partner, had outwitted Octavian. To Antony the chance of power and glory; to Octavian the odium of reconstruction, which inevitably meant the dispossession of many and general disaffection. Moreover, despite the Triumvirate, Octavian did not hold supreme power in the Italy where he had to work. That had to be shared with the Senate and the traditional magistrates. He had 100,000 veterans to re-settle; the disaffected soon found a willing audience in Antony's brother, Lucius, consul in 42, Antony's wife, the powerful and violent Fulvia, and even Lepidus. Friction was imminent.

Nevertheless, against this unpromising background, Octavian pursued the work of reconstruction. Where State land was available, the business was simple, but little State land was free. Accordingly Octavian marked down nineteen Italian municipalities and confiscated one-third of their estates for his re-distribution. Compensation was promised, though the ejected had frequently long enough to wait since Octavian was short of the funds which Antony was supposed to be raising from the East. In addition, there were further confiscations from such obstinate adherents of the Republican party as had somehow escaped the proscriptions. Octavian walked a narrow line: on the one hand he had to satisfy the legitimate aspirations of his soldiers; on the other he did not dare, and had no desire, to alienate the Italians, on whose support he already saw the stability of the State depending. In this work he displayed a supreme administrative competence that distinguished him from Antony.

Such competence alarmed Antony's family. Protesting that Octavian had favoured his own veterans at the expense of Antony's, Fulvia and Lucius appealed to arms. They raised eight legions. Octavian may have welcomed this recourse to war; it gave him the chance of at last fixing his grip on Italy. He despatched Agrippa, his closest friend and lieutenant, after Lucius. Agrippa drove the enemy into the hill-town of Perugia. The siege lasted throughout a harsh winter (41/40). Agrippa's tactics of investment recalled Julius' at Alesia; no doubt there were old Caesarean centurions who had fought there and could offer reminiscent advice. When the town fell Octavian spared the Antonian leaders – Lucius indeed was made Governor of Spain. He had no choice over this, no desire to break yet with Antony. But the Republican remnants and senatorial refugees who had rallied to Lucius *faute de mieux* were put to death, and the town was burned and its lands confiscated. Octavian was demonstrating his mastery of Italy.

Antony meanwhile had been reorganizing the East with his eye on the Parthian war. First he had to make sure that the client kings, through whom Rome exercised indirect rule over large territories (rather as the British Raj used native princes in India), were obedient to the Triumvirs. Only when authority had been perfectly secured in this way could he turn farther east. Among these client states was Egypt, whose queen, Cleopatra, he summoned to meet him at Tarsus in the late summer of 41.

They already knew each other well, for Antony had been in Egypt with Julius after Pharsalus. They had met also when Cleopatra had lived in Rome as Caesar's mistress. But she had never turned her remarkable attentions to him; they had been reserved for his master. Now, with Caesar dead, politics – Cleopatra's keen awareness of the interests of Egypt – dictated that she set out to captivate Antony, whom she took, understandably, to be the new ruler of the Roman Empire. Her arrival at Tarsus was meticulously and splendidly stage-managed. Shakespeare's description of her progress up the River Cydnus in a barge is derived from Plutarch and remains one of the great set-pieces of literature. Pointless to paraphrase it; Antony fell. While Fulvia and Lucius starved and froze in Perugia, assailed by the leaf-stripping Tramontana wind, Antony reclined on Egyptian cushions, feasting. Probably he knew nothing of the Perugian campaign till it was well advanced. He could not fail to be displeased; the action of his wife and brother was purest folly. It had a further unfortunate consequence; Octavian made it his excuse for seizing Gaul and assuming command of its legions. Suddenly Antony's position seemed

Part of a mosaic found at Praeneste, representing the Nile and other
Egyptian scenes

precarious, as all the West, save for the islands held by Pompey, and Africa allotted to Lepidus, came under Octavian's sway.

At once Antony sailed for Italy to restore the situation. First refused entry at Brindisi (by Octavian's orders as he thought) he then landed troops and began to manoeuvre through southern Italy. Octavian despatched an army against him. All Italy paused, dismayed. It seemed as if the accursed Civil War was about to break out again, this time within the Caesarean faction and in Italy itself: new war, new proscriptions, new seizures of land; all were imminent. Even the soldiers were reluctant to fight: it was needless; what was to be gained? Diplomacy saved the moment. Maecenas, on Octavian's part, and Asinius Pollio, on Antony's, averted hostilities. A new agreement, the Treaty of Brindisi, was formalized. Octavian kept the Gallic provinces, Antony the East; slight unmeritable Lepidus, still hovering on the fringes of power, trusted by neither of his colleagues, yet still a buffer, still a means of holding a section of the nobility, was confined in Africa, though the time was not far distant when he could be dispensed with. Antony warned Octavian that his old friend Salvidienus Rufus was plotting against him; Octavian, grateful, put him to death. The new compact was sealed by a marriage alliance. The unspeakable Fulvia had fortunately died; Antony therefore married his colleague's much-loved sister Octavia. The news was greeted with joy: Virgil's *Fourth Eclogue*, written that year, looked forward to a Golden Age to be heralded by the birth of a prince, possibly the looked-for offspring of this marriage.

Slowly, clarity was emerging. That did not mean that problems were disappearing; rather that, after the utter confusion of the late forties, it was becoming possible to identify them. Octavian, first simply fighting desperately for position, had now a goal in sight: power, peace and prosperity. The boy was becoming the representative of what all Italy longed for: the restoration of a fruitful order. His prestige steadily grew: in 42 the Senate had been persuaded to declare Julius a god; Octavian was now therefore *divi filius*, son of a god.

His character, still in many respects inscrutable, was becoming clearer. He had a calm, a resolution and resilience, beyond his years. He displayed fortitude in adversity and was ever quick to snatch advantage from a new development. In tenacity of purpose he may be compared to William of Orange in his long struggle against Louis XIV, but he had a charm of character which William lacked. With this went a capacity to win friends and retain them – Salvidienus was an exception. No soldier himself, he knew how to use military genius like Agrippa's, and how to do so without losing respect; that was a mark of character too. Not without personal vanity and conceit in small matters – the *Res Gestae*, the account of his reign which he drew up at the very end of his life lists all the honours accorded to him – he had yet already shown a grasp of reality, firmly rooted in a common sense that was rare. Astonishing how he never over-reached himself, even in these tyro years; and he was still only twenty-three when the Treaty of Brindisi was made. Yet he also allowed himself warm affections. He might be head of a party, but he longed to be head of a family too. His first two marriages were brief, political, loveless affairs. Clodia, Fulvia's daughter by her first husband the scoundrel Publius Clodius, he had married when she was scarcely nubile; the marriage had been dissolved unconsummated. Then he had allied himself to the elderly Scribonia, previously married to two ex-consuls; it was an alliance that won him political influence. She bored and irritated him. Eventually, 'I divorced her,' he said, 'because she nagged me.' (In fact on the day when she bore his daughter, Julia.) But a more important reason had emerged. Octavian had fallen in love.

The girl was only nineteen, already married, mother of one child (the future Emperor Tiberius) and pregnant of another. She was called Livia. Her husband was Ti. Claudius Nero, member of a great aristocratic house: and she was indeed a Claudian herself. Nero had been a Pompeian, an obstinate Republican who had even fought at Perugia. It didn't matter: Octavian was in love. Livia was beautiful, intelligent and wise. They married, and she gave birth to a son three days later. (There were those of course who claimed Octavian was the father, but that was impossible.) They remained in love for fifty years. Octavian wasn't always faithful – Romans did not regard the sexual act as of very great importance – but he never lost his love and respect for her, a respect without which true married love is perhaps impossible. He consulted her on political as well as family matters. The tone of the surviving correspondence has the easy intimacy of equals accustomed to discuss whatever is important to either. There were political advantages too, though they were not the cause of the marriage. Livia belonged to the highest aristocracy; she brought many conservative families into her new husband's party. As virtuous as she was beautiful, Livia was a great woman; she was however to be horribly traduced, and portrayed as insensately ambitious in the advancement of her own children, Tiberius and Drusus. In old age, after her husband's death, she may have become difficult. Tiberius certainly resented her attempts to interfere in the management of affairs, and eventually stopped seeing her. In her prime however she was worthy of the love Octavian gave her. Unfortunately, modern impressions of her too often derive from Robert Graves' *Claudius* books; the figure presented there is a compound of venomous and unhistorical slanders.

Octavian had met her while engaged on the unfinished business of the West, dealing with Sextus Pompey. The son of the man who had cleared the Mediterranean of pirates had in effect become one himself. From his Sicilian stronghold he could dominate the western seas. Most dangerous of all, he lay across the route that brought Egyptian corn to Italy. Without the assured supply of corn, political stability was impossible in Rome. It was necessary to deal with Pompey.

The Triumvirs tried diplomacy first. Meeting him near the promontory of Misenum in the Bay of Naples in 39, they offered terms: a proconsular command over Sicily, Sardinia, Corsica and Achaea (the Greek Peloponnesus) for five years; a consulship after that. Those Republican partisans who had taken refuge with him were to be pardoned, Livia's ex-husband among them. It was a compromise, a

Livia as a priestess: a statue found at Pompeii

buying of time, that everybody recognized as offering no lasting solution. The conference provides the memorable scene in Shakespeare's *Antony and Cleopatra* when Pompey's lieutenant, Menas, offers to kidnap and murder the Triumvirs on his master's behalf; and Pompey's nerve fails. Psychologically true, since politics at this level did amount to a matter of nerve, the old analogy with poker holding good. At any rate, Menas, convinced by Pompey's scruples that he had backed a loser, soon deserted him, handing over Corsica and three legions to Octavian.

That was the prelude to Octavian's last major campaign in the West. The war with Pompey lasted three more years. (In the course of it the Triumvirate, which had technically lapsed in 38, was prolonged for another five years.) Antony was busy in the East (with unsuccessful invasions of Parthia, in 40 and 36), though he sent some ships in exchange for the promise of legions; a promise not fulfilled. After an initial disaster in 38 when he lost half his fleet, Octavian relied principally on Agrippa to manage the war. Reversals were at first frequent. Lepidus was summoned from Africa to assist, in 36 landing twelve legions in western Sicily. Intensive combined operations followed; and Octavian suffered yet another naval defeat. At last Pompey, finding Sicily slipping from him, risked all on a major sea battle, in which Agrippa triumphed, thanks partly to a new device called the harpax, a grapnel shot from a catapult. Sextus fled to the East, where he was eventually put to death on Antony's command.

The sequel clarified Western politics still more. Many of Pompey's legions had surrendered to Lepidus, who accordingly now found himself apparent master of no fewer than twenty-two legions – almost a hundred thousand men. In the seven years since the Triumvirate had first been formed, Lepidus had felt himself to be losing influence. The noblest-born and most experienced of the three, he had been condemned by character and capacity to a subsidiary role. These new circumstances seemed to offer him a chance of reassertion. He claimed possession of Sicily, and ordered Octavian to leave. Such a command from such a man could be disregarded, and Octavian called his fellow-Triumvir's bluff. Troops began to trickle from Lepidus, whose power was suddenly revealed as being without substance and who had to throw himself on his rival's mercy. The incident is instructive: the material advantage had lain with Lepidus, the moral with Octavian – and the moral prevailed. Lepidus was allowed to live and retire into private life. Octavian permitted him to retain the great honorific position of *pontifex maximus*, a shrewd move: nothing could have better displayed the young man's respect for ancient Roman tradition than this evidence of his reverence for the supreme priestly office. It was indeed a respect of which he remained proud himself, recalling it in the *Res Gestae*. He could afford his self-satisfaction. The Triumvirate was at an end; and the Roman world was now divided between two masters.

Ostensibly they continued to work together. Each had complaints against the other; different priorities led to accusations of self-interest. Still, while Antony lived with

Octavia at his headquarters in Athens for three years, relations could be maintained. In the winter of 37 however he had sent Octavia, who was expecting a child, back to Rome. A few months later he was joined by Cleopatra, whom he hadn't seen since his affair with her four years before. Now however he needed Egypt's wealth for his Parthian campaign, while she looked to him to promote her dream of a Hellenistic empire based on Egypt. Political considerations therefore drew them together; sexual attraction cemented the bond. Sometime – the date is not certain – Antony married her, according to either Macedonian or Egyptian law. The marriage was not valid in Rome – no Roman could legally wed a non-citizen – and so Octavia remained Antony's legal wife till he divorced her in 32. What is certain however is that his separation from Octavia and his return to Cleopatra marked the deterioration of his relations, never of course good, with Octavian. And the failure of his Parthian campaign in 36 weakened his position in Rome while increasing his dependency on Egypt.

In contrast Octavian's position had never been stronger. When he returned from Sicily he was granted an ovation (a triumph was impossible since the campaign had been undertaken against fellow-Romans) and, more important, the sacrosanct status of a tribune. It was an honour which acknowledged the strength of the Republican tradition on the one hand, or at least the Popular variety of it, and on the other pointed the way to a means by which Octavian could unobtrusively initiate or control legislation. His standing with the army had already been enhanced by his assumption of the title *imperator Caesar*. A golden statue of him, set up in the Forum, proclaimed that order had been restored by land and sea. That was Italy's wish and necessity; Octavian had recognized it early. The wisdom of his acceptance of the Italian commission after Philippi was growing ever more apparent. Italy was now ready to associate itself with him, while Antony lost himself in alien Eastern extravagance.

First though he had business to do on the frontiers. It was a measure of Caesar's success in Gaul that Rome had endured almost ten years of civil strife since his murder without trouble there. But the north-east frontier of Italy was insecure and Octavian undertook a campaign against the Illyrian mountain tribes. It reinforced his popularity in Italy; that frontier had been too close to civilization for security.

Back in Rome he and his lieutenants, Agrippa, Maecenas and Statilius Taurus, began what was to be a lifelong work of beautifying the city and making it more agreeable and more splendid. Agrippa undertook the responsibility of repairing aqueducts and building new ones; no easy task to bring a sufficient supply of fresh water from the Alban and Sabine hills to satisfy the public and private needs of a city that certainly now topped the million mark. The efficient organization of cheap food remained a perennial problem. In the countryside the reconstruction embarked on after Philippi was beginning to be fruitful; the break-up of many huge estates and the restoration of peasant proprietors was encouraging a local patriotism and the elaboration of that idealized picture of rural Italy epitomized in the question posed by the geographer and antiquarian Varro, 'have you who have travelled widely ever seen a land better cultivated than Italy?' The celebration of Italy and of the moral superiority of country life was to find its finest and most mature expression in Virgil's *Georgics* and Horace's *Odes*. Love of this rural Italy was a formidable part of Octavian's political armoury, but it was only formidable because it reflected a reality. Octavian spoke for Italy, its small towns and farmers.

At the same time anti-Eastern sentiment, always strong in conservative Rome, was being exploited. Astrologers and the practitioners of Eastern cults were banished from the city; old Roman shrines and temples were repaired. (In the *Res Gestae* Octavian was to boast of having restored eighty-two temples in Rome itself.) Everything was being got ready for the final struggle.

The contest between Octavian and Antony was personal, a fight for supremacy. But it was more than that, too. The Roman world could not abide division, and their developing enmity threatened that. The West depended economically on the East, on the rich treasury of Asia and the abundant grain of the Nile valley. But the East's dependence on the West was no less great. Only Rome could bring stability, curb the dynastic ambitions of princes, allow the cities to develop in prosperity and guard the frontier. In these circumstances it was not surprising that Romans had learned to believe in their destiny, their imperial mission:

> . . . pacis imponere morem
> parcere subiectis et debellare superbos . . .

('To impose the habit of peace, to spare the humble and subdue the proud' . . . Virgil.)

Octavian's achievement was now to convert the last stages of a civil war into a national and imperial mission. His cause, essentially an unremitting quest for personal supremacy, became identified with Rome's, with Italy's, with, in the fullest sense of the word, Virtue. He directed attention away from Antony, decadent and renegade Roman, and towards his mistress, Cleopatra. Rome, symbol of virtue and decorum, of peace and piety, was matched against the corrupt, licentious and superstitious East. It was a remarkable triumph of political intelligence and will.

In 33, with the Triumvirate about to expire, Octavian became consul for the second time. He would hold that magistracy for the next seven years, always going through the formality of re-election. Even though he could not at first arrange that his colleague was also his creature, the consulship assured his authority in the State, giving him legal command in the city and also of the armies. Next year, desperate for money, he imposed heavy taxation on Italy, risking disaffection. Propaganda helped to make it tolerable; threats did the rest, letters being sent out guaranteed by his personal seal of the Sphinx or by Maecenas' seal of the frog, urgent and terrifying. Italy was in danger from the East and must pay and pay heavily for

Roman galley. The crocodile suggests this may represent one of Antony's
ships at Actium

victory. Though Octavian had discarded the name of Triumvir, he still had legions
to support his personal authority. The taxes were paid.

Then, as a reinforcement, he organized an oath of personal allegiance. All Italy
should bind itself to him, personally, directly, not simply as an officer of the State.
As he put it in the *Res Gestae*, that document that records with marvellous lapidary
exactitude the official version of his history, the Augustan truth: 'all Italy swore in
my name of its own free will and chose me as leader in the war in which I conquered
at Actium. . .' This was the dynast, the revolutionary leader in action; the oath was
a sort of plebiscite. So also Napoleon was to link the French people to his own
person, speaking directly over the heads of the normally politically articulate
classes. No mention either of Antony; it was a national war. All the same, even now,
he showed rare tact: Bologna was not required to take the oath because the

Antonines had long been patrons of the town. To drum up feeling he caused Antony's will, deposited as was the custom with the Vestal Virgins, the most respected order of Roman priestesses, to be published. It horrified the people, for it listed as Antony's principal heirs the children he had fathered on Cleopatra, bastards in the Roman view. (And Antony had already proclaimed that Cleopatra's boy Caesarion was indeed as she claimed the child of Julius Caesar; if this was true, Caesarion, not Octavian, was Julius' true heir.) The will fed the rumours that Antony was planning to transfer the capital of Empire to Alexandria. The Senate responded correctly: Antony was outlawed. Even so he retained support there, and Octavian permitted his friends and relatives to join him in the East. It looked generous; it was prudent. Octavian had no mind to leave dissidents behind him in Rome, and he had no desire to expunge the reputation for moderation which he had recently been at pains to cultivate, by indulging in new proscriptions.

The war itself was brief; of immeasurable historical importance but little military interest. Antony's fleet was destroyed at Actium on the west coast of Greece. He fled back to Egypt with Cleopatra. Octavian followed hard on him, besieged Alexandria and destroyed it. Antony fell on his sword. That pleased Octavian who had no desire to embarrass himself with his defeated rival, colleague and brother-in-law. Cleopatra was a different matter; he hoped to display her in triumph. She cheated him however by having asps smuggled to her in a basket of figs, and dying of their fondling bite. At Octavian's orders the lovers were buried in the same tomb and the mausoleum they were building was completed. Octavian put both Antony's son by Fulvia and young Caesarion to death, but spared the children of Antony and Cleopatra. Egypt was annexed; it became the private possession of Octavian, jealously guarded and administered by his own agent. Its first prefect was G. Cornelius Gallus, a knight. The choice was significant. Egypt was too valuable to be risked to the hands of anyone of senatorial rank; indeed senators were forbidden to enter the province. A mere knight lacked the authority to set himself up as an autonomous rival. (Nevertheless Gallus over-stepped the mark. The elevation went to his head; he was dismissed and ordered to kill himself.) Meanwhile Octavian had laid his hands on what he most immediately needed: the treasure of the Ptolemies, kings of Egypt; his armies, mutinous since Actium, could now be satisfied.

He spent some months tidying up affairs in the East, but in general left most of Antony's dispositions untouched. Learning from his rival's failure in 36 he made no move across the Euphrates against the Parthians; for the moment Crassus would have to go unavenged. The eagles lost at Carrhae and the others, more recently, by Antony would have to remain in Parthian hands. Octavian, showing a realism and grasp of priorities that Julius had lacked, knew there was other work to be done. But first, he must signify his achievement. The doors of the temple of the two-headed God Janus were closed, a symbol of peace rare in Roman history. (They had been shut in the legendary reign of King Numa and once later, in 235, after the First War with Carthage.) In the summer Octavian returned to the city and celebrated his triumph for the victories in Illyricum, at Actium and over Egypt. It was just fifteen years since Caesar's murder. Now, at the age of thirty-four, Julius' adopted son had attained a position equal to his own.

What was he to do with it? He was supreme, but Sulla had been supreme, Pompey too and Julius; they had built nothing lasting. Could the young man do what they had failed to achieve, effect a durable reform of the State? As Sir Ronald Syme puts it, 'the attempts of earlier statesmen had been baulked by fate – or rather by their own ambition, inadequacy or dishonesty'. Now certainly, 'peace had been established. There was one faction left – and it was in power'. But could Octavian continue to control it? Would it break in his hands? There had been a century of crisis, since Tiberius Gracchus became tribune and launched the Reform programme, a century certainly of unprecedented Roman expansion, but also of atrocious internecine struggle. Octavian had triumphed in war, but the real test was only beginning.

Two urgent problems confronted him: the army and the Constitution. Though they were necessarily connected – it was the existence of huge armies attached to great quasi-independent proconsular commands which had wrecked the Republic – they could be tackled separately. Octavian started with the advantage that there was only one army left in the Roman world and he commanded it. Antony's legions had, in the manner of armies in the Civil Wars, crossed over and put themselves at his disposal. Disposal was indeed the word. Most of the soldiers clamoured for demobilization and therefore for land. Settling this new crop of veterans was once again the prime task, urgent and awesome. After Actium Octavian found himself at the head of seventy legions. Had these been at full strength they would have represented a force of 420,000 men. In the *Res Gestae* he claimed that 'about 500,000 Roman citizens were under military oath to me. Of these when their term of service was complete, I settled in colonies or sent back to their own municipalities a little more than 300,000, and to all these I allotted land or made cash payments as a reward for military service.' These figures extend of course over the length of his reign and refer to men whose time had expired naturally as well as to the forty-odd legions disbanded after Actium. To settle these veterans he paid Italian municipalities a little over 600 million from his own resources, and also 260 million for provincial lands. It was an astonishing administrative feat, performed in little more than three years. With the reduction of the huge army and the satisfaction of the disbanded legions came the possibility of a lasting peace.

The historian of the Roman army, Graham Webster, has stated that 'the most important decision made by Augustus was the size and distribution of the army'. He now retained twenty-eight legions, a force of about 150,000 men. They were stationed on the periphery of the Empire: five legions in Spain (where mountain tribes still had to be subjugated), five or six in Germany, five on the Danube frontier of Illyricum, three or four in Macedonia to guard the lower Danube and the Balkan passes, three in Egypt, three in Syria, one in Africa and either one or two in the

Alpine region called Vindelicia. Italy itself had only the nine cohorts (600 men to a cohort) of the Praetorian Guard, not yet based in Rome.

It was to be no longer an army of proletarians; instead an attractive career was offered with regular pay and a retirement bounty. At the expiry of their original period of enlistment, NCOs (the centurions) could remain in the army on high pay or enter the ranks of civil officials as personal agents of the Emperors. Colonies of veterans also formed a sort of reserve, frequently planted near frontiers where they could exercise control and influence over the local inhabitants and deter raiding tribesmen. In addition to the legions were the forces known as *auxilia*, drawn from non-Roman citizens but officered by Romans. The *auxilia* also numbered about 150,000 men, so that the total strength of the military establishment of the Empire was around 300,000. Auxiliaries now enlisted for a period of twenty-five years and – the great attraction of the service – were granted Roman citizenship on discharge.

Fixing the size of the army was one thing; stationing it on the frontiers another; ensuring its obedience a third. Octavian knew well how time and again in the preceding century civil order had broken down when an army commander felt himself slighted or endangered, or simply grew ambitious, and then moved against the State backed by troops who felt intense loyalty to him, and felt also that their interests depended on his success. Octavian was taking the first step to guard against this by attaching the soldiers' expectations, and therefore loyalty, to himself, rather than to their immediate commanders. Nevertheless other safeguards were needed.

Clearly he himself must remain supreme commander. The army was bound to him by a personal oath of loyalty, and the removal of patronage from the generals diminished their importance. Even so he supervised them closely and jealously; only those of whose loyalty he was absolutely certain could retain command; and they were expected to practise self-abnegation. In later years he used whenever possible members of his own family; he had that Italian feeling that family is all you can really trust. He bound Agrippa, his greatest general and closest friend, still more securely to him by marriage alliances. As for the other generals they must not be allowed to shine too brightly. Of twenty-seven men of consular rank in 28, eleven of whom had been designated *viri triumphales* (men worthy of a triumph) and three others of whom might be identified as great nobles in the prime of life, only one, Sextus Apuleius, was to command an army again. That was significant; military glory must be reserved for the imperial family and its intimates. Finally, as a constitutional measure, Octavian retained proconsular command in almost all those provinces where legions were stationed. Nobody else could be permitted to hold independent command of any military force, command that is from which he could not be legally and without difficulty dismissed. That was the rock on which the Augustan peace was founded.

This was part of the constitutional settlement of 27 (revised in 23). Its exact significance had been a matter for intense argument. The *Res Gestae* gives the official version:

In my sixth and seventh consulates, after having extinguished the civil wars, and having by the consent of all attained supreme power, I transferred the state from my own power to the control of the Roman people. For this service of mine I received the title of Augustus by decree of the Senate and the doorposts of my house were publicly decked with laurels, the civic crown was fixed over my doorway, and a golden shield set up in the Julian Senate House, which, as the inscription on it bears witness, the Roman People gave me in recognition of my valour, clemency, justice and devotion. After that time, though I excelled all in authority I had no more power than those who were my colleagues in any magistracy.

So runs the official interpretation, backed up by the imperial historian, Velleius Patroclus, who said, 'the old form of the Republic was restored'.

Certainly normality was back. Vitruvius, in the preface of his great work on Roman architecture, spoke of the Senate and the Roman people 'having been set free from fear'. Even Tacitus, ever suspicious of imperial assertions, Tacitus, who had dismissed the whole period between Pompey's consulship in 52 and this year of Octavian's sixth consulship as one when there was 'no custom, no law', recognized that the events of 27 January marked the end of civil strife and the establishment of civil order.

But as to what had happened and what it signified there has been keen dispute, not concord. Was the Republic restored? Was a monarchy established? Or did the settlement take the form, as the great nineteenth-century German historian Mommsen thought, of a dyarchy?

There is a case for contending that the restoration of the Republic was intended to be genuine. From 27 there was again open competition for the traditional magistracies with elections held annually in the old way. It is true that Augustus (as he must now be called) continued to hold one consulship every year till 23, and he might exercise the right his 'authority' gave him to recommend candidates for other offices; and of course his recommendations were never refused. Still, elections did take place; competition existed; the noble families could be satisfied with the honours they received. It was evident that the old constitution was functioning again.

The Senate, which had never of course been in abeyance but which had certainly been overshadowed during the Triumvirate, when decisions had been made without any Senatorial consultation, resumed its ostensible power. Indeed it was soon to enlarge its sphere of action, becoming a court of law also. Augustus was granted the old Republican title of *princeps senatus* (chief of the senate); but this too recognized his *authority*, not *power*. He took his place in ordinary sessions and spoke frequently in debate. It was natural that, as a member of such distinction, he should claim the right of initiating discussion, like a Front Bench spokesman in the House of Commons; but he was treated with no special ceremony. His speeches were often interrupted; no servility was shown, at least in the early years. The

Roman nobility remembered that many of them were better born than Augustus, and expected to be treated as his equals. 'It happened more than once,' says Suetonius, 'that he would be interrupted by cries of, "I can't understand you" . . . and that, exasperated by arguments which lowered the tone of debate, he left the house angry and was followed by shouts of 'you ought to let senators say just what they think about matters of public importance'. In the Senate Augustus was first among equals, no more; but his authority diminished the sense of equality as he grew older.

Government of the provinces was divided between Senate and Augustus. The Senate appointed governors and controlled taxation and administration of the heartland of empire. (It was this division of responsibility that led Mommsen to speak of dyarchy.) In this way the nobility saw posts of public utility and honour open to them, posts moreover for which they would be indebted to no single person. Yet the division of provincial responsibility in fact showed more clearly than anything else how limited was the restoration of the old Republic. Augustus remained proconsul – admittedly by decree of the Senate and people – of almost all provinces where there was a military establishment; to the Senate, the rest. Political realism could not be more grimly and effectively expressed.

By this proconsular command and the direct oath of the soldiers, Augustus ensured his ultimate ability to control the State. Nevertheless it could not give him legal power in Rome itself; nor in Italy; the power of a proconsul lapsed when he crossed the city boundary. Since 36 he had possessed the inviolability of a tribune (he could not actually become one, of course, because he was a patrician). In time he was to see the tribuniciary power as a means of establishing direct authority in Rome; tribunes could veto any proposed law, and initiate legislation in the Assembly. More important, the tribuniciary power was to give him a direct claim to be the representative of the people; whose interests the tribunes had traditionally guarded. John Buchan has indeed suggested that the mediaeval kingly claim to defend the common people against the baronage in fact stretches back to the tribuniciary power of Augustus.

In 27 however Augustus was still feeling his way towards this. Meanwhile he was consul. That gave him power in Rome as chief magistrate – and he was re-elected annually till 23. There was a precedent for combining the office of consul and proconsul – Pompey had held both ranks in 52 – but it was not an entirely happy one. The next few years were to reveal disadvantages. For the moment it was a power he felt necessary to him. In 28, preparing for the settlement, he had taken Agrippa as his colleague; together they had been granted the power of the old Republican magistrate, the Censor, so that they might purge the Senate of undesirable and unsuitable members, reducing it in the process to just under six hundred members. This was a more workable body; but Augustus still considered a Senate half that size would be more efficient. However the temptation to exercise patronage by securing the elevation of new senators was to prevent Augustus and his successors from further pruning on any great scale.

This settlement of 27 was careful and elaborate. It had been preceded by an edict of 28 which had proclaimed an amnesty and annulled any illegal or unjust orders given during the Triumvirate. It was preceded too by close debate among the leaders of the Caesarean faction. The Greek historian, Dio Cassius, writing in the third century but drawing on contemporary documents now lost, records a debate between Agrippa and Maecenas as to whether the Republic should be restored or a monarchy established. The argument is a fiction, an exercise in rhetoric – there is no evidence that Agrippa ever held the Republican view assigned to him; but it probably reproduces the sort of arguments that were bandied about. The case for the Republic is simple: the Romans loved their old institutions, identified them with the practice of political virtue, and could not be happy without them. Maecenas, scion of Etruscan kings, argued with more historical penetration; his analysis of the situation may be taken to reflect what Augustus and his intimates believed. He said:

> The cause of our troubles is the multitude of our population and the magnitude of the business of government; for the population embraces men of every kind, both of race and endowment, and both their tempers and desires are manifold; and the business of the State has become so vast that it can be administered only with the greatest difficulty. . . As a result our city, like a great merchant-vessel, manned by a crew of every race and lacking a pilot, has now for many generations been rolling and plunging, as a ship without ballast. . .

It would be absurd then to drop the pilot who had appeared on the bridge and saved the ship from the rocks. So he emerged from the reorganization with a new name, Augustus, redolent of religious and primaeval associations, and a modest title, Princeps; chief, or first man. (Properly speaking, the Augustan Empire is called the Principate.) It was an inspired choice, for it avoided the historic unpopularity of 'king', the suspension of the traditional constitution inherent in the title 'dictator' and the military associations of the word *imperator*. It could be translated as 'president', but that word's meaning is so various that its use could have little value; and it is best simply to call Augustus the Princeps.

But, first, a comedy. On 13 January 27, Octavian, speaking in the Senate, proclaimed the restoration of the Republic and offered to retire into private life. The offer was refused; he had, after all, 'first briefed his most intimate friends among the Senators', as Dio puts it. These knew their parts; and, as for the rest, most of them were appalled by a glimpse of the void that might open before them. So followed the grants of honours and offices already described; and he emerged Augustus and Princeps.

The year 27 did not see the final settlement; that was reserved for 23. In the intervening years, Augustus had been mostly out of Rome, soldiering in Spain and compelling the reluctant mountain tribes to accept the benefits of Roman rule. On his return in 23 he first faced a dangerous aristocratic conspiracy, aimed at a restoration of a more real Republic; then he fell ill, handing his signet ring over to

Agrippa as the only man who could replace him at that moment. On recovery he resigned his consulship, the first time he had not been consul since the lapse of the Triumvirate; he had realized how unpopular was his monopolization of the office every year. There were two clear advantages in this decision: it freed him from a good deal of routine business, and, while satisfying the aspirations of the nobility by making the chief post available to them, it would in a stroke double the number of ex-consulars available to take up important administrative posts.

It created a problem however; his legal exercise of power in Rome had depended on the office. The matter was easily resolved. First the Senate voted that his proconsular *imperium* should not lapse when he crossed the city boundary. Second he was granted a superior *imperium* which permitted him to interfere in the administration even of senatorial provinces, and indeed over-rode the *imperium* of any other magistrate. Third, and most important, he was now invested with the full power of a tribune (he was to date his rule from 23, in terms of the number of years that he had held the tribuniciary power). All these powers were granted him by the Senate; and almost certainly they were sanctioned by a law passed in the Popular Assembly.

Augustus had not restored the Republic. That was impossible, for there had never been a Republic to restore. Since the Romans had no written constitution, there was no one moment in their history which could be taken to represent the Republic in full perfection. An attempt at restoration would have been purest folly. What he had done was, by contrast, intelligent and durable, because it was an empirical construction, contemptuous of theory. His authority rested on two foundations: the tribuniciary power which gave him command in Rome itself and gave his rule a popular aspect, and the over-riding *imperium* which gave him control over all armies and provinces. With the tact of a master of propaganda he paraded the first power, which was Republican, and concealed the second, not even mentioning it in the *Res Gestae*; a true measure of the enduring Republican sentiments of people and nobility. His political work, then, did not consist of a restoration of what had existed before the Civil Wars; rather it was a consolidation and re-ordering of what those wars had created, and it was in this that he displayed his genius.

Dangers remained however. Inherent in the settlement was the threat of military tyranny – for such a tyranny in fact existed, shadowing the constitutional state that had been renewed. In theory moreover, it was possible for the army to replace its supreme commander by another, if the first lost its confidence and affections; failed, that is, to nurture its affection and sense of duty. The skill and intelligence of Augustus and his successor Tiberius concealed this peril, and the army was slow to realize its strength; it was not till exactly a hundred years after Actium that, in Tacitus' bodeful words, 'the secret of the Empire was made public, that the Emperor could be made somewhere other than in Rome. . .'

Thus, effectively, would the Augustan façade have screened the truth.

The Principate therefore satisfied the conservatives by leaving the institutions of the

Republic apparently untouched, so that throughout the long reign of the first Princeps they were hardly sensible of their continuing decadence. It satisfied the Italians and the provincials by substituting good government for bad; peace, security and prosperity replaced the chaos of the last years of the Republic. Even Tacitus had to confess its merits – for the provincials, as he admitted, had, 'distrusted the government of the Senate and the People on account of the struggles of the powerful and the rapacity of officials; while the laws offered no protection'.

Few things, meanwhile, are more impressive in Augustus' character than his moderation, his sense of the possible. It marked him out as a greater man than his dazzling uncle: greater because constructive. He cared nothing for the appearance of power – not for him the high red boots of the Alban kings, which Julius had affected – indeed he even disdained it, all the while feeling its reality. So the monarchy rested hidden by its Republican screen.

As an aid to understanding we may look for modern parallels. The American presidency affords some similarity; for one thing, the President may claim, like the Princeps, to be the repository of the interests of the people taken as a whole, against the special and sectional interests speaking through Congress or the Roman Senate. Yet inasmuch as the United States is in no sense a military tyranny, the comparison is inept, and cannot be pushed too far, the American President having none of the arbitrary authority of the Roman Princeps. A closer resemblance may exist between the reality of the Augustan Principate and the location of power in the Soviet Union. There too one finds quasi-autonomous bodies dominated by secret authority: the First Secretary of the Communist Party, though lacking the formal attributes of a head of State, exercises effective control in a manner not unlike the Roman Princeps; the Red Tsar recalls Moscow's claim to be the third Rome. And attempts to maintain that the Roman Republic had actually been restored – that, since the Princeps derived his power ostensibly from the free grant of the Senate and the Roman people, he was a servant, not supreme ruler – may be parallelled, in ironical spirit, by those now accustomed pleas put forward by the apologists and blind enthusiasts for the Soviet system: as, for example in this effusion from Sidney and Beatrice Webb: 'let it be noted that, unlike Mussolini, Hitler, and other modern dictators, Stalin is not invested by law with any authority over his fellow subjects . . . he has not even the extensive power which the American Constitution entrusts for four years to every successive President. There is from every decision an effective right of appeal – this appeal may be pursued right up to the Central Committee in Moscow.' Precisely: in the words of the *Res Gestae* again: 'after that time I excelled all in authority, but I possessed no more power than the others who were my colleagues in each magistracy. . .' A soothing assertion; yet Augustus well knew, like Stalin, that authority is the acceptable and effective face of power; and power clothed can be no less ruthless than power naked.

In 23 Augustus was still only forty; he had another thirty-six years to live. He had laid the foundation of his work; he had now to build the edifice as a habitation in which the Roman people could be given that experience of peace which alone could reconcile the nobility to the loss of liberty, and which would allow Italy and the provinces to bloom in prosperity. He had to create an administration for the Empire, restore the Roman ethos, and establish secure frontiers.

The Roman peace was internal. Though the doors of the Temple of Janus were to be closed three times during the reign, great campaigns continued to be fought on the bounds of empire. Wisely Augustus abandoned the dream of a Parthian war. Crassus' expedition had shown what could be the fate of a Roman army caught by a swift-moving lightly armed force in the Arabian sands. Mark Antony, a general of the first rank, had fared little better in 40 and 36. Enough, for Augustus, to gain diplomatic success. Taking advantage of a disputed succession to the Parthian throne, he contrived to obtain the return of the standards and spoils lost in these campaigns.

The north however was a different matter. First, no land route linked Italy to Macedonia, save the slow tortuous one around the Dalmatian coast; and the whole of the Balkan land-mass was hostile territory, inhabited by warlike tribes and dangerously near the north Italian municipalities. Augustus' marshals waged a succession of campaigns by the end of which his stepson Tiberius had pushed the Roman frontier right up to the line of the Upper Danube; an enormous gain for security. Similarly, to the north-east the Rhine was established as the frontier. For much of the reign the intention was to push on through the wild forests of Germany and fix the line of empire on the River Elbe. This policy was abandoned when the Governor of the German province, Quintilius Varus, was annihilated with three legions in AD 9. Accordingly Augustus left his successor the advice that he should be content with the limits of empire already achieved. All the same Augustus, the Prince of Peace, annexed more territory than any of the great generals of the Republic; it is not the least of the ironies that shadow his career.

War and administration reveal what common sense would tell us anyway: a great empire is never only a monarchy, just as it can never be more than nominally a democracy. Search closer and you will find an oligarchy, the chiefs of the ruling party, regardless of whether this be concealed or open. So Augustus relied on the support and cooperation of senators and knights who had attached themselves to his faction and who demanded their rightful share in its triumph. And he had his coadjutors, of whom Agrippa and Maecenas are only the best-known.

The part these two played in Augustus' life bears witness to the subtlety and depth of his own character, for they were themselves clear opposites; Agrippa, the low-born rough man of action; Maecenas the aristocratic dandy-connoisseur.

Agrippa, soldier and administrator of supreme competence, had become aedile in 33 to help Octavian win the Roman people to his side by a series of practical measures: for example by repairing and extending the system of aqueducts which brought water to the city. He held this position as commissioner of public works till his death in 12 BC. He determined how much water should be allotted to public and private consumption, and assured its supply; and he kept a private squad of slaves to maintain aqueducts, reservoirs, collection basins and drains. On his death they passed to Augustus as Agrippa's heir, and he made them over to the State.

This was an example of the new professional competence animating the Empire. Between them Augustus and Agrippa undertook a great building programme, in Rome especially. It was to be Augustus' boast that he found the city of brick and left it of marble; a fair claim, since the opening of the Carrera quarries afforded an abundant supply of the finest white marble. Among many buildings, Augustus built the Temple of Apollo on the Palatine (long vanished) and the Theatre of Marcellus, which still stands at the base of the Capitol. Agrippa built the first version of the Pantheon, and though the present dome is the work of the Emperor Hadrian, Agrippa's name still decorates the portico.

The same efficiency extended to provincial administration. Republican administration had been haphazard. Lacking in method, it had depended too much on the character and capacity of individual governors. The slow growth of the imperial civil service, originating in the household staffs of Augustus and Agrippa, changed all that. The collection of most taxes was taken from the rapacious companies of private-enterprise tax-collectors. Uniformity was established; the ultimate appeal to Rome, made most famously by St Paul, came to extend its protection to provincials. Taxes were not high, for much of the business of government was still financed by the Princeps from his own resources; it was not till AD 6, for instance, that provision for the soldiers' demobilization gratuities and pensions became a charge on the public purse. In the same way, it was Augustus himself who paid for the reconstruction of the Via Flaminia, stretching north from Rome and across the Apennines to Rimini.

Moreover within the Empire there remained a great measure of local autonomy; the administration of cities continued to be the responsibility of local councils. Indeed the Roman Empire may be regarded as an association of city states. It was partly to maintain the value and self-respect of local citizenship that Augustus was so sparing in his grants of the superior citizenship of Rome itself. At the first census he took, in 28, there were 4,063,000 Roman citizens; at his last, forty-one years later, 4,937,000 – little more than the natural increment over such a long period of peace. This forbearance contrasted with Julius' wholesale granting of the coveted status – and it reflected more than the difference in temperament between uncle and nephew; it also showed the care Augustus took to foster a strong sense of Italian patriotism; the Italians were the elite of empire.

Such a concern also animated his social legislation. For a long time, conservatives had deplored the decline in Roman moral standards. Luxury, vice and all such self-indulgence offered clear evidence of how the Romans had fallen away from the austere standards of the early days of the Republic. Almost inevitably, the establishment of the Principate was accompanied by attempts at reform. (If his political settlement suggested he was the heir of Pompey as much as of Julius, here Augustus seemed to have inherited Cato's mantle.) Nothing surprising about that of course; political renewal is naturally accompanied by moral reform; a common characteris-

Virgil between his two Muses, Clio (on the right) and Melpomene

tic of revolutionary regimes being the attempt to promote a stricter and more
elevated code of behaviour: Cromwell, Napoleon, Mussolini, Hitler, Lenin, Mao,
and on a descending scale Fidel Castro and Dr Arnold: the theme is common —
moral austerity rules.

Augustus was no exception. By a series of laws, extending from the Julian laws of
17 BC to the *Lex Papia Poppaea* of AD 9, he attempted to restrict private

expenditure on luxuries, to make divorce more difficult, to provide heavy penalties for adultery and seduction, and, by privileges granted to fathers of large families, to encourage marriage. If in this Augustus appears as the heir of Cato than of Julius, it was part of his effort to incorporate all that was best in Roman history and tradition in the new regime, and to promote a serious and responsible public spirit among the upper and middle classes. In detail the laws were a failure, as legislation of this kind almost always is; yet they contributed to a revived seriousness, decorum and sense of mission among the Roman people.

For the Principate was a New Order, and as such it produced propaganda that was more than mere bolstering for the new institutions. Augustus, having himself a lofty sense of his mission, worked unremittingly to create a new climate of opinion, in which cause he associated himself closely with the two great poets of the age, Virgil and Horace. Both were brought into his circle by Maecenas, whose chief contribution to the Augustan regime was as an introducer of such talent and as an interpreter of public opinion. (Maecenas himself however was no great advertisement for the new sober propriety. He was a dandy and epicure; his dress was fantastic; and he is credited with having introduced as a novel delicacy to Roman cuisine the flesh of young donkeys. Moreover his passion for the actor Bathyllus was notorious, while the patriotic historian Velleius Patroclus described him 'as going almost beyond the feminine in his love of luxury'.) It was Maecenas who reconciled the two poets to the regime. They both became personal friends of the Princeps; Augustus himself suggested the subject of the *Aeneid* to Virgil, and heard readings from the work in progress. He also invited Horace to become his personal secretary – nor did he resent the poet's disinclination to take the post or allow this to change his regard for him. Augustus went beyond a recognition of both men's usefulness to the regime; they shared his own values, and for this reason their works provide a means of understanding his own mind and interpreting the age itself.

In his *Eclogues* and the *Georgics*, Virgil sang the beauties of Italy and the nobility of rural life, themes echoed by Horace in many of his odes. Both poets celebrated the homely pieties of the country-dweller, and saw mystery and divinity in the progress of the seasons and the working of a beneficent Nature. Augustus, himself of a reverent temperament, felt the beauty of such devotion. Neither poet approved extravagance, whether of conduct or emotion; nor did the Princeps, whose own way of life was of the simplest. But what also inhabited all three was a sense of the glory of Rome, the enduring miracle of the Roman Empire.

No regime has had its origins, nature and mission more finely celebrated than was the Augustan by Virgil. The *Aeneid* linked Augustus with the earliest memories and legends of Rome. It gave Rome and the Roman people a sense of their transcendent mission which had come to its fullest fruit in the Principate: Aeneas and his descendants, fleeing from the burnt towers of Troy, were yet promised '*Imperium sine fine*' – 'limitless empire'. Of even more immediate and greater purpose was the promise already quoted:

Augustus Caesar, divi genus, aurea condet
Saecula qui rursus Latio regnata per arva
Saturno quondam. . .

Such lines were no simple flattery; they represented the sense of what was happening. That was the measure of the Augustan achievement: propaganda and fact could indeed be reconciled.

In 17 BC a great demonstration of how health had been restored to the body politic was planned. This was the *Ludi Saeculares* – games which had been instituted in the year of the Republic's foundation and repeated every century. The fifth celebration should have taken place in 49, but had been prevented by the Civil War. That difficulty could be circumvented, for it was conveniently remembered that the old Etruscan century had lasted a hundred and ten years, so that four hundred and forty years had in fact elapsed since the Games were first held. (This Etruscan connection helped to emphasize the holy and immemorial aspect of the proposed Games; much of Roman religion had Etruscan origins, albeit that the Etruscans were already mysterious even to the Romans, who drew so much directly from them.)

The Games were to have a manifold symbolic purpose:

The ceremony must reunite in picturesque harmony the belief in the regeneration of the world, the social ideas of the oligarchy who governed the Empire, the Etruscan doctrine of the ten centuries, the Italic legend of the four ages of the world, the oracles of the Sibyl which announced the approaching reign of Apollo (God of the regenerating, life-giving Sun, God of the powers of Light, to whom Augustus had built that noblest of his temples in white Carrara marble shining on the Palatine Hill), the recollections of Virgil's *Eclogue* which had predicted the returning Golden Age, the Pythagorean doctrine of the return of souls to the Earth, which taught that after four hundred and forty years body and soul lived again in their former state, and society returned to its former condition. (Ferrero, *Greatness and Decline of the Roman Empire*.)

This last Pythagorean teaching was peculiarly appropriate, for here, exactly four hundred and forty years after the Republic had come into being, the wheel of time had come full circle and Augustus had restored the Republic to its pristine virtue.

The ceremonies extended over four days and were the result of exact preparation and stage-management. For weeks before, heralds had travelled all over Italy calling the country people to Rome. Now at last, under a full summer moon in the Field of Mars (formerly a swamp but now made splendid with temples, monuments and public buildings), the Princeps sacrificed nine lambs and nine kids to the Fates; and repeated a strange archaic prayer to those goddesses who controlled the destinies of men and nations. Then a blaze of torches turned the silver of the moonlight to a deep red and hymns were sung to Juno and Diana.

Next day, on the Capitol, Augustus and Agrippa each sacrificed a bullock to Jupiter on the steps of the great marble temple, where, seventeen hundred and eighty years later, Edward Gibbon 'sat musing amidst the ruins, while the bare-footed friars were singing vespers . . . and the idea of writing the decline and fall of the city first started to my mind. . .' All that day, and for the next two thereafter, games and plays were given in the Field of Mars. At night another midnight sacrifice honoured the goddess who gives fertility to women. On the second of June, again on the Capitol, Augustus and Agrippa sacrificed anew, this time to Juno, in the presence of one hundred and ten matrons from the noblest families of the city; and at night, in a ceremony of the greatest antiquity, Augustus, in the Field of Mars, sacrificed a pregnant sow to Mother Earth, calling for blessings on her children. Virgil had described Aeneas himself performing the same action for the same purpose; here the Princeps was establishing himself as the second father of the Roman people.

The ceremonies culminated on 3 June, a day consecrated to Apollo and Diana, divinities of Light. Augustus and Agrippa offered bloodless sacrifice in the gleaming new temple on the Palatine, and then, in contrast to the awkward Latin of the archaic prayers, twenty-seven boys and twenty-seven girls sang the *Carmen Saeculare*, composed by Horace for the occasion.

Impossible to escape the religious seriousness of these ceremonies. There are those who see Roman religion simply as a thing of convenience, of outward forms which the sophisticated observed while enjoying an inward sense of sceptical superiority. That element existed certainly enough; but to see only this is to be superficial. Practical men like Augustus and Agrippa are never mere actors. The ceremonies had a profound meaning, for without such they would have been only empty farce. Though the ancient temper was averse to theology, it experienced mystery: and from mystery grew, on occasion, devotion. As a young man Augustus had been initiated into the Eleusian Mysteries in Greece; four years after the *Ludi Saeculares*, he became, on Lepidus' death, *pontifex maximus*: Caesar and Pope simultaneously; the same title was to be inherited by the Bishop of Rome. Augustus was not only capable of reverence; he felt also that some divinity worked in, and through, himself. He could not fail to believe that in restoring health to the Roman State he was in tune with the spirits that nurtured the universe; he was indeed Aeneas come again – and the adjective Virgil consistently applies to Aeneas is *pius*.

When four years later the Altar of Peace was inaugurated, the full meaning of Augustus' work was complete; everything that he offered the Roman people had been displayed. On the practical level, he had ended the Civil Wars: he had also established a state so subtle in its lineaments that it could be accepted by all but the most stubborn Republican, and so flexible in its institutions that it was to survive in one form or another for over a thousand years and was to offer inspiration to Europe for even longer; the greater mediaeval dream of a Universal Empire, so fervently expounded by Dante, harks back to Augustus. On the ideological level he had provided a wholly satisfying reinterpretation of Roman history and the Roman world. He was the great synthesiser, reconciling Pompey with Caesar; bringing into being Cicero's dream of a *concordia ordinum*; uniting past, present and future. The appearance of the children on the frieze of the Altar not only very beautifully introduced the child into Western art; it spoke eloquently of what Augustus offered the world: a future. Thirty years earlier he had been proclaimed 'the son of a god'. Now few could fail to see that he was a god himself, though his prudence, good taste and keen sense of the ridiculous forbade him to allow himself to be presented in this way in Italy. (The East was a different matter; he knew the Asiatics' propensity for deities, and was content to have temples built to his divinity, recognizing that Emperor-worship was a solvent of Roman rule.)

Yet no one could have lived less like a god than Augustus, no one more simply. True, he was immensely rich; but his way of life remained frugal and decorous. Even his house on the Palatine, though growing larger all the time, as new wings were added, sometimes by other members of the family, was simple. The courtyards were supported by columns of humble *peperino* stone; no marble to be seen. He slept in the same bedroom for forty years, on a camp-bed. His clothes were made by his wife or daughter. He drank little, never taking more than half a litre of wine, usually mixed with water, and he seldom touched wine between meals, preferring if thirsty a piece of cucumber or a sour apple picked straight from the tree. He ate with equal simplicity. Though his position required him to give formal dinners, his own preference was for the simple food of the common people: not for him the extravagances that we associate with Roman eating. He liked coarse bread, whitebait, pecorino cheese, green figs. Like many busy men he often lived on snacks: 'on the way back from King Numa's palace on the Sacred Way I munched an ounce of bread and a few hard-skinned grapes,' he notes in one of his letters. 'I had a snack of bread and a few dates, when out on my drive today,' he says in another.

His health, which had been poor in his youth, improved as he grew older. All the same he had to take care of himself. He disliked extremes of temperature, wearing as many as four tunics, and a heavy woollen gown and woollen underpants in winter, and always a broad-brimmed straw hat to protect him from the sun. He suffered from catarrh when the scirocco (that harsh south wind that is the curse of the Roman climate) was blowing.

Always handsome, he was frequently careless of his appearance. He so disliked wasting time over haircuts that he would have three barbers work on him simultaneously, and would read or dictate when having his hair cut or being shaved. He worked very hard and his relaxations were simple: conversation with his family, especially the children; playing dice for small stakes; walking; even going for runs and playing handball. He couldn't bear lying awake at night; if he woke up he would send for slaves to read to him.

Augustus as a priest of Jupiter: despite stylization, a very human and
sympathetic portrait

Like all educated Romans he took an interest in language and literature. He had worked hard to perfect his oratory, cultivating an easy and simple style, the style of a man with something important to say. A man of taste, he made fun of the extravagance of Maecenas' way of speaking, and he had no time either for the archaisms that his stepson Tiberius was fond of introducing into his speeches. As for Antony's windy rhetoric, it filled him with amusement: Antony wrote 'as if he wanted to be admired rather than understood'. He advised his grand-daughter Agrippina 'to avoid affectation in writing and talking'.

His own speech was salty and idiomatic. He had a number of favourite expressions which reveal his character: 'quicker than boiled asparagus' was one, 'don't be a beetroot' another. In his desire for absolute clarity he broke a number of grammatical rules; for instance he regularly used a preposition with names of towns to avoid any possibility of misunderstanding. He wrote an autobiography which unfortunately has not survived, and made a collection of epigrams. He also wrote a verse tragedy, *Ajax*, but had sufficient discrimination to realize its faults, and destroyed it: 'Ajax has not fallen on his sword but has wiped himself out on my sponge,' he said.

Like all Roman nobles, too, he had numerous country houses – Rome was considered unhealthy in summer, and everyone who could do so left it. Augustus would spend the hot weather either in the hills or at the sea. He had a number of villas in the Castelli (the Pope still retires there to his summer palace at Castel Gandolfo after the Feast of Saints Peter and Paul on 29 June). He also loved to go the Bay of Naples and enjoyed sailing off that enchanted coast of Siren Land. He bought an estate on Capri, built a villa there and delighted in his visits to the island. There was nothing of the stuffiness of royalty about his way of life; he lived rather as a gentleman of means and good taste. Indeed he detested servility and liked to be treated as an equal, but one whose dignity commanded respect. The tenor of his private life resembled the constitution he had made for the Empire; nothing was overstated, all absurd extravagance was excluded. He would offend no one by arrogance or excessive display. It was, in short, mannerly, distinguished by good sense and good taste.

Though accorded divine honours, Augustus was human, susceptible to the buffets of Fortune (a goddess in whom all Romans profoundly believed). So, for all the religious aura with which he invested it, was the Roman State. The Principate itself was not something fixed. The habit of Augustus' supremacy became ever more deeply ingrained. The length of his days consolidated, and at the same time corrupted, the regime. The nobility grew slowly accustomed – whatever exceptions to the rule might exist – to the loss of liberty. When Augustus died in AD14 the younger generations consisted of those who had been born after Actium, and even many of the older generation had been born during the Civil Wars. 'How few were left who remembered the Republic,' sighed Tacitus. Consequently, for all the

Republican façade, the fact of monarchy became ever more apparent, and accordingly the question of the succession was raised.

The problem was acute. Augustus' position was personal: 'though I excelled all in authority, I had no more power than my colleagues in each magistracy'. Yet a Principate demanded a Princeps; how was the authority to be transferred, and to whom?

Augustus and Livia had no children, a bitter blow to one so imbued with the Italian sense of family as the Princeps; but there it was – his only child was his daughter Julia, born to Scribonia in 39.

She was married first to her cousin Marcellus, son of Octavia by her first marriage. Marcellus was a favourite of his uncle; he had ridden on the right-hand trace-horse in the triumph of 29. Probably Marcellus was the original intended successor; as a member of the highest nobility with extensive connections on his father's side, he could look for widespread support. Certainly Augustus built him up as a substitute son. His elevation displeased some of the Caesarean faction, possibly even Agrippa. As Marcellus rose, Agrippa was despatched to the East on a mission. It may have indicated pique; on the other hand the mission was important; one version of events was that Agrippa was happy to accept the post because he did not wish his lustre to outshine the boy. Agrippa could hardly at that point have been considered as a possible heir – his birth was against him. All the same he had already been attached to the imperial family, his daughter Vipsania being betrothed to the Princeps' stepson Tiberius, Livia's boy by her first marriage.

However Marcellus died suddenly in the critical year of 23. Augustus was profoundly distressed. Virgil honoured the dead youth and the Princeps by 'the noblest lines ever dedicated to an inheritor of unfulfilled renown, when Aeneas in the underworld meets the slender shade with Night fluttering about its brow'. Augustus built a theatre in his memory which still stands, below the Capitol at the entrance to the old ghetto, one of the ruins of imperial Rome to have been made a fortress in the Middle Ages – the top flight is still used as apartments. Marcellus died; and Augustus' own illness that year made the question of the succession critical; the Princeps passed his signet ring to Agrippa, the only possible choice. Augustus knew well enough how reluctant the nobility would be to accept this plebeian upstart; yet who else could command the support of the armies? There was no adult male within the family itself. A solution was found; Agrippa must enter the inmost ring of the family circle. Accordingly, at the age of forty, he was married to the sixteen-year-old Julia, becoming his old friend's son-in-law. It was a strange but necessary alliance: the girl was flighty and loved luxury and parties; yet politics required it. It seemed to work. They had five children – Gaius, born in 20; Lucius three years later; Julia; Agrippina; and Agrippa Postumus. Augustus was delighted; the swelling family appealed to all his strongest instincts as a man as well as a politician. He adopted the two boys, Gaius and Lucius, to ensure that they should be his heirs; they thus became simultaneously sons and grandsons. The proposed course was now clear. Agrippa was granted the tribunician power in 17 and an *imperium* over the provinces on the same terms as the Princeps. In effect he was co-Regent; but Augustus held the greater authority. For the moment the question of the succession was resolved. If Augustus died, Agrippa would step into his place, for he already held the same legal powers. That would ensure the eventual succession of Gaius. By the time the boy was an adult Agrippa would be an old man, happy to associate him in the regency on similar terms before handing over the reins of power to him; after all Gaius and Lucius were his own children by blood. It was both neat and satisfactory.

It didn't work out like that. First Agrippa died, in 12, when Gaius was only eight and Julia was pregnant with their last child (hence his name, Agrippa Postumus). A new arrangement was necessary. Augustus himself was fifty-two, the same age as Agrippa, though his health, so poor in youth, was now generally good. He turned to his stepsons, Tiberius and Drusus. Both were now in their late twenties and showing military and administrative ability.

Both were married; Tiberius to Agrippa's daughter Vipsania, Drusus to Antonia, daughter of Mark Antony and Octavia. Vipsania was dispensable; since her father was dead the marriage no longer possessed any political value. Showing the ruthlessness of a *mafioso*, which always survived beneath his benign demeanour as Princeps, Augustus commanded Tiberius to divorce his wife and marry Julia. He was to take the place of Agrippa. Reluctantly Tiberius obeyed. The arrangement subsisted. Tiberius stood out as the support of his stepfather, now also his father-in-law, and as the protector of his stepsons. He received the tribunician power in AD 6 for a period of five years.

Then Tiberius rebelled. He refused his stepfather's order to take up a command in Armenia and, pleading that he was weary of public life, retired to Rhodes. (The reasons for this withdrawal are fully discussed in the next chapter.) Augustus was angry and tried to make him change his mind, but eventually had the good sense to accept Tiberius' stubbornness. Anyway, the boys were growing up; for the moment, however inconvenient, the Empire could manage without Tiberius. To honour the boys on the years of their introduction into public life, Augustus accepted the consulship in 5 and 2 BC. Gaius and Lucius were named as *principes iuventatis*: 'princes of the youth movement.' This was an association of the sons of the equestrian order, designed to encourage morality, patriotism and public spirit. It was the sort of organization that self-consciously imperial movements tend to spawn: Boy Scouts, public schools' OTC, Hitler Youth, the Soviet Pioneers or Komsomol, the Fascist Giovanezza. Nothing could have made it clearer than this elevation how the Principate was moving towards royal status.

Yet again, however, Augustus was to be defeated by events. The young men died within three years of each other. It was a shattering blow, which turned him into an old man. Not only were his political hopes dashed, but his love for the boys had been his mainspring in the last twenty years. He had always enjoyed the company of children, and liked to have them around him – like many Italians he made a cult of the child. He doted on the boys: 'Light of my eyes,' he wrote to Gaius in AD 2, 'I miss you desperately, especially on a day like this. Wherever you are I hope that you have kept my birthday in health and happiness, for, as you know, I have passed the grand climacteric, which for us old men is the sixty-third year. I have prayed to the gods that I may spend the time that is left to me in a prosperous Rome while you are playing the man and are learning to take up my work.'

He never fully recovered from their deaths. These years of Tiberius' absence were politically troubled too, and disturbed by scandal. Men became restive as the Princeps aged. His old coadjutors were dead, and he had lost touch. There was a new temper; the sense of relief at the passing of the Civil Wars, and the high sense of purpose that this relief had engendered, were fading. Virgil had been dead for almost twenty years; the new fashionable poet was Ovid. Not for him moral exhortations and the consciousness of a high calling; on the contrary, his most popular poem, 'The Art of Love', scoffs at morality and at seriousness in anything except the sexual chase. Augustus detested the work, but Ovid spoke for fashionable Roman society. And one leader of society whom he delighted was the Princeps' daughter, Julia.

Julia was a product of affluence, one who, living for pleasure, found simple pleasures stale; she demanded ever more intense excitement. Her appetite for sex grew, and grew coarser with the years. She had found satisfaction in none of her marriages. Marcellus had died when she was only sixteen. Agrippa, twenty-four years older than she, had given her five children, but little else. He had often been away, and in his absence Julia sought lighter pleasures. This pattern was repeated in her marriage with the dour Tiberius, who may himself have been sexually timid or at least inactive. When he went off to Rhodes, Julia abandoned any restraint. She took part in orgies held in the Forum itself, and even solicited passers-by like any common prostitute.

That was bad enough, and unspeakably displeasing to one of Augustus' sense of dignity. It flew in the face of his own attempts to improve morality; it mocked him. There was worse to come however. For a long time no one dared to tell Augustus what was happening. When they did, he acted. It was not just a question of immorality; the names of Julia's lovers spoke of a graver danger – Iullus Antonius, grandson of Mark Antony, a young member of the Gracchus family, the aristocracy that he had thought subdued. Possibly the wretched Julia was being used for political purposes. The plot revealed (it is said by Livia), Augustus was ruthless. Julia was banished to the island of Pandateria off the Campanian coast, where she was kept under close arrest and forbidden wine and male company. Antonius was compelled to kill himself; other lovers were exiled. It was bitter fruit for the Princeps. Hearing that one of Julia's freedwomen, called Phoebe, had hanged herself, he remarked 'I should have preferred to be Phoebe's father.' When a delegation from the people begged that Julia be recalled, he said, 'if you mention this matter again, may the Gods curse you with daughters as lecherous as mine; or let your wives turn out that way also.'

That was 2 BC, when the boys were still alive and his hopes rested securely in

The Boscoreale cup: on one side, Augustus is shown as master and pacifier
of the world; on the other, he receives the submission of barbarians

them. He himself put through the divorce of Tiberius and Julia. The award the same year of the title 'Father of the Country', given him by the Senate, was some compensation for the misery of the Julia affair. But family troubles continued to afflict him. Lucius died in AD 2, Gaius in 4. His other grandchildren proved disappointing: the younger Julia followed her mother's career, and in 9 she too was exiled. The last grandson, Agrippa Postumus, proved to be a brute and mentally deficient; he too had to be confined. Only Agrippina, married to Drusus' son Germanicus, seemed to be turning out well. But Germanicus, born in 15 BC, was far too young to be considered as a successor: their first children, Nero and Drusus, were born only in AD 6 and 7.

In the circumstances Augustus turned back to Tiberius, the one man of proven talent. He could no longer be regarded as a makeshift or temporary Princeps, someone who could hold the fort till Augustus' grandsons were old enough. And so, to mark his recognition of the inevitable, and prepare the transition of power, Augustus, in AD 4, adopted Tiberius as his son, and had him granted tribunician

Cameo: the 'Gemma Augustea'. Augustus is shown seated beside Rome, crowned by Cybele and attended by Neptune and Fortuna. The young Germanicus stands to his right, while Tiberius is descending from a triumphal chariot

power for ten years (the previous grant had lapsed and had not been renewed). All the same his hankering for the succession of his own blood persisted – Tiberius was compelled to adopt Germanicus at the same time, even though he already had a son of his own, Drusus, Vipsania's child; at least Germanicus was married to Agrippina, and their children were therefore in direct descent from Augustus.

Tiberius was badly needed. Augustus, never a great soldier, had not for a long time been able to withstand a campaign, and there was trouble in the north. The Germans were restive, and in 6 a revolt broke out in the recently conquered Danube province of Pannonia. It took Tiberius three hard years' fighting in suppress it. No sooner was that done than Varus rashly led his legions into the reign's greatest disaster in the German forests. There was alarm in Rome; fears of a coup d'état; Augustus ordered the Praetorian Guards to parade the city by night. He himself took the defeat bitterly to heart, leaving his beard and hair untended as a sign of grief. Yet, within two seasons' campaigning the good sense, thoroughness and exemplary resolution of Tiberius had restored calm and order in the north. The lesson was learned, however; it was Varus' disaster which led Augustus to append a note to his testament that the Empire should be confined within the existing frontiers. It was a decision that Tiberius was to regard as binding.

Augustus was an old man now and it was clear that he was failing. After Tiberius had celebrated his triumph, he was joined with his father in the management of the Empire, as Agrippa had been almost thirty years earlier. His tribunician power was renewed; he was granted a superior *imperium*; and together they conducted a census. Over these years Augustus had been growing closer to Tiberius; he had come to respect him for his fortitude and sagacity; and he knew how much he depended on him. His letters are warm and friendly; the fact that this awareness of his dependence bred such feelings rather than resentment says much for both men. Yet he was never really intimate with Tiberius; he found something chilling in his long silences, and he never ceased to regret his lost Gaius and Lucius: 'since cruel fate has robbed me of my sons Gaius and Lucius,' he had said when adopting Tiberius, and the same phrase stood out in his will. He knew too that Tiberius would have a hard job, for he lacked that conversability that was so disarming a feature of his own character. Tacitus indeed records a conversation in which Augustus discussed other possible candidates for the Principate: 'he had described Marcus Aemilius Lepidus as suitable but too proud, Gaius Asinius Gallus as eager but unsuitable, and Lucius Arruntius as both fit and capable of making the venture if the chance arose. . .' If the chance arose; it was the intention of both Augustus and Tiberius to ensure that it shouldn't. Augustus knew that a smooth succession was necessary if his life's work was to endure; his last service to the Roman people was to achieve it.

Yet rumours of other purposes were rife. It was said that Augustus had made a trip to the island of Planasia to see Agrippa Postumus, and that a reconciliation had taken place. No evidence of such a journey exists, and the idea that he might have considered handing over the government to a brutish idiot may be dismissed. Such rumours were intended to serve another purpose, to breed uncertainty and give the chance of disruption; they are evidence also of the alarm that the prospect of the Princeps' death occasioned. In Tacitus' words, 'a few people started talking of the blessings of freedom. Others, more numerous, were afraid of the prospect of civil war; others welcomed it.' All were to be disappointed: Augustus had placed all the controls of the State in Tiberius' hands; he was the one man the army would accept, and whom therefore the Senate could not avoid.

In the summer of AD 14 the Princeps made a trip to his beloved Bay of Naples. He spent a holiday on Capri, giving dinners and enjoying picnics. His light-heartedness was remarked on. He invented lines of bogus Greek poetry and teased Tiberius' astrologers to say where they came from; he spent a whole day watching games given in his honour. Then he travelled south as far as Benevento, where he said goodbye to Tiberius who was about to set out for Brindisi and the armies in Illyria. Augustus turned north again, along the same road that he had travelled in mixed hope and apprehension in that distant April after the murder of Julius. He reached Nola, eighteen miles from Naples, where he had a family villa. He fell ill, and died there in the very chamber in which, when he was five years old, seventy years before, his own father had died. It was August, his lucky month, the one named after him. Almost his last words were: 'how have I played my part in the comedy of life?' His temper remained cool, sceptical, yet serious to the end. Tiberius, hastily summoned, arrived in time for a last discussion, and the Princeps died, trying to kiss Livia, with the words, 'farewell, Livia, live mindful of our marriage.'

The body was carried to Rome by night, since the days were too hot for travel. It proceeded from Nola to Naples, thence to Cumae, to Formiae, across the Pontine Marshes and the Latin plain to Bovillae in the Alban Hills. In each town the magistrate took charge of the bier and it rested during the hot day in the local court-house. At Bovillae, the family shrine of the Julians, twelve miles from Rome, the principal ceremonies began. The body was now taken under the care of the equestrian order, which Augustus had been so careful to encourage, and on an evening of early September, one of those velvet evenings of the late Roman summer, it proceeded on the last stage along the Appian Way to the Palatine.

Rome had never seen a funeral like it. The great procession made its way from the Palatine, along the Sacred Way, into the Forum, past the Temple of Janus, whose doors the dead Princeps had seen closed three times, to the Rostra where Tiberius' son Drusus, dressed all in black, read the panegyric on Augustus' virtues. At the Temple of the Divine Julius, Tiberius pronounced a second tribute, sober and factual.

On, beneath the deep azure of a September noon, under the rock of the Capitol, where now stands the National Monument to King Victor Emmanuel and the heroes of the Risorgimento, and through the triumphal gateway, now vanished, that led to the Field of Mars. There the body was laid on a pyre on which the citizens threw down decorations they had won in war; a last tribute to the father of the country. Centurions applied the torches. The flames mounted; an eagle was released, symbol of the soul of the Princeps ascending to the gods. At last the fire died, and the great crowd, senators, equestrians, common people, melted away; only the praetorians departing in order. Livia remained beside the pyre, her head hooded; the last smoke climbed and lost itself in the twilit sky, against which the pines of the Palatine and the Pincian Hill stood out hard black in outline. She continued there till on the sixth day some of the leading members of the Equestrian Order accompanied her, all of them barefoot, to place the ashes in the nearby imperial mausoleum, which already housed the remains of Octavia, Marcellus, Agrippa and the young princes, Gaius and Lucius.

A few days later the Senate formally decreed that the late Princeps had become a god, an ex-praetor, Numerius Atticus, obligingly swearing that he had seen him ascending to the skies.

He had found Rome of brick and left it of marble. His boast may be applied to State as to city. The most remarkable feature of the Augustan revolution was its capacity to endure, to shed its revolutionary aspect and appear natural. The constitution he had so deftly constructed from the rubble of Republic and Civil War was to prove all the more durable for its imprecision. Within its framework the nobility were allowed to enjoy the pleasure of self-delusion, the cities of the Empire to prosper in

Seventeenth-century view of Augustus' mausoleum, then used as a garden and summer palace by the Soderini family. Originally it had supported a pyramid and a huge statue of the Emperor

The Roman Forum

security, the majesty of Roman peace, Roman law and Roman civilization to spread across the whole middle world.

Romans, and Christians after them, saw the divine hand in Augustus' work; the habits of peace and uniformity which he spread were to allow the Jewish heresy associated with Jesus of Nazareth, born in that year when a decree went out from Caesar Augustus that all the world should be taxed, to develop into the majestic structure of the Church of Rome. Without Augustus it is hard to imagine that the conquests of the Republic could have survived, and that the Empire would not have broken, as Alexander's had done, into a myriad of petty states and satrapies.

Of course there were losses. The work was indeed imperfect. Born of fraud, violence and civil war, the regime never wholly lost the marks of its origins. Cruel reason of state continued to disturb the Augustan sunlight with its icy blasts. At the end of the Sacred Way still lurked the dank death-chamber of the Mamertine; the

Cameo, showing the apotheosis of Augustus

Reconstruction of the Forum of Augustus and the Temple of Mars

little islands of the Mediterranean can be wet and windswept in winter as they are sun-smacked and parched in summer, and they made chill homes for political prisoners. Still, when that is said, it cannot efface the humanity and reason of the Augustan Principate. True, the enigma of the Princeps' character to the end defies certain elucidation; we cannot say just how the 'icy and bloodstained' Triumvir, controlled and ruthless, transformed himself into the benign father of his country. But we can recognize the profound good sense and humanity of the man, his imperviousness to the potential corruption of power – did ever anyone so disprove Acton's dictum? When all is said and done, his achievement speaks for itself. He was a great man, and a wise man; of later emperors only Trajan may be held his equal.

Tiberius. Pride and sensitivity can be read in the features

TIBERIUS

WHEN GILLES DE RAIS, sometime colleague of Joan of Arc, confessed in 1440 to crimes which included the seduction or rape and subsequent murder of some eight hundred children, he accounted for his atrocious conduct in the following way: he had read Suetonius, he said, and had been so impressed by his *Life* of the Emperor Tiberius that he had succumbed to a desire to emulate him. Such was the mediaeval reputation of the man whom the great German historian Mommsen was himself to call the most capable of emperors.

Nor did it stop there. The first six books of the *Annals* of Tacitus were discovered in 1510. His portrait of Tiberius, a masterpiece of historical writing as dramatic and as trustworthy as Macaulay's depiction of Stafford or Marlborough, immediately delighted Renaissance Europe. The lessons in the arts of dissimulation and pretence, of which Tiberius seemed so great a master, were to the taste of princes schooled by Machiavelli. Though there was an eighteenth-century reaction against Tacitus – Voltaire of course was sceptical and Napoleon called him a 'traducer of mankind' – the Roman historian's view of Tiberius prevailed. Charles Dickens, sailing past Capri in Victorian sunshine, shuddered at the memory of 'this deified beast'. All the efforts of academic historians could not efface the deeply etched picture that the great Roman had presented. At best it was acknowledged that Tacitus was guilty of exaggeration, bias and suppression; that he drew Tiberius, whom he hadn't known, in the guise of Domitian, whose awful reign he had survived. Norman Douglas might write in 1906 that 'no scholar of today, with a reputation to lose, should stake it on the veracity of Tacitus and Suetonius'; others were less certain. Tiberius at least remains what he was to his contemporaries: an enigma.

It is no wonder that he should be so. He was a withdrawn, silent man, given to long periods of brooding; indecisive till the moment of action and then prompt; so gnomic in utterance that Tacitus easily portrayed him as a consummate hypocrite; a

Republican who ruled as Princeps for a quarter of a century; a principled cynic; a man forced to the centre of the stage who was yet dominated by a desire to withdraw; one who showed a love of islands and seclusion incomprehensible to his urban contemporaries; the author of a reign of terror who left the Empire stronger than he found it. There is no single key which will unlock his character.

One has to go back, to look first at heredity and upbringing.

Tiberius belonged to one of the greatest of aristocratic families, the Claudii. His ancestors had been men of the utmost distinction throughout Roman history. Yet for all that, the Claudian reputation was equivocal. They could not be called a typical or predictable part of the Roman nobility. Even their aristocratic enemies had long berated them for pride and denounced them as the oppressors of the people. This Claudian pride resounds through Roman history. There was the Claudius Pulcher for example who took the auspices in his capacity as consul before a naval battle off Sicily. Finding that the sacred chickens had refused their food, he cried, 'If they will not eat, let them drink', and threw them into the sea. The battle was lost. Such recklessness was typical of one Claudian strain, exemplified also by Publius Clodius, the enemy of Cicero and the brother of Catullus' Lesbia. He disguised himself as a girl to attend the Sacred Festival of the Great Mother, from which men were excluded. Sometimes the Claudians did great service to the State, like the Claudius Claudex who expelled the Carthaginians from Sicily or the Tiberius Nero who defeated Hannibal's brother Hasdrubal; sometimes their violence seemed rather directed against it. What was constant was an aristocratic recklessness; they were utterly careless of public opinion, which they genuinely despised. There were indeed two types of Claudian – the haughty and dignified and the wild and violent; it was the same attitude in fact, expressed according to temperament. The Emperor Tiberius belonged to the first category. His pride made him taciturn; to explain himself seemed degrading; consequently communication with others was difficult, and he was frequently misunderstood and as often distrusted.

He was indeed doubly a Claudian, his father being descended from the original Tiberius Nero, and his mother, the beautiful Livia, from Appius Pulcher, who long ago had advised the Senate against an alliance with King Pyrrhus and so gained a reputation for wisdom. Tiberius' father, Tiberius Claudius Nero, was a man whose twists and turns well indicate the problems of trying to keep a footing in a revolutionary era. First a partisan of Julius, he had commanded the fleet in the Alexandrian campaign. Then he turned against the Dictator. After the Ides of March he even made the provocative suggestion that the 'Liberators' be rewarded. He held his ground briefly and was praetor in 42. The following year he joined Antony's brother, Lucius, in his ill-starred war on Octavian. The surrender of Perugia in 40 rendered Nero's position precarious. He fled to Sicily and threw in his lot with Sextus Pompeius. He was however too coolly received for his pride to endure; he departed thence and rejoined Mark Antony. The Peace of Misenum, concluded between Antony, Octavian and Pompey in the spring of 39, offered an

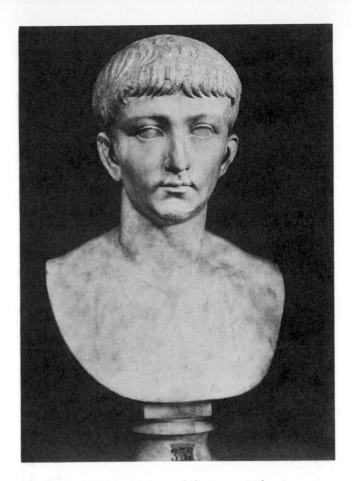

Tiberius as a young man

amnesty for refugees. Nero returned to Italy with Livia and their son Tiberius, now in his third year. In all this there was no sign of principle or political conviction: Nero was fighting for advantage. He lost and it turned into a struggle to survive.

Now came the marriage of Livia with Octavian that was to shape Tiberius' life and eventually make him Princeps. It was of course scandalous, for she was months pregnant at betrothal. Tiberius' only brother, Drusus, was born in fact just three days before the marriage. The suggestion that Octavian may have been the father has to be discounted.

Tiberius' childhood was spent under the shadow of war. His father, who had abandoned all political ambitions when he surrendered his wife, died in 33, and Tiberius, aged nine, pronounced the funeral ovation. Whoever wrote it must have strained veracity and rhetorical skill to find something laudatory to say of that shifting and unsuccessful figure. Two years later Actium ended the Civil Wars in which almost two generations had suffered and been corrupted. But while some endure, others profit. Octavian became Augustus, and his supporters settled down to enjoy the rewards of victory. Tiberius appeared in his stepfather's triumph of 29, riding on the left-hand trace-horse; the position of honour on the right-hand horse was reserved for Augustus' blood-nephew, the young Marcellus.

91

Augustus had, as we have seen, all the Italian sense of family; family also was what you could trust, and therefore it was family that had to be employed in affairs of State. The fact that the Princeps had no sons of his own, only a daughter, Julia, by his first marriage, meant that the succession was open, a matter of choice. This question dominated the next forty years. Tiberius was past middle age before he was accepted as Augustus' heir; and then only with apparent reluctance.

Meanwhile the young must be married and set to work. Tiberius was betrothed therefore to Vipsania, the daughter of the great Agrippa, perhaps as early as 33, perhaps later. The marriage does not seem to have been celebrated till 20, when he was twenty-two. It was designedly a family compact, one of the two by which Augustus bound Agrippa to him, but it was to prove happy. A son, Drusus, was born in 14. All the evidence suggests that Vipsania was one of the few – and the only woman – with whom Tiberius felt at ease. For a man as reserved and secretive as Tiberius, as unwilling to expose, even perhaps admit, his feelings, an understanding wife may be more than a pleasure; she may offer a means of communication which is otherwise denied him. So Macaulay was to stress the part Mary Stuart played in sweetening William of Orange's connections with the English political world. Vipsania could have played such a role for Tiberius; he was to be deprived of her by the demands of dynastic politics.

One place for the young princes was with the armies. Tiberius first saw service in Spain where he was military tribune (a junior officer) at the age of sixteen. That was necessary experience under the eye of Augustus himself, as the Romans strove to bring the mountain tribes of the north under their rule. He learned typical imperial warfare, the kind of thing that generations of the British Indian Army were to know. Tiberius showed himself an apt pupil.

It was also necessary that he acquire experience of civil administration. He was quaestor in 23, having been given the right to stand for each magistracy at five years below the legal age. (Significantly the exception made for Marcellus, now married to the Princeps' daughter, Julia, was evidence of greater favour; he was excused *ten* years' seniority.) As quaestor, Tiberius tackled the problem of corn supply at Rome and the port of Ostia, and headed a commission which investigated the slave barracks throughout Italy to ensure that no free men were wrongfully confined or military deserters harboured. He conducted cases in the law courts too, for it was a peculiarity of Rome that there was no class of lawyers as such. There was no Public Prosecutor either – a lack which was to have a baneful effect on Tiberius' reign and reputation. Tiberius himself therefore conducted the prosecution of one Fannius Caepio, accused in 22 BC of treason for allegedly conspiring against Augustus. Thus early does the *Lex de Maiestate* cast its malign shadow over him.

In all these tasks he showed a welcome efficiency; he was a young man on whom Augustus could rely. The trust the Princeps had developed was displayed in 20, when Tiberius was sent to Armenia on a military-diplomatic mission. Armenia was a state of vital importance as a buffer between Rome and the Parthian Empire. It played an even more important part in Roman-Parthian history than Afghanistan in Russo-British relations in the nineteenth century. Mark Antony's vain intrigues had resulted in the establishment of an Armenian regime hostile to Rome. Augustus now judged that diplomacy, backed by a show of military force, could restore the situation. Tiberius was put in command of the expedition; he was just twenty-two. An internal coup simplified his task; he crowned a Roman client king with his own hands. A triumph of far greater symbolic value followed. This was the restoration by Parthia of the Roman standards lost by Crassus in his disastrous war of 55 BC and of more eagles subsequently lost by Decidius Saxa in 40 and Mark Antony himself in 36. Tiberius received them on the banks of the Euphrates. His success was widely celebrated; honour had been restored; Augustus must have been pleased by the way his stepson was shaping.

Three themes, connected yet capable of being treated separately, dominate the thirty-four years that were to elapse before the death of Augustus and the accession of Tiberius to the Principate: Tiberius' military career, the succession problem with all that implied for him, and his retirement to Rhodes from 6 BC to AD 2.

For most of this time, except those years spent in Rhodes, Tiberius was employed on the northern frontiers of the Empire. A brief record is sufficient. Augustus' aims were first to conquer the Alpine lands whence the mountain tribes were wont to raid Italy and Gaul; then to push the Illyrian frontier north to the Danube. This would link the province of Macedonia with Italy. Success here would make the Rhine and the Danube the boundaries of the Empire. The third theatre of war was Germany, where an effort would be made to push the frontier as far north as the Elbe. All this meant a considerable extension, comparable to Julius' conquests of Gaul.

Tiberius was first employed in a subordinate role, but in 15 BC he set out with his younger brother Drusus to subdue Rhaetia and Vindeliciae, Alpine territories on the south bank of the Danube, the modern Swabia. He did so successfully. After Agrippa's death in 13 he took over command in Illyricum. It was a gruelling and prolonged campaign punctuated by frequent rebellions. Nevertheless the job was done by the year 9. Drusus died that year – Tiberius accompanying his corpse from Germany to Rome, walking beside the bier – and Tiberius had to assume command on the Rhine. The sojourn in Rhodes then interrupted his military career after he had been granted a triumph in 7. Finally from AD 4 to 12 he was constantly engaged on the northern frontier, first suppressing a most serious revolt in Pannonia, then pacifying the land right up to the Danube and raiding beyond; then, with the greatest care and devotion, restoring the situation in Germany after the destruction of Varus and his three legions.

It was not a spectacular career. Tiberius was no Napoleon or Alexander, not even a Julius Caesar. There were no great victories, tactical or strategic masterstrokes; he fought campaigns rather than battles. He belonged in fact to a recognizable military type: the imperialist general who brings law and order to savage regions. Kitchener is perhaps the best-known British equivalent. And indeed a comparison may fairly be made between the two. Like Kitchener, Tiberius was meticulous in planning and careful with the expenditure of both blood and money. No doubt Napoleon would have accorded both the contempt he showed towards Wellington whom he dubbed 'a Sepoy general'. But Tiberius, Kitchener, the young Wellington are the generals an empire needs. The joy with which the troops greeted Tiberius' return in the year 4 was neither feigned nor sycophantic. They knew they had a professional back, one who would not squander their lives in the pursuit of glory – a quality more often admired by historians than by enlisted men.

His carefulness showed itself in the precautions he took when he returned to Germany after the Varian disaster. He strictly limited the baggage that could be carried on any crossing of the Rhine and issued all his orders in writing. Any officer who was uncertain as to their precise meaning was urged to consult him at any hour of day or night. Moreover, he showed himself ascetic, sleeping and eating in the open, sharing his men's privations. One may speculate that he was never happier; there was clearly a job to be done and he knew how to do it. His military achievement was substantial. He reduced the whole of Illyricum, a territory comprising all modern Yugoslavia and Hungary, to complete submission.

Yet there were certain aspects which might perturb and which boded ill for his Principate. It was not that he imposed the severest discipline on his men, even to the extent of reviving obsolete punishments, so much as his tendency, only corrected in his last German campaigns, to withdraw into a brooding seclusion. This is not only a mark characteristic of a certain type of intuitive political or military genius, shown for instance by both Bismarck and Ulysses S. Grant; it was also a sign of a character that was secret and inscrutable to a fault. It was no wonder that contemporaries found him difficult to read; what struck them most was his absolute impenetrability.

He had need of it during these long years. The death of Agrippa in 13 destroyed, or at least imperilled, Augustus' careful plans for the future. It left the young princes, Gaius and Lucius, without a stepfather, and his daughter Julia without a husband. Neither princes nor daughter were safe in that condition. A solution of the most beautiful symmetry and economy presented itself to the Princeps. Tiberius should divorce Vipsania and marry Julia. The fact that Vipsania was pregnant made no difference; she was after all now superfluous. She had been a means of attaching her father Agrippa to the Julio-Claudians, and now Agrippa was no more. Accordingly Tiberius should, as it were, become Agrippa, the support of the regime, the guardian of the young princes, the husband who should keep the Princeps only daughter, the beloved Julia. No action of his reign more completely shows how the *mafioso* survived in Augustus. Whether Tiberius was consulted or not, he obeyed. Doubtless it was presented to him as a matter of duty; what the safety of the State demanded. That he regretted it is certain. He only once saw Vipsania after the divorce; his eyes filled with tears and his gaze followed her about the room. Measures were taken to prevent a repetition of this distressing scene. Vipsania was married off to Asinius Gallus, a senator of high repute.

If Vipsania had understood Tiberius, Julia tormented and embarrassed him. She was warm, greedy, sensual, drunken and promiscuous. She was also beautiful. It is averred that she had long desired Tiberius, a childhood playmate, and had felt an adulterous passion for him even while she was married to Agrippa. It may well be true enough; at that point she had been unable to have him, an attraction in itself. Moreover Tiberius was now in his prime, tall (he stooped a little), broad-shouldered, with a fresh complexion, not yet disfigured by the skin disease that afflicted him in later life; his reddish-blond hair grew low down over the nape of his neck, a family characteristic. More important perhaps was his reputation. He was a mystery and a celebrity, Rome's greatest general, whose silences represented a challenge for Julia. Finally, he would be away on frontier-duty much of the time; any wife of his would easily find opportunity for other adventures. Accordingly Julia wanted him; her wishes chimed with her father's; the marriage took place.

For some years it went well enough. Appearances at least were maintained. A son was born in Aquileia in 10. Presumably he died in infancy. Had the baby lived he would have complicated the succession problem further. Hard to believe though that the child's existence would have held the marriage together. Julia was reckless, and greedy for new pleasures; her pride now centred in her shamelessness. Soon lovers were admitted in droves. She careered through the city and the Forum on nightly orgies. By the statue of Marsyas she accosted passers-by like any common prostitute. She chose the Tribune itself, where her father had proclaimed laws against adultery, as her coupling-ground. For a long time her behaviour was hidden from Augustus; Tiberius knew of it well enough, and suffered.

No doubt he felt it as a reproach to his manhood – an illogical response, even given that he may have been sexually timid or indifferent, a hypothesis supported by the fact that, in later years, he neither married again nor maintained a mistress. However Julia had long passed the stage when any husband could have satisfied her. That knowledge could not diminish Tiberius' shame and resentment; and there was little he could do about it. He could hardly divorce and disgrace the daughter of the Princeps. He drew aside. It appears that by 7 BC they were no longer living together. The failure of his marriage, and the peculiar circumstances of that failure, must have contributed to his disillusion with public life and his decision to retire to Rhodes the following year, even though he had just been granted tribunician power.

No wholly satisfactory explanation has ever been given for his retreat. He himself put forward two reasons. At the time, he merely said that he was seeking a rest from his labours and claimed that he had had enough of honours. Later he explained that he had wished to remove himself from the public eye, so that his own renown would not overshadow the rise of the young princes, Gaius and Lucius. Hostile critics on the other hand asserted that he was in fact jealous of the favour Augustus showed the young men, that he felt slighted, believed his own services to the State had been insufficiently regarded. They would ascribe his decision to 'high disdain and sense of injured merit'. Certainly he had reason to find Augustus' plans for the young princes offensive. Sir Ronald Syme suggests that they must have seemed criminal to

Tiberius. 'Illicit and exorbitant power, *regnum* or *dominatio*,' he writes, 'was no new thing in the history of Rome, or in the annals of the Claudian house. The hereditary succession of a Roman youth to monarchy was something very different.' And certainly there was no other interpretation that could explain the Princeps' plan for his elder grandson, Gaius.

Yet we delude ourselves if we think that human actions can be accounted for by straightforward schematic reasons. The power of the irrational also shapes our conduct. Tiberius himself may have been puzzled by his behaviour. One thing alone is certain: he didn't want to go on. So he stepped backwards into the limelight. Something else is evident too: the Princeps was furious. He had determined that Tiberius should go to the East – there was trouble in Armenia again – and, occupied there, he wouldn't overshadow the young princes. Augustus wasn't accustomed to defiance. Tiberius had to go on four days' hunger strike before Livia obtained permission for him to depart. It says something for Tiberius that permission was granted at all. It says something for Augustus too. He knew his man and sensed that he might need him again later.

Tiberius was probably happy on Rhodes. He had first visited the island on his way back from Armenia in 20. It seemed, in the Hellenic sunlight, ideally sympathetic. He lived there quietly, enjoying the lectures of philosophers and debating with them on equal terms; for Tiberius was an intellectual. He wrote poetry (in Greek) and later, on Capri, his memoirs. He studied the great science of the day, astrology. Thrasyllus, one of the foremost of contemporary mathematicians and, hence, astrologers, was a member of his household, at least from these Rhodian years to the end. Tiberius' tastes were suited to the simple life. He was fond of asparagus, cucumbers and radishes, which he ate with honey and wine. He liked fruit, especially pears. He was a great lover of trees, a sign of a sensitive nature but one which finds the expression of emotion difficult. He had no taste for the luxuries popularly associated with imperial Rome, any more than Augustus had. True, he had a reputation as a hard drinker. His troops, punning on his name, called him Biberius Caldius Mero, meaning 'drinker of hot wine without water'. A less temperate culture may find this affords evidence of Italian sobriety rather than of hard drinking on his part. Pliny says he drank a lot in youth, less later. There were other stories of drinking-bouts and commendations of others as good fellows and hard drinkers, none very well substantiated. Probably Tiberius drank a bit more than most, dourly and morosely; he may even have been given, like General Grant, to solitary bouts. It would fit his character; but evidence is insufficient.

One recorded incident of his life at Rhodes testifies to his breeding and courtesy. He expressed one day a desire to visit the sick of the island. His staff misunderstood his intention and officiously had them collected and arranged, in groups according to their various ailments, in the public colonnade. Tiberius was taken aback, offended and dismayed by this evidence of the working of the official mind.

Eventually he went round the invalids, apologizing to each – even the humblest and least important, Suetonius tells us – for the inconvenience to which they had been subjected. It is a revealing glimpse of the man, secure in himself, needing no public display to bolster him.

The years of retirement slipped away. Meanwhile the young princes held the centre of the stage. Tiberius became aware that he was being relegated to history. His consequence was disappearing, even though senators sailing by the island were accustomed to stop and pay their respects. Soon it became clear that he might even be in danger. In the year 2 BC Julia was at last disgraced. Her behaviour, long notorious, apparently became so overt that even her father learned of it, so the received version ran. Julia was exiled; her lovers, who included Iullus Antonius, the grandson of the Triumvir, were put to death. Their distinction was such that historians have suspected their real offence went beyond immorality; that there was in fact a conspiracy against the Princeps. Tiberius wrote to Augustus, pleading for leniency towards Julia; evidence, his critics assert, of hypocrisy. Yet it need not have been so. Tiberius required no affection for his wife to feel for her disgrace and to see moreover that her fall might endanger him. It severed the link that bound him to the princes, Augustus' destined successors. His letter was ignored. The Princeps himself pronounced the divorce in Tiberius' name.

The following year the tribunician power, which rendered Tiberius inviolable, expired and was not renewed. He appealed to be allowed to return to Rome, now that the princes were established in their careers. The weakness of his position was shown by the appeal itself; he had gone to Rhodes of his own will and there was no formal reason why he should have to seek permission to return. Yet his request was rejected. Livia's pleas on her son's behalf were in vain. All she could gain for him was an appointment as legate for Augustus. As a cloak to hide his disgrace it was transparent.

He paid a visit to his former stepson Gaius, now on a mission to the East. He found him advised by an old enemy, Marcus Lollius. Lollius, a self-made man, had lost a legion in Germany in 16; Tiberius' criticism had made him an enemy for life. Now Lollius enjoyed revenge. He accused Tiberius of tampering with the loyalty of Gaius' troops. All Tiberius could do was request that a check be kept on all his words and actions – a request that was certainly superfluous. But the accusation had done its work. Gaius received the great general coldly. Tiberius returned to Rhodes fully sensible of his peril.

He took what precautions he could. His efforts were directed to convincing Gaius that he had indeed withdrawn utterly from public life. He no longer exercised on the parade ground as had been his custom; he even wore a Greek cloak and slippers instead of the toga. Meanwhile his standing continued to decline. A young blood, one of the prince's entourage, offered at the dinner-table to sail to Rhodes and bring back 'the Exile's head'; boastful but dangerous talk. The citizens of Nemausus overthrew his statues. Tiberius could not doubt that he might not long survive the death of Augustus. It was necessary to strengthen his position before that happened.

He renewed his appeals to be permitted to return. Augustus turned the decision over to Gaius.

Now Fortune intervened. Tiberius, sceptical as he was in most things, had long been assured by astrological science that his future would be glorious. Accordingly, with his fortunes at their nadir, his position was quickly transformed. First, Lollius fell from favour. With him removed, Gaius consented to the return of Tiberius, only imposing the humiliating condition that he abstain from public life. It was a first step to rehabilitation. A few days before the news arrived, an eagle, a bird never before seen on Rhodes, had come and perched on the roof of the house where Tiberius was living. Silently, Tiberius noted the omen. When he came back to the city, he moved his house from the neighbourhood of the Forum to the less fashionable Esquiline Hill, evidence of his compliance with the conditions of his return.

Then in the space of three years the world turned upside down, and Augustus' plans were shattered. First, the younger of the princes, Lucius Caesar, died in Spain. (Tiberius employed his retirement in composing an elegy; unfortunately it has not survived.) Then in AD 4 Gaius also died. Tiberius became again the necessary man.

His adoption by Augustus settled the issue. True, Augustus also adopted his only surviving grandson, Agrippa Postumus, at the same time; but Agrippa soon showed himself boorish and stupid to the point of imbecility, and perhaps beyond; another island was found for his exile. Augustus had accepted the reality of the position: Tiberius was the only possible successor. At the same time however Tiberius was constrained to adopt the young Germanicus, the son of his own brother Drusus and of Antonia, the Princeps' niece. The succession would thus revert to the Julian branch of the imperial family. It was the best Augustus could contrive. Neither of them really had a choice. By becoming the Princeps' son Tiberius abandoned the position as head of the Claudians that had ensured him an independent status and powers. Now he was theoretically in pupillage to his adoptive father. He took his position seriously: made no more gifts, freed no more slaves and accepted no inheritances.

The relations between Augustus and Tiberius have been the subject of much more conjecture and argument. Clearly Augustus never found him *simpatico* – he used to stop chattering when Tiberius entered the room – and, not being a blood-relation, Tiberius was a late choice as successor. Augustus mocked the pedantry Tiberius sometimes showed in his speeches, and he apologized to the Senate for some of his stepson's mannerisms. It is evident though that he respected him, he was after all Rome's foremost general. The fragments of letters which Suetonius has preserved show this respect clearly enough. . . 'if any business comes up that is unusually demanding, requiring careful thought, or that irritates me, then I swear I miss my dear Tiberius more than I can say. . .' 'your summer campaigns, my dear Tiberius, deserve my warmest praise. I am sure that nobody else alive could have managed them better, considering the difficulties and the war-weariness of the soldiers. . .' '. . . if you were to fall ill, the news would kill your mother and me, and the whole country would be in danger. . .' And he wrote too about more intimate matters, friendly little letters about gaming and meals, which suggest a degree of affection. All the same the terms of his will are evidence of his continuing regret at the course of events: 'Since cruel fate has deprived me of my two sons, Gaius and Lucius, Tiberius shall inherit two-thirds of my property.' It sounded reluctant, echoing the remark he had made at the time of the adoption: 'I do this for the sake of the State.' Even that, though, was capable of more than one interpretation. Wasn't it perhaps a compliment? Velleius Paterculus, a historian always favourable to Tiberius, certainly understood it in that sense. Something of the same dubiety surrounds the adoption of Germanicus. It may have been a sign that Augustus only accepted Tiberius reluctantly, *pro tem*; on the other hand, the knowledge that Germanicus would succeed could be held to strengthen Tiberius' position. Tacitus thought so. Tiberius was not by birth a Julian and had never made any effort to acquire popularity. He could only gain from an association with Germanicus.

As for Tiberius himself, it would be surprising if his attitude to Augustus was not ambivalent. With the exception of the years spent on Rhodes, he had submitted his will and his entire life to his stepfather. He had shown himself Rome's greatest general; his loyalty had never for one moment been in doubt; and Augustus could point to no other occasion when Tiberius had put his will or his personal ambition before public duty. Certainly Tiberius had nothing with which to reproach himself – yet the man without self-reproach is the man who will be prey to resentment. Despite his loyalty and efficiency, Tiberius had seen himself set aside for other members of the family, individuals with no achievement to justify his stepfather's preference. At crucial moments he had had to depend on his mother to safeguard or advance his position. Even now, when he had been acknowledged as the heir to the Principate, he found his freedom shackled; he was compelled to adopt Germanicus and set aside his own son, Drusus. Yet there is no evidence that he repined. Augustus remained his model; he never deviated in intention from the line he had drawn. Still, this acquiescence introduced a new element of strain. Tiberius retained the sentiments and opinions of a Roman aristocrat – now that he was in power, for instance, the consulate was dominated by members of the old nobility. But he must know that Augusuts' boast of having restored the Republic was a sham; and he was soon to experience the full weight of that *imperium* of which he could not approve. Moreover he was advanced in middle age; he had passed a long adult life, thirty-five years, in dutiful submission, the mind assenting, the heart reluctant. He owed everything to Augustus, yet Augustus would have played him false; the legacy was tainted.

In AD 13 Tiberius was formally associated with Augustus as a full partner in his *imperium*. The next year the old man died, out of Rome, at Nola. Tiberius, on his way to the armies, was fetched back by news of the illness, and there was probably time for a day spent in talk. Augustus had left instructions for the disposal of his grandson, Agrippa Postumus. The unfortunate brute was despatched on his island prison. Tiberius disowned responsibility for the murder, probably with justice, but it was to be held significant that blood had marked the beginning of his reign.

And a reign, however reluctantly so, it was to be. That fact had to be recognized; and Tiberius effectively did so by calling on the Praetorians to furnish him with a bodyguard. The consuls meanwhile swore an oath of loyalty, and administered it to Senate, equestrians and people. Yet Tiberius still hung back, unwilling to make the final commitment. No man ever showed less eagerness for empire; no wonder the legend of hypocrisy established itself.

The comedy was played out in the Senate that September. The extent of the powers Tiberius already possessed is uncertain. He did have the tribunician power, by virtue of which he had summoned the Senate; and proconsular *imperium*, probably valid within Rome itself. What he certainly lacked was the control which Augustus had possessed over the imperial provinces. That power had been personal to him; Tiberius could not automatically inherit it, but would have to have it conferred by the Senate. A motion was brought to define his position; and Tiberius pleaded that he should not be asked to take up the burden carried by the now deified Augustus. It exceeded his capacity, as it would that of any other single person. The

The Via Appia Antica, along which the body of Augustus was borne back
to Rome

responsibility should not therefore be placed upon one man, but should rather be divided. The Senate shrank back appalled; they could not believe in his sincerity. It must be a trick, something to catch them out. One senator, G. Asinius Gallus, called the bluff. What part would Tiberius want? Tiberius was silent, taken aback perhaps. It was not a matter for him to decide, he said at last. Gallus now backed down. He had only put forward the question to show the impracticality of what Tiberius, no doubt with the best of intentions, had seemed to suggest. The Empire was one and indivisible. He was of course quite right. Yet it is possible to see Tiberius' speech as something a good deal more interesting than hypocrisy; as either a desperate attempt to avoid his fate, or, at the very least, as showing a gloomy determination to make the senators understand what they were piling on him. It was for this reason that he had read out the *Breviarium*, the document in which Augustus had catalogued the military and financial resources of the State. But there was no escape. Gallus, whom Tiberius already disliked (he was Vipsania's second husband, and one of three men whose capacity for empire Augustus was known to have discussed), had made that clear. Tiberius shouldered his load, accepting power 'until such time as you judge it fair to grant me some rest in my old age'. With these words he played out the bitter comedy to the end. From now on he was Atlas.

He would have liked to involve the Senate in the government of the Empire, and to that end he made every effort. He attended debates, he showed courtesy to the magistrates, he spoke often and modestly, he besought the Senators to assume responsibility, referring to them many matters which Augustus would have settled by himself. It was all in vain, he was too late. The Senate had lost any genuine independence of will and become accustomed to subservience. 'O generation fit for slavery,' Tiberius was soon heard to mutter as he left its august portals. He had forgotten, among other things, or had not yet learned, how greatly the Senate had been corrupted and debased by his stepfather; and it is here that the failure is rooted of his attempt to rule as a constitutional monarch.

Other factors operated. First, he lacked the qualities of his predecessor. The Roman nobility had certainly resented Augustus' power; they had perforce accepted it. They might see him as an adventurer, but he was one who had risen from civil war to become master of the world; his authority was something personal and undeniable. Not so with Tiberius. He was an aristocrat, recognizably one of themselves, Princeps by inheritance rather than by achievement – by the will of another rather than by his own volition.

Second, Augustus had employed an affability, a sweetness of manner, that rendered the immediate exercise of his power acceptable. He cast a sheen of charm over the naked fact, he was a master politician, a fixer, an arm-squeezer, a cajoler. Tiberius, remote, austere and awkward, both lacked and despised these political arts. He could not disguise what he was – despite all the talk of hypocrisy and dissimulation – and it became worse when he eventually retired to Capri. It was to be then that the Senate learned to feel its true position.

Finally Tiberius was out of touch with the Roman political world. It was thirty years, during his praetorship in 16 BC, since he had regularly frequented the Senate. A new generation had arisen, with standards unfamiliar to him; even at the beginning of his reign, Tiberius was out of date.

Meanwhile there were more immediate problems, and ones peculiarly painful for Tiberius. The legions had mutinied. The succession was the occasion rather than the cause of the mutinies; nevertheless they were dangerous and shameful to the Emperor. The men had cause enough; they complained of poor pay, brutal centurions, service prolonged beyond the period of their original engagement and the provision of worthless land-allotments in marshy or mountainous country – if they were ever actually permitted to retire. The first revolt, of the Illyrian legions, stopped there. Tiberius sent his son, Drusus, to quell the mutiny. He succeeded by an adroit combination of promises and firmness.

Things were different in Germany. There Germanicus, heir and potential rival, was in command. That gave the mutiny a political complexion, for the men offered the Empire to him. He refused it; the day had not yet come when the imperial title was in the gift of the legions, though it was not far distant. Germanicus instead responded to this gesture with one of equal theatricality. He proclaimed that the soldiers had insulted him, that he could not live in such disgrace; and he held a sword to his throat as evidence. (A ribald soldier offered him a sharper one; he paid no attention.) This theatricality ran through his whole handling of the mutiny. He made lavish promises in the name of the Emperor, without authority. He sent his wife Agrippina, grand-daughter of Augustus, and their children out of the camp amidst great publicity; among the children was the soldiers' playmate and mascot, Caligula (Little Boots), the future Emperor Gaius. Their departure broke the soldiers' hearts – or so it was said . . . that they should not be trusted with their playmate . . . the mutiny ran out of steam, bad weather helping. The popular Germanicus continued in character. Instead of resuming his authority, he encouraged the soldiers to punish the ringleaders themselves, thereby rooting them out without loss of popularity himself. It was not a performance which could have impressed Tiberius.

Yet relations between the two were of the first importance. There is no evidence that Tiberius resented Germanicus or disliked him; he was after all the son of his own brother Drusus, to whom he had been devoted. But there was inevitably a clash of interest; in the eyes of many they could not fail to be rivals. Moreover, Germanicus, cheerful, friendly, handsome and young, was popular with the people. Tiberius, who even despised the Games in which the populace delighted, never achieved or sought their favour. (It is to the credit of his humanity that he disliked gladiatorial shows and attempted to impose a limit on the number of bouts.) Within the family too there were strains, generally identified as between Claudians and Julians. They were expressed by the women at least. Agrippina was intensely ambitious, intensely virtuous, proudly aware of her

Julian inheritance. She at least cast the aged Livia and Tiberius himself as enemies.

Tiberius and Germanicus were at odds on policy too. The Emperor had accepted the lessons of the *Clades Variana*. Augustus himself had concluded that the limits of empire had been reached in the north. Tiberius concurred, not simply out of deference. Experience had taught him that the conquest of Germany would be difficult and of little value. Moreover the resources of the Empire were already fully extended. Recruitment of the legions was still restricted to Roman citizens, in effect to Italians. The loss of Varus' legions had only been repaired with difficulty – the mutinies were exacerbated by the poor quality of some of the recently enlisted men. A period of consolidation was necessary. Tacitus was to lament this: 'peace was scarcely broken – if at all,' he wrote of the reign. 'Rome was despondent, the ruler uninterested in expanding the Empire.' In this the Princeps was wiser than his historian.

Germanicus however disagreed with Tiberius: Augustus' precepts meant nothing to him either. He was headstrong, vain and greedy for military glory. It is a measure of the delicacy of the relationship that for three years he was given his head and an attempt was made to conquer Germany. Accounts of the campaigns of 14, 15 and 16 are hard to follow in detail; the pattern though is clear enough. Each year Germanicus assembled a powerful force, laden with equipment, and marched into the forests. He pursued the enemy, gained great victories and then withdrew, always with difficulty. Imminent disaster brooded round each year's retreat. In the third campaign he still found himself fighting the Marsi, a tribe settled just to the north of the Rhine, whom he had first defeated in 14. His sycophants compared him to Alexander.

Tiberius called a halt. He did so with circumspection, but effectively. Germanicus had achieved great things – that was the public version; privately Tiberius spoke in other terms. Meanwhile Varus had been revenged (the account of the legions' discovery of his fatal battlefield is one of the great dramatic and macabre scenes of Tacitus), and Germanicus was awarded a triumph. He was lavishly praised and appointed to a mission in the East – there was another outbreak of the recurrent Armenian trouble, another disputed succession. Germanicus objected, begged to be allowed one more campaign in which he would bring the affairs of Germany to a triumphant conclusion: but in vain. Tiberius knew that raids, battles and retreats would never conquer the northern forests. Instead, the slow steady advance of an occupying army would be needed; and he judged that the expense and danger outweighed any possible reward. Accordingly, still protesting and loaded with honours and proconsular *imperium*, Germanicus, with Agrippina, proceeded eastwards. Their partisans did not hesitate to say that Tiberius had been prompted by jealousy.

They were soon to have some cause. Tiberius felt his position to be difficult, he distrusted Germanicus – at the very least he can have had little opinion of his judgement, even if he did not doubt his loyalty. He feared lest the young man might embroil the Empire in a Parthian war. Accordingly he took steps to check his independence while apparently leaving his *imperium* untouched. He appointed Gn. Calpurnius Piso legate of Syria; a move whose significance was twofold. First Piso, the son of an ardent Republican who had refused ever to accept the Principate, was a man of high social standing – the Pisones were among the great families of the old nobility – and of fierce independence of mind. Second, the legate of Syria had direct control over four legions, by far the largest army based in the East. Tiberius could therefore rely on Piso, an old friend, to exercise a restraining influence on Germanicus.

The plan, testifying to such distrust, had obvious weaknesses. Yet it is difficult not to feel sympathy with Tiberius. The problem after all was real enough. He did not trust Germanicus' capacity and judgement; yet he could not avoid employing the heir to the throne. He had to accord him public honours, while privately ensuring that the colt was bridled. Yet, however wise, and necessary the conception, Tiberius had blundered. He chose the wrong man in Piso, gave him orders that were open to misconstruction, and so prepared the catastrophe which would work itself out to the ruin of his reign.

Piso from the first took a delight in thwarting and insulting Germanicus. He made efforts to attach the legions to himself by the relaxation of discipline and the scattering of favours, being rewarded by the appellation, 'Father of the Soldiers'. He refused to send troops to the young prince; he disregarded his communications. When Germanicus returned from a trip to Egypt (in itself probably illicit, for there was an Augustan edict which forbade senators to enter that imperial province) he found that Piso had countermanded some of his instructions. Exercising his *imperium*, he ordered the legate out of the province. Piso reluctantly obeyed, protesting that he would lay the whole matter before the Emperor.

Up to this point the dispute had been petty and squalid, but hardly dangerous. Now however Germanicus fell ill, of a wasting fever. He began to believe that he had been poisoned; obviously his enemy Piso was the villain. In the gathering hysteria Agrippina set slaves to work to seek evidence of poison and magic; they found what they had been instructed to discover. Prudent slaves and agents know better than to return from such a quest without satisfactory evidence. No sooner had they done so than Germanicus died. Agrippina and her partisans swore he had been poisoned. The common people, always ready to believe scandal and jealously fond of Germanicus, agreed with enthusiasm. Piso and his wife, Plancina, well known as a friend of Livia, showed foolish joy at the news of the death. Even more stupidly, Piso made an attempt to regain control of his province, despite the prudent warnings of his son. Events moved fast. Agrippina, returning to Brindisi with the body of her dead hero, had a triumphant reception all the way to Rome. The citizens thronged the mourning city; Tiberius and Livia however held aloof and did not attend the funeral. It was in character for Tiberius; he despised public manifestations of emotion. It was a sad mistake all the same. The fact that Antonia, Germanicus' mother, also stayed away from the funeral, counted for nothing; everyone knew that Tiberius had coerced her.

Piso's attack on Syria failed, and he was arrested and charged with treason. His whole conduct since his appointment was included in the charge, his quarrel with Germanicus being deemed part of his offence; most serious of all, he was accused of poisoning the young prince. The case was sent to Tiberius, who remitted it to the Senate. His own position was fraught with embarrassment. He had given orders to Piso, which, if produced, would justify the fact of Piso's obstruction of Germanicus, if not the manner. More seriously, he could not fail to be aware of the rumours. Agrippina's friends had let it be understood that Piso's instructions had extended to murder: some said Tiberius himself was responsible; others favoured Livia.

Tiberius' speech to the Senate was a model of good sense such as he had already displayed in the few treason-trials of the reign to date. Piso, he pointed out, had been Augustus' friend as well as his own; he himself had made him Germanicus' helper in the East. Admittedly things had gone wrong; and the Senate now had to decide whether, having upset the prince by disobedience and quarrelsomeness, Piso had then merely rejoiced at his death, or whether he had indeed murdered him. If he was guilty of no more than rejoicing, then he, Tiberius, would be content with withdrawing his friendship from him and closing his doors to him henceforth. It was not fitting that a ruler should use his power to avenge private wrongs. If however Piso had murdered Germanicus, it would be the Senate's duty to give proper satisfaction to the State and to the imperial family. He then asked them to consider the other charges against Piso: bribery of the troops and incitement to mutiny, and making war to recover his province; he urged too that the trial be conducted fairly and energetically. Finally he told the Senate to disregard his own tears and those of Drusus, his son; to disregard also any slanders invented against them.

He could not have done more; but it was not enough. It was of course impossible to make out a case for murder, but Piso could not produce an effective defence against the other charges. He hinted that he had instructions he might produce. This was obviously the moment of danger for Tiberius; that Piso had some such instructions can hardly be doubted. The Emperor's description of him as 'the helper of Germanicus' was a euphemism. It was possible to avert the danger however; and a compromise was effected. Piso did not produce the orders; Tiberius limited the attack to him alone and protected his family. Accordingly Piso submitted to the realities of fate and politics; his suicide bore witness to the power of reason. His wife Placina meanwhile escaped punishment; Tiberius himself pleaded on her behalf; explaining that Livia had besought him to do so.

The death of Germanicus and the trial of Piso together mark the first turning-point of the reign. Hitherto Tiberius had been respected, though never popular. Henceforth he was an object of suspicion; of detestation also in some quarters. A rift had been torn through the imperial family with Agrippina the living symbol of the Empire's loss. Tiberius might commend the children of Germanicus to the care of the Senate; it was another mark of hypocrisy. The rift widened gradually. While his son Drusus lived, Tiberius had a partner who could share the labours of empire without arousing too much suspicion and resentment. His death in 23 isolated the Emperor further, and plunged him deep in gloom. Josephus, the Jewish historian whose information came by way of Herod Agrippa, at that time a frequenter of the court, stated that Tiberius 'could not bear to see people about the court who reminded him of his son'. The decade of the twenties saw gloom and fear encroach on the city and the court. Treason-trials began to proliferate. Conspiracies and rumours of conspiracies abounded. The succession was doubtful. In 26 the aged Emperor withdrew from the city; the following year he established himself on Capri, a recluse, almost an exile, but still supreme. The decade that began with the death of Germanicus was to end with the imprisonment of his wife, Agrippina, and their two elder sons, Nero and Drusus. It saw the rise to influence, and then to apparent supremacy, of the enemy of the house of Germanicus, the Prefect of the Praetorian Guards, the plebeian adventurer L. Aelius Sejanus.

The intensity of political life in Rome can easily distract the historian. Tacitus indeed concentrates on it to the exclusion of the provinces. With reason; it was there that history as he understood it was made – the history of the struggles for mastery in the Empire. Yet it is as well to remember that the Roman Empire was also a matter of administration; of administration moreover of the whole Mediterranean world. It was at this task that Tiberius toiled unremittingly and with consistent success. If the Roman State was able to withstand the convulsions of the forty years that followed his death, it was in no small degree due to the peace and prosperity he maintained and extended. There were exceptions of course, revolts in Gaul in 21 and 28, and in North Africa from 17 to 24. For the most part however, peace prevailed. This *pax Romana* was an especially notable achievement considering the size and constitution of the Empire and how recently much of it had been acquired. The revolts just mentioned had been sparked off by Roman greed, the excessive exactions of provincial governors. Such behaviour was in sharp contrast to Tiberius' precept: 'I want my sheep shorn, not shaved.' In general however administration improved; in particular corruption declined. Several governors were brought to trial for cruelty or extortion; an encouragement for the rest. Good governors were maintained in office for a long time – partly as a reflection of Tiberius' dislike of change and partly through his reluctance to make new decisions. This also represented an end of the old Republican practice whereby ambitious politicians founded their fortunes on the yield of provincial governorships. The general success of Tiberius' rule may be measured by the progress of Gaul: twenty years later Claudius found the Gauls ready for citizenship.

Moderation, good sense and retrenchment were the Emperor's mottoes. Financial stability was achieved without an increase in taxation. Tiberius was not only able to grant compensation for public disasters – fires on the Caelian in 27 and the Aventine in 36 for instance – but left behind a treasure of 2,700 million sesterces (Gaius soon dissipated that). Good sense marked his public pronouncements, at least whenever his own safety was not threatened; often even then. He refused to accept deification: when delegates came from the province of Further Spain seeking permission to dedicate a temple to him, he declined, saying: 'I must stress that I am human, carrying out human tasks and happy to occupy the first place among men.' In similar style he deprecated a proposed law which would have enlarged the sphere of executive action: 'Emperors,' he said, 'have enough power and enough burdens. If you strengthen the executive, you weaken the law. When the law will suffice, it is a mistake to use official authority.' He was indeed always sceptical of the efficacy of government. Although of simple and frugal tastes himself, he had little time for attempts to compel others to practise such virtue. 'The remedy,' he said, 'lay with the individual. If we are decent we shall behave well.' Example was better than exhortation: he served up a mere half boar at dinner one day, and sardonically observed that one half tasted just as good as the other. A particularly fine fish was offered to him. He sent it out to be sold, remarking that some rich idiot like Apicius or Octavius would be sure to buy it. He was right; Octavius paid 5,000 sesterces.

Flattery annoyed him. One day when an ex-consul came to apologize for some fault and fell pathetically to his knees, Tiberius retreated so quickly that he fell over backwards himself. He regarded the address 'Lord and Master' as an insult, and when it was proposed on one occasion that he enter Rome to an official ovation, he replied sourly that, having conquered so many great nations in his youth and been rewarded with so many triumphs, he was hardly likely to be pleased by the honour of a suburban parade. With this honesty and Johnsonian hatred of cant went a preference for free speech. Indeed he used to say that the liberty to think and speak as one wished was the test of a free country; an impeccably Republican sentiment. He acted on this principle too: when the Senate dealt abruptly with the equestrian Clutorius Priscus, who had slandered the Emperor, he reproved them, and decreed that henceforth ten days should elapse between the passing of sentence and its execution. (It was a decree the Senate were nevertheless to disregard.)

These qualities, to which that of industry must be added, ensured that the government of the Empire was wise, just and efficient. When Tiberius died, a judgement has gone, 'he left the subject peoples of the Empire in a condition of prosperity such as they had never known before and never knew again'. Yet the felicity of the provinces is obscured by the drama that centred on Rome, as a great black-purple thundercloud blots out a golden summer afternoon; and the Emperor's good sense, intelligence, public spirit and cool aristocratic disdain were insufficient to avert his personal tragedy.

The tragedy is inescapably linked with the name of Sejanus, the evil genius of Tiberius; 'the Partner of my Labours', as the Emperor termed him; his protégé and support and ultimately the destroyer of his peace of mind. All rulers need coadjutors. Augustus had used Agrippa, Maecenas and the members of his own family. He had been well served. Tiberius was less fortunate, as his own position was less strong. Augustus had won the Principate in civil war, a title to possession that gave him a priceless, because unchallengeable, authority. It had enabled him to associate others with him in the management of the Empire without the fear that they might supplant him. (Though there had been moments when Agrippa had seemed a threat.) But Tiberius had come to power by a different route. Certainly he had proved himself as general and administrator, but always in a subordinate role. His power, reluctantly held, could be impugned; his very reluctance weakened his position. Germanicus had been not only heir, but rival. Drusus, as heir, had been satisfactory; but now that he was gone, any nobleman closely associated with Tiberius would be seen as a possible emperor; the days of the triumvirates were not yet so far distant. On both occasions the rule of three had ended in the supremacy of one; and in neither case had the man apparently strongest at the start lasted the course. Pompey and Antony had perished; the two Caesars prevailed. It could happen again. Hence, when Tiberius looked for a minister, he prudently looked beyond the nobility. He sought a man whose power would derive from him, who by himself would be nothing, a political nonentity, a *novus homo*; he found Sejanus.

L. Aelius Sejanus was not quite nobody in fact. His father, L. Seius Strabo, was an equestrian from Etruria who had been a personal friend of Augustus. He had been Prefect of the Guard and Viceroy of Egypt and had married into a patrician family, the Cornelii Maluginenses. The young Sejanus had therefore consular relatives and had himself been adopted into the Aelian family. All the same his standing was respectable rather than distinguished. He was not someone the Roman nobility could accept as their equal; and certainly they could never have regarded him as their master.

Sejanus had first come to notice on Gaius Caesar's staff in the East; possibly he did Tiberius some service then. At any rate in AD 14 he was associated with his father in the command of the Praetorians, and soon he was sole commander. It was he who concentrated the Praetorians in a camp just outside the city – hitherto they had been quartered on householders – and so made them a political force. (They were the only branch of the armed forces stationed in Italy; it would not be long before they chose an emperor.) Sejanus was energetic and competent, and impressed Tiberius by his administrative skill and by his loyalty – once he reputedly saved Tiberius' life, preventing a boulder from falling on him during a picnic dinner in a cave near Naples. Here was someone who identified his interests with the Emperor's; moreover he was a hard worker, a quality Tiberius admired. Tacitus says that Sejanus 'hid behind a modest exterior an unbridled lust for power. Sometimes this drove him to excess but more often to incessant work. Which is just as dangerous when it aims at the throne.' Whether that was in fact his target must be doubtful; certainly, however, he was greedy for power. While Tiberius lived his position seemed secure; but afterwards?

Drusus was the first obstacle, for Drusus detested him. Once indeed he struck Sejanus on the mouth; and he complained that Tiberius seemed to prefer an outsider to his own son. The claim was ill founded; in 21 Drusus had shared a consulship with his father and the next year had received the tribunician power, promotions that marked him out as successor. Indeed, coupled with Tiberius' disenchantment with, and withdrawal from, public affairs, they suggested that the old man might soon make way for his son. That would be the end for Sejanus.

One ambitious attempt to secure his position by forming a connection with the imperial family had already come to nothing. He had contrived to have his daughter betrothed to another Drusus, the grandson of Germanicus and son of the future Emperor Claudius. That had failed when the young prince died in a ludicrous accident: he threw a pear in the air, caught it in his mouth and choked. Even so, no alliance of that sort could secure the favourite's power in a new reign, or even guarantee his safety. Sejanus had to look for other means.

He found them in the wife of Drusus. It was an unlikely association, perhaps the most unlikely of all. Livilla (or Livia Julia; she is known by both names) was Germanicus' sister and therefore also the grand-niece of Augustus. Unattractive as a young girl when she had been betrothed to Gaius Caesar, she had become a great beauty in her maturity. Sejanus now laid siege to her; she succumbed. Although she would have shared the Empire with her husband Drusus, she yet, in Tacitus' matchless words, 'degraded herself, her ancestors and her descendants with a small-town adulterer'. Sejanus proved his devotion by divorcing his wife, Apicata; Livilla hers by plotting against her husband. Her motives have given rise to much inconclusive argument. It is said, for instance, that believing Drusus would honour Augustus' intention and set aside his own children in favour of the heirs of Germanicus, she turned against him to safeguard her children's future. Perhaps; but the truth may be rather that she had come to hate Drusus and was now infatuated with Sejanus. She may have felt neglected or insulted; Tacitus tells of a eunuch, Lygdus, 'whose boyish good looks had endeared him to his master Drusus'. What is certain is that Livilla became Sejanus' mistress and was ready to become his wife. And, after all, it may be that the shameful nature of their love made it all the more obsessive.

Drusus died in 23. The death was accepted as natural; and not till later, when such revelations were safe, was it asserted that he had been murdered by the command of Sejanus and Livilla. The slaves then accused of acting as the agents of the guilty pair confessed under torture. One may wonder that they had survived so long; it would have been safer for Sejanus to have disposed of them years before. Moreover the fact that the Emperor's informant was Sejanus' discarded wife, Apicata, renders the story suspicious. All the same the death could not have been more convenient; and as to the question of murder, one may say, with countless generations of Italians, 'se non è vero, è ben trovato'.

Agrippina, herself proud as any Claudian and consciously possessed of a virtue rare in the imperial house, also hated and despised the upstart Sejanus. He meanwhile could hope for nothing if her children succeeded. From 23 to 29 Rome was excited, awed and made to tremble by the struggle between the two factions. It was now that the *Lex de Maiestate* came into its own. All treason laws are necessarily vague, for it is hard to separate intention from performance. Disaffection itself becomes quickly treasonable. Words endanger security; suspicion is epidemic. Such was the condition of Rome in the twenties, rendered worse by the peculiarity already referred to; that the Roman State made no provision for the office of Public Prosecutor, even in affairs which threatened its security. Prosecution was the work of private individuals, who might profit from their work; for, to exacerbate the situation, it was the rule that the property of a convicted man should be divided among his accusers. Accordingly there flourished numbers of professional informers – *delatores* – who maintained offices, files and agents, functioning indeed as private-enterprise bureaux of espionage. Not surprisingly such activity bred real conspiracies. Nothing encourages conspiracy like a secret police.

One example will suffice. An equestrian called Titius Sabinus was an adherent of Germanicus, continuing to pay close attention to Agrippina and her children. Four senators, said to be ambitious for the consulship, resolved to trap him into treason; in this way they could demonstrate their loyalty. Sabinus was easily tempted into rash words and tearful complaints, for, as Tacitus says, 'misery is demoralizing', and the exchanges of forbidden confidences seemed a basis for friendship. The four partners arranged that three senators should be concealed where they could overhear what Sabinus had to say, cramming them in a space between roof and ceiling. Sabinus spoke in a way that clearly revealed disaffection, and the senators laid the information before the Emperor, who demanded retribution. The miserable gull Sabinus was put summarily to death on New Year's morning 29.

Such is the version according to Tacitus, an episode perhaps more sinister and symptomatic of the general corruption because this time the accusers were amateurs and well born. It may be true. Agents provocateurs have always worked in this way. But such agents can normally only provoke what is already there; and Sabinus, as even Tacitus admits, was in truth disaffected; doubtless with reason. He may himself have sought out allies. The fact was, two parties were locked in a struggle for power. The prize was empire; the penalty for failure, death. It would be naive to suggest that the plotting was all on one side.

Certainly Tiberius believed his life was in danger; and Sejanus worked sedulously on his fears. Such apprehension was rife. Tiberius knew for example, of Agrippina's enmity. 'Is it my fault,' he said to her once, quoting a Greek verse, 'that you are not queen?' (The true answer was 'yes'; he was still alive and her husband Germanicus done to death.) In turn she feared Tiberius. When she came to dine at his table, she refused to eat, in such a way that he could not mistake her meaning. He commended some apples, offering her a dish and she handed the apple, untouched, to a slave. There was a blow for pride: to be accused of attempting to poison his niece at his own table. No wonder Tiberius turned to his mother and asked if it was surprising that he should envisage taking harsh measures against a woman who made her mistrust of him so terribly clear.

The Praetorian Camp on a gold coin
of Claudius, AD 44–5

Agrippina the elder, the wife of
Germanicus. A commemorative coin
issued by her son Gaius Caligula

Three years after his son's death Tiberius left Rome for a villa in Campania. The
following year, 27, he removed to Capri. He never entered the capital again. With
this retreat the Emperor crossed the boundary that separates history from legend.
So 'after a youth of exemplary virtue, and half a century more of public life, during
which the manners and morals of Tiberius were an honour to his age, he retired in

his sixty-ninth year to the island of Capri, in order at last to be able to indulge his latent proclivities for cruelty and lust'. He had entered on that part of his existence that was to feed the imagination of Gilles de Rais. . . He built himself a private brothel where sexual perversions were engaged in for his voyeuristic delight. Boys and girls, skilled in unnatural practices, were collected from all over the Empire – selected doubtless in competition – and brought to Capri for his delectation. Nooks of lechery were planted throughout the island, so that Tiberius might divert himself when the mood took him on a country stroll. Youths dressed as Pan were stationed at the entrances to the famous grottoes. The Emperor trained little boys, designated minnows, to chase him when he went swimming and get between his legs and nibble him. Handsome young sprigs of nobility were summoned to the island, debauched, and never seen again. Once, when sacrificing, Tiberius took a fancy to the acolyte who carried the casket with the incense. Naturally he could hardly wait for the ceremony to end before hurrying the lad off with his brother, the sacred trumpeter, out of the temple, and assaulting the pair of them; energetic work for a septuagenarian. When they protested, he had their legs broken. Unfortunately, Suetonius, so fertile in such details, omits to tell us their names – or those of any other victims of his aged lust.

Tacitus, less satisfactorily, gives no details at all, merely talks of secret orgies and idle malevolent thoughts. And so on and so forth. The accusations are not of course absolutely incredible; cases of senile dementia of this kind are hardly unknown. Nevertheless the lack of precise evidence and the fact that the charges are so exactly what one would expect gossip to invent – gossip of the islanders if first-century Capriotes in any way resembled their descendants, and gossip of Rome itself – that scepticism is natural. Scepticism is reinforced by the list of companions who accompanied the Princeps to the island: the Senator M. Cocceius Nerva; a man of letters, Curtius Atticus; Thrasyllus; and numerous other scholars and mathematicians, mostly Greeks, in whose discourse he had always found relaxation. It was the same sort of entourage as he had had at Rhodes thirty years before; jolly company for an orgy!

It is not necessary to invent elaborate or scandalous reasons to account for his retirement. The longing to withdraw had always been there. Indeed, 'in retiring at the close of an arduous life to enjoy the tranquil beauties of nature on fabled Siren shores, he was only doing what any civilized person might be expected to do'. And why not? Buffeted by fate; finding the incessantly public nature of Roman life oppressive; disillusioned in his efforts to persuade the senators to assume a Republican degree of responsibility, and disgusted by their servility; encompassed by plots and rumours of plots; wearied by his aged mother and by the obdurate antagonism of Agrippina; fearing for his life and fatigued of his labours, what more natural than retirement to the most beautiful of Mediterranean islands. Capri can claim that title even today, after almost a century of despoliation; in Antiquity it must have been paradisal. It was a secure Eden moreover; there were only two landing-stages, both easily overseen.

No doubt Sejanus encouraged Tiberius in his decision; but he had no need to implant the idea. The advantages for himself meanwhile were evident. He became the necessary link between Tiberius and Rome, the channel for all communication. He could control the information which reached the Princeps, as well as his visitors. By withdrawing to Capri, Tiberius had delivered himself to Sejanus.

Moreover his withdrawal, whatever his intentions, marked a change in his relationship with the Senate. Whereas he had been accustomed to attend the Senate without an escort, taking his seat and making his speeches like an ordinary, if distinguished, member of the house, relations now were clearly those of master and servant. He communicated by letter; the courtesy and deference he had shown in person were replaced by these missives, often cryptic but always requiring that the Senate comply, and inevitably the nakedness of the Senate's position was displayed and felt. Nothing made the sham of the Augustan restoration of the Republic more evident than Tiberius' retirement to Capri.

Sejanus now proceeded to act against Agrippina and her children. Speed was of course imperative since the old Emperor might die. Agents were therefore employed to betray their friends into treasonable words and acts, so that friendship to the house of Germanicus would begin to seem dangerous. The family thus found themselves increasingly isolated. Men began to shun Nero, the eldest of Agrippina's sons. Sejanus sent his agents to urge Agrippina and Nero to flee Rome and take refuge with the German legions, where the memory of Germanicus was especially revered, or to appeal to the people; to do something, in short, that would incriminate them. They prudently rejected the suggestions, but the discussions were reported to Tiberius as if these courses were being considered. Suspicion clouded his mind. At last, in 29, just after Livia's death (Tiberius did not attend the funeral), he wrote to the Senate attacking Agrippina and Nero in general terms.

Possibly the letter was less than Sejanus hoped for. Neither was accused of treason, Agrippina merely of general hostility to the Princeps, and Nero of immorality – homosexual indecency, says Tacitus. The Senate hesitated, unable to interpret the letter. Their agony of doubt is clear enough. They were ready to do whatever the Princeps wished – if only he would make it clear just what he desired. Meanwhile outside the Senate-house a crowd demonstrated in favour of the accused, something that Sejanus was able to represent as evidence of sedition. What could Tiberius do but believe? Sejanus had even enlisted the help of Nero's younger brother, Drusus, promising that he would help him to the throne. The third brother, Gaius Caligula, was to say later, when Emperor, that Tiberius had been bound to believe the charges – with so many accusers about.

The Princeps sent a second letter, more explicit; and the Senate's doubts were removed. Nero was declared a public enemy. No account of these proceedings is extant; but it seems likely that the charges were now more explicit, political rather than moral; if all homosexuals had been termed public enemies, the upper ranks of society would have been thinned indeed. Loaded with chains, the accused were taken off to islands, Nero to Pontia, Agrippina to Pandateria. The latter was an example perhaps of the Emperor's bitter humour; her mother, his ex-wife Julia, had been imprisoned there too.

The following year Sejanus turned against his dupe, Drusus, and he too was accused and imprisoned, this time in the dungeons of the Palatine. Sejanus now stood supreme. Only two male members of the Julio-Claudians were still at liberty – Gaius Caligula and the Emperor's grandson, young Tiberius Gemellus. Sejanus moreover was now betrothed at last to Livia Julia, and the Emperor publicly hailed him as his partner. His birthday was officially celebrated, and in 31 Tiberius was to share a consulship with him. Tiberius had only held the consulship twice in his reign, each time with his acknowledged heir, Germanicus in 18 and Drusus in 21. All the same it is hard to believe that Sejanus really hoped for the Empire. His best hope of continued power would be as guardian to Tiberius Gemellus, the son of Livia Julia. It was still unlikely that the aristocracy, tamed but not completely broken, would accept the small-town adulterer as Princeps; nor was there any reason to expect the armies to back him. His position therefore, though magnificent, was still fraught with danger. He stood over the Roman world like a man perched on a high column, dizzy with the view.

The one obstacle was Gaius Caligula. At this moment a forgotten figure intervened, the young prince's grandmother, Antonia. She wrote to Tiberius, with whom she had always maintained good relations, apparently warning him that Gaius was in danger. She did more; she let Tiberius feel that Sejanus had been using him, that he was no longer in full command. That was enough. Tiberius, out of touch with Rome, could no longer be sure of the feeling there. It might be that Sejanus had designs even against him. His creature had become autonomous; like Baron Frankenstein he had breathed life into a monster.

He moved cautiously, continuing to heap honours on Sejanus, lest he arouse suspicion, and still lauding him in letters to the Senate. Possibly the shared consulship itself was a snare for the over-mighty favourite. Meanwhile Tiberius sounded out the Senators, and confused Sejanus and Senate alike by letters that were more bewildering than ever. (It is clear from the manoeuvrings of the year 31 that Sejanus had not quite succeeded in controlling all access to the Princeps.) Tiberius' actions became increasingly unsettling. One day the favourite was praised; the next, mild criticism was inserted. He was appointed to the priesthood, and so was his son; but so, on the same day, was Gaius. Hints were dropped that Tiberius saw Gaius as his successor. The trial of L. Arruntius, an old enemy of the favourite, was stopped by imperial command; yet, at the same time, Nero was put to death. It was rumoured that Sejanus was to be granted the tribunician power.

In fact Tiberius was preparing his counter-stroke, in desperate secrecy. He despatched an officer of the Guard, Macro, from Capri to Rome with a commission as the new Prefect of the Praetorians. Macro entered the city by night and made his mission known to one of the consuls and to the captain of the night-watch. Early in the morning of 18 October he mounted the Palatine, where the Senate was to meet in the temple of Apollo. There, in the crisp yet evanescent light of a Roman autumn, he met Sejanus. The favourite was worried by the absence of news. In secrecy Macro assured him that he had just delivered a letter to the Senate that contained the grant of tribunician power. Sejanus relaxed, and entered the Senate like a great purring lion. Macro placed a guard round the Senate and hurried away, across the city, to the camp of the Praetorians, in the site of the modern Borghese Gardens. He revealed that he was their new commander and promised them a donative. He cannot have been certain that they would accept him; every officer, every centurion had been appointed by Sejanus; it was seventeen years since he had become Prefect. Yet to a man they deserted him.

Back on the Palatine, inside the temple, the consul read the Emperor's long and wordy letter. For some time its drift was unclear. Tiberius confessed his fears. He begged the senators to send a military guard to escort him in his old age, grief and loneliness to Rome. He uttered some trivial complaints against Sejanus, such as he had occasionally made in the last year. The Senators listened silently, none daring to applaud or even glance at the favourite. He, conscious of where the letter was heading, tolerant of his master's epistolary vagaries, in themselves a sign of his years and of the decline that required a partner, sat back in patience. The moment would come. But the letter ended abruptly with a request that the Senate arrest Sejanus. For minutes no one moved or raised his head. It might be a trick; they might not have understood. The silence prolonged itself. Then the consul Memmius called Sejanus forward. He did not move. The call was repeated. The favourite sat still, immobile, stricken. At the third call he stumbled to his feet to find Laco, the captain of the night-watch, at his side. Abuse broke out all round. Still the consul did not dare risk a general vote or propose the death penalty. Instead, with a caution that speaks of Tiberius' own instructions, he asked one senator only, one who could be trusted, whether Sejanus should be imprisoned. The fallen favourite was hustled out, under the azure sky that stretched away to the Alban Hills; down, among a guard of soldiers, the ilex-fringed Clivus Palatinus; along the Sacred Way, where the mob, wont there to hail triumphal processions, now pressed hard on his escort, shrieking execrations; and across the Forum to a little building crouched under the Capitol. This was the Mamertime Prison, a dank cell built into the hill, where State prisoners came to execution. Hurled down a narrow twisting staircase, or, desperately resisting, thrust through a hole in the floor of the upper room (now covered by a metal grille), he found himself, who that morning was a prince among men and master of the marble sun-drenched city, confined in a foetid den a few paces wide, the walls damp to the touch. If there was any light he could see the ring to which the great African prince, Jugurtha, had been fastened, at which he had gnawed his arm to stay his hunger. Sejanus would not live long enough to feel hungry.

The news of his fall sent the mob wild. They tore down his statues and clamoured for revenge. Their reaction and the acquiescence of the Praetorians gave the Senate courage. They met again in the afternoon and condemned Sejanus to death. The sentence was executed at once. Sejanus was strangled, and his body dragged to the Gemonian Steps, where for three days it was exposed to the insults of the populace. Those who had most servilely praised him were now most assiduous in insult. On the third day the mutilated corpse was chucked into the Tiber.

Meanwhile Tiberius waited on Capri in extreme anxiety. He had no confidence that Macro would succeed, and kept ships ready so that he could take refuge with the armies if he had failed. Nothing more clearly shows the power Sejanus had wielded than the Emperor's fears. He had brought them on himself by his isolation and misplaced trust. The isolation was something he could not now change, but he would never trust again. While he was preparing his counter-stroke the exigencies of the moment had kept him nervously keen. It is not surprising that there was to be a reaction. He had always resented the burdens of the Empire he had never sought. For seven years, since his son's death, Sejanus had been the one man he could trust to share the intolerable weight and the one man who had protected him against his enemies. He was now completely alone.

Worse was to follow. In just over a week he received a letter from Apicata, Sejanus' ex-wife, in which she told her story of the murder of Drusus. Of course Tiberius believed her; how could he fail to? One way or another Sejanus had destroyed his peace of mind for ever.

For nine months, Suetonius asserts, he did not leave his villa. In Rome the enraged people and insulted Senate embarked on an orgy of revenge. First, Sejanus' family and closest adherents were put to death. The killing continued into December, when the favourite's younger children suffered, his little girl being first raped by the executioner, since the law forbade the execution of virgins. And though Tiberius was to declare that he had turned against Sejanus because of the favourite's attack on the children of Germanicus, there was no reprieve for the members of that family: Agrippina and Drusus remained in prison. Agrippina lost an eye in a fight with a centurion before starving herself to death on the anniversary of Sejanus' fall. Drusus, confined in the Palatine dungeons, either went mad or simulated insanity. Hunger drove him to chew the stuffing of his mattress. All his words, mostly directed against the Emperor, were noted down. When he died, Tiberius ordered that the complete record of his sufferings and ravings be read to the Senate; it was as if he was determined finally to involve them in the meaning of this sort of empire.

The killing continued. It was a time for private revenge to masquerade as public duty. It was a time too when suspicion could not be lulled; there had been so many conspiracies, so many treasons proved, so many vicious prosecutions undertaken. Who could believe anything? Who could refuse to give credence to everything? As for the Princeps, his deception had been complete. He had nothing more to give, nothing to hope for but the release of death, which his obstinacy yet forbade him to seek. His agony of mind is fully shown by the opening of his best-known letter to the Senate; 'If I know what to write to you at this time, Senators, or how to write it, or what not to write, may heaven plunge me in a worse ruin than I find overtaking me every day.'

There was only one solace – work, the surest anodyne. He continued to attend in the most meticulous detail to the affairs of the Empire. Where his own safety was not concerned his mind was as sharp as ever. New alarms on the eastern frontier were skilfully calmed. A financial crisis, resulting from a shortage of liquidity, was circumvented when Tiberius made interest-free loans available. Even in some criminal cases he showed his former craggy honesty. When Fulcinius Trio committed suicide to avoid prosecution in 35, and left a will in which he denounced the Emperor as an old madman, Tiberius ordered it to be read in the Senate. It was in character; this was what Trio had felt, and such truth should be published whatever the consequences.

That was all he had left to cling to, the shreds of his integrity. The question of the succession he treated with fatalism: it would have to be Gaius, unpromising though his character seemed. As for his own grandson, young Tiberius Gemellus, his future was clear. 'You will kill him,' he said to Gaius, 'and another will kill you.' But there was no alternative, and perhaps he was past caring.

He could not settle even in Capri. Yet neither could he bear to return to Rome. Thrice he reached the outskirts of the city, gazed on the hills and palaces and withdrew. The Senate still sat and fearfully awaited his letters. The people groaned at the name of this Emperor who gave no Games, who gained no glorious triumphs, who hid from them.

He died at Misenum on 16 March 37. Even the manner of his death is obscured and legendary. Tacitus recounts that he lapsed into unconsciousness and was presumed dead. All the courtiers therefore surrounded Gaius with congratulations. But word came that the Emperor had recovered, and was asking for food. The crowd paled and slid away one by one. Macro however kept his head. They had gone too far, hailing Gaius as Emperor. It was better there should be no turning back. A slave was summoned and despatched with orders to smother Tiberius with his own bedclothes.

The news of his death was received with glee in Rome. 'To the Tiber with Tiberius,' they cried. There were even suggestions that his body be exposed on the Gemonian Steps. The Senate took pleasure in agreeing with Gaius that the late Emperor's will be set aside; he had been of unsound mind.

He would have been surprised by none of this. He had never thought much of mankind; in the end even his cynicism had been unable to support him or offer equanimity. The last picture is of the wandering Emperor forever vainly seeking rest. He had tried to do his duty for over sixty years, and everything had fallen apart. The taste of life was bitter. The elder Pliny called him the saddest of men: 'tristissimus homo'. It was a fair judgement. Whatever the terror that spread over his last years, it was but a reflection of the wasteland of his own mind.

Gaius Caligula

GAIUS CALIGULA

THE YOUNG MAN wandered through the colonnades of the Imperial Palace, waiting for the dawn. Sleep had long vanished. Three hours a night was the most he ever achieved, and that with the help of wine. Then he would wake from painful and frightening dreams, his body twitching and mind racing. With the first light he looked down from the heights of the Palatine, either over the slowly stirring Forum, where the street-sweepers were mixing with the last revellers, or across the Tiber to where his private Circus was being erected in gardens which he had inherited from his mother. Before then, to while away the night or calm his fears, he would ponder his plans: throwing a bridge over the Forum to join the Palatine to the Capitol; cutting a canal through the Isthmus of Corinth, constructing harbours for the corn-fleet in the Straits of Messina; building new aqueducts; conquering the remote misty island of Britain. There was nothing he could not do, for this strange, bald, lanky hollow-eyed young man, whose body was so hairy that some called him 'the goat', was Emperor, and as such he felt his power. At a banquet he had once broken into peals of laughter, and when the consuls asked him if they might share the joke, had replied, 'it just occurred to me that I have only to nod my head once and your throats will be cut straightaway'. And he was fond, it was said, of quickening the pleasures of his embraces by imparting the same pleasantry to his lover. And why not? He was a god, conscious of divinity, capable of all; he had even threatened to make his favourite horse, Incitatus, consul. What could stop him? Nothing was beyond his imperial divinity; except sleep.

Gaius was the youngest son of Germanicus and Agrippina, born at Antium, the modern Anzio, on 31 August AD 12. He had been the soldiers' favourite, the pet of the camps; and the legionaries had bestowed on him the nickname Caligula, Little Boots, by which he is best known to posterity. Still, his earliest memories were of the mutinies of 14 and of the fear they had occasioned. He was bred indeed in

119

apprehension. His father died when Gaius was seven, and he grew up first in the suspicious and vengeful atmosphere of his mother's house, where he was educated to regard Tiberius as the monstrous enemy of his family. The twenties saw this atmosphere thicken and darken, as Agrippina and his elder brothers, Nero and Drusus, either involved themselves in plots against the Emperor, or were trapped in the snares laid for them by Sejanus. Gaius, apparently too young to be accounted a danger, alone escaped. For a few years he lived with his grandmother, Antonia, the daughter of Mark Antony, widow of Tiberius' brother Drusus, and mother of Germanicus. In her household he learned to feel tenderness for the memory of Antony; so that when he became Emperor, he abandoned the festival which Augustus had inaugurated to celebrate his victory at Actium. He associated there too with a group of Eastern princes, the Thracians Polemo, Rhoemetalces and Cotys. From them he imbibed ideas of what it was to be a prince, ideas to which Antony himself had not in his later days been averse. Gaius was to be the first Emperor who felt himself royal, set apart from other men by his birth.

Then, when he was nineteen, Tiberius summoned him to Capri. He celebrated his coming of age and was admitted to the priesthood. On Capri he was safe from Sejanus' machinations. If he felt regret for his mother and brothers, or anger at their fate, he concealed such dangerous emotions. He showed himself modest, careful and subservient. When Sejanus fell, and a year later young Drusus starved himself to death, Gaius was left almost alone as a possible inheritor of the Empire. The only rival was Tiberius Gemellus, and he was a child, seven years younger. The aged Princeps would have to live long for his grandson to be a serious rival to Gaius; even then, the popularity of the house of Germanicus, a popularity which their misfortunes had only enhanced, would make Gaius the likely successor.

Tiberius accepted the fact, though he made the two boys joint heirs of his property. Equally important, Macro, the Praetorian Prefect, was quick to recognize Gaius as the next Emperor, the young man who must be cultivated. (It was reported that he permitted him to enjoy his wife.) Gaius himself remained circumspect. Some courtiers tried to trick him into complaints against Tiberius; but without success. The young man knew better; he also knew how to wait. As for Tiberius, he was tolerant of others' alleged opinions. When the dissipated and roguish Jewish prince, Herod Agrippa, a close crony of Gaius, was reported to have expressed impatience at the old man's clinging to life, Tiberius found it natural.

He did his best for Gaius. The Jewish writer, Philo, states that he was careful not to let him be spoiled by flattery, and certainly he attended to his education. Gaius became fluent in Greek, and his speeches both in Latin and Greek, delivered extempore, showed eloquence and quickness of mind. For all his later vagaries, Gaius was no fool. His observations were acute, his judgements to the point. Certainly his taste in literature was doubtful; but it was at least his own. He had no time for poets like Homer and Virgil. He used to say that the best thing he knew about Plato was his decision to exclude Homer from the *Republic*. He found Livy's patriotic history verbose and yet insubstantial; generations of schoolboys would

The Palatine: the Clivus Victoriae, and the entrance to Caligula's house

agree with him. More surely, he dismissed Seneca, rhetorician, moralist and dramatic poet, with utter contempt – his writings were 'sand without lime'; he was 'nothing but a text-book orator'. There can be little doubt that Gaius Caligula had the makings of a critic.

But if Tiberius did not neglect Gaius' education, seeing to it too that he studied mathematics under the best tutors, he was unable to do something equally vital. Up to now, both Tiberius and Augustus had associated their prospective successor with them in the management of the Empire. Now the evil effect of Sejanus' deceptions was felt. Tiberius could not trust Gaius away from Capri. He had to keep him there under his eye. Historians were to invent explanations. Tiberius, they said, had gauged the young man's vicious inclinations. 'I am nursing a viper in Rome's bosom,' he was quoted as saying, 'a Phaeton who will lose control of the sun-chariot and scorch the whole world'. To support this view, Suetonius asserts that even then 'Caligula could not control his natural brutality. He loved watching tortures and executions.' But the stories of tortures and executions were a Capri fable, and, even if they had taken place, it is unlikely that Tiberius, who deplored gladiatorial contests, would have permitted young Gaius to indulge in such amusements. Moreover, if he had discerned this radically vicious nature, it can hardly be believed that he, whose care for the Empire continued unremitting to the last, should voluntarily have passed it on to such a man. It would not have been difficult to dispose of Gaius. The real explanation is simpler, and, in its way, more terrible. Tiberius was afraid. Gaius could therefore go neither to Rome nor the armies, lest he become the focus of discontent, conspiracy and insurrection.

At last the old man died, amid a welter of the usual rumours. The news came to Rome like the torrents of spring after a prairie winter. Nobody spared a thought for his devoted service over so long a life. Instead all eyes were on the young man. His progress to Rome was a triumph. Nothing had been seen like it since his mother had brought the dead body of Germanicus on its melancholy journey from Brindisi – only this time, instead of cries of lamentation, the air of the Via Appia resounded with paeans of joy. Crowds clustered gleefully round him, shouting endearments such as 'star', 'chicken', 'baby' and 'pet'. The Senate, without hesitation and with no debate, conferred absolute power on him. It seemed, Suetonius says, 'like a dream come true'. Even the non-Roman world evinced pleasure; Artabanus, King of Parthia, made overtures of friendship to Gaius and paid homage to the Roman eagles.

Everything the young man did gave pleasure and promised good. He staged a magnificent funeral for Tiberius, to the gratification of the mob, delighted equally by the show and its occasion. Immediately afterwards he sailed for Pandateria and the Pontian Islands to bring back the remains of Agrippina and his brother Nero. It was reported that he reverently transferred the ashes to splendidly engraved urns with his own hands. They were received in Rome with pomp. Games were decreed in memory of Agrippina, and the rehabilitation of his family proceeded with the award to his grandmother Antonia of all the honours that Livia had won in her lifetime, and with the choice of his eccentric uncle Claudius as his fellow-consul. It could hardly have been made more evident that, after so many vicissitudes, the House of Germanicus had at last come into its own.

In the public realm his actions were likewise popular. Exiles were recalled, banned books published. He abolished the sales-tax, gave lavish games and distributed largesse. Not only the mob rejoiced. He checked the practice of delation and announced that treason-trials would no longer be encouraged. Potentially incriminating documents were publicly burned. The batches of written evidence prepared against his mother and brothers were among these. The Emperor swore he had not read them and that no copies remained extant. Thus no revenge could be taken against those who had testified in these cases. This was magnanimity of a high order; in fact other copies did exist, but Gaius may have been ignorant of this at the time, and so can be given credit for his generosity of spirit. He promised to consult, and co-operate with, the Senate. It seemed as if a golden age had returned.

Disillusion was not long in coming. In October 37 Gaius fell ill. Crowds thronged the skirts of the palace, praying to the gods that he might be spared. The gods listened, and, acting with habitual irony, granted the request. Gaius recovered, but his brain was diseased; he emerged from his sickroom as a monster.

So at least the legend runs, a legend hard to substantiate, inconsistent as to dates and strangely at odds also with those other legends which ascribe inherent vice to the young man even on Capri. At any rate, the tradition has it that thenceforth he exhibited unprecedented lust, cruelty and depravity. For instance, he habitually

Coin issued by Caligula showing his
sisters Agrippina the younger,
Drusilla and Julia Livilla the younger

123

Gaius Caligula sacrificing a bull
before the Temple of the Divine
Augustus

committed incest with his three sisters, one after the other. His love for one of them, Drusilla, was extreme. As usual the legends contradict each other, for some place the incestuous relationship years back; it is also alleged that their grandmother had caught them in bed together when they were both minors. Perhaps; it is certain that he loved Drusilla, whatever form his devotion may have taken. His grief at her death in 38 was marked. Henceforth whenever he had to take an important oath he would swear by her holiness, and indeed he decreed that she was to be worshipped as a goddess. At first Gaius was certainly devoted to all three sisters – they were included in the oath of allegiance to the Emperor. Such affection was a feature of his family, and the deaths of his brothers and the loneliness of his own upbringing naturally enough encouraged the sentiment. It did not last however. Soon the two other sisters were involved in plots against him, and suffered the fate of so many of the women in the Julio-Claudian family: they were consigned to an island prison and their lovers executed.

The Emperor's own appetites could hardly be satiated. It was affirmed that he treated the respectable married women of the city as an Eastern sultan might his harem, having them paraded before him that he might select whichever pleased his momentary fancy; he would then immediately withdraw with the chosen one, even from a public banquet. On his return he would treat the company to a critical description of her attributes and performance. Though he had banished a horde of catamites from the city, he indulged a passion for the actor Mnester, covering him with kisses even in the theatre in full view of the audience. He demanded the utmost respect for his lover's performances. One equestrian, who chattered while Mnester was acting, found himself straightway despatched, doubtless in trepidation, as the bearer of a sealed message to King Ptolemy of Mauretania. When opened, it was found to read, 'do nothing, either good or bad, to the bearer of this message', a stroke of humour not without its sadistic element. Nothing was found incredible; a young man of consular family, Valerius Catullus, boasted that he had sodomized the Emperor to a point where they were both utterly exhausted. As for wives, Gaius ran through them with theatrical speed. Three were acquired and discarded (one ripped from a wedding feast with another husband) before he found satisfaction with Caesonia, who was neither young nor beautiful. She compensated for these failings by being extremely lustful. Suetonius says that the Emperor loved her 'with passionate fidelity'. He would dress her up in military uniform or parade her naked before his friends, and enlivened their hours of love-making by wondering whether he should have her tortured so that he might discover why she loved him. Her experience – she had been notoriously promiscuous – enabled her to cater to his immature sadism, and her energy matched his. It was a happy marriage.

Sadism was an inescapable feature of his character. 'Bear in mind that I can treat anyone exactly as I please,' he told his grandmother Antonia, and proceeded to do so. 'Kill him so that he can feel he is dying' was his most celebrated instruction. Yet many of the stories recounted by Suetonius, in particular, indicate wayward humour, though of a perverse and nasty kind. 'Kill every man between that baldhead and that one,' he laconically observed, gazing at a row of prisoners. A man who had sworn to commit suicide was found to be still alive; the Emperor compelled him to fulfil his vow. Finding butchers' meat too expensive for his lions, he fed the beasts criminals instead. He ordered the tragic actor, Appeles of Ascalon, famous for his honeyed voice, to be flogged, and gave instructions that it should be performed slowly, so that he might longer enjoy the melodious sound of his shrieks. Learning that the priest of Diana at Nemi, by law a runaway slave who had acquired office by killing the previous incumbent, had met no challenger for years, he at once despatched a young hopeful to remove him. Such stories may be apocryphal; yet it is in anecdote that an impressionistic truth may be discerned.

Gaius was fond of Nemi (a redeeming feature of his character, for it is a place of delight), and it was the scene of some of his most lavish and least baneful extravagances. He had a villa nearby, just over the hill at Aricia, and had constructed a huge pleasure-galley, in which he would picnic on the lake, magically still in its bowl of thyme-scented hills. In this, as in other ways, he anticipated Nero. Both had ambitions to make art of life. Like him, Gaius was a great builder, even though most of his plans failed to advance beyond the conceptual stage. All the same he completed and dedicated the Temple of the Divine Augustus, which Tiberius had neglected to finish. He extended the imperial palace on the Palatine, and built his private Circus across the river, a Circus destined to be the scene of the first Christian martyrdoms in Nero's reign (the Colosseum was a construction of the Flavian Emperors) and eventually to be absorbed in the great Basilica of St Peter.

His personal extravagance was enormous, and Tiberius' carefully accumulated treasure was soon dissipated. His gifts were prodigal: two million sesterces to a favourite charioteer, another million to one Livius Geminius, who swore he had seen the beloved Drusilla soaring heavenward; money easily earned, one might think. Before long this extravagance was to have political consequences. Shortage of money contributed to the decision to reintroduce treason-trials; they gave enormous opportunities for confiscation of property. It eventually encouraged him to impose as many as forty new taxes, some of them grotesque – on prostitutes and the daily earnings of porters and carriers, for instance.

Yet it was only one aspect of a general extravagance of behaviour that developed as he came to feel the power of his position, and as his equilibrium, both physical and psychological, was disturbed. Philo, the acute Jewish observer, remarked, 'heavy drinking and a taste for delicacies, an insatiable appetite even on a swollen stomach, hot baths at the wrong time, emetics followed immediately by further drinking and the gluttony that goes with it, indecent behaviour with boys and women, and all the vices which destroy body and soul and the bonds which unite them, attacked him simultaneously'. No wonder that his judgement became uncertain and his conduct utterly capricious.

The most celebrated example of such caprice was the building of a bridge of boats over the Bay of Baiae, a distance of more than three Roman miles. Suetonius described it as being 'on so fantastic a scale that nothing had been seen like it before'. Merchant ships were collected from all quarters, anchored, boarded over, with earth piled on the planks, so that 'he made a sort of Appian Way', 'along which he trotted to and fro for two days'. On the first day he crossed on horseback, gaily caparisoned in cloth-of-gold cloak and wearing the breastplate of Alexander the Great. His second day's progress was more ambitious, for, dressed as a charioteer, he drove a team of two fiery steeds, and was followed by the entire Guards division, also in chariots. All sorts of explanations for the folly were suggested. Gaius was emulating, even seeking to surpass, Xerxes. He was contradicting a prophecy of the astrologer Thrasyllus who had told Tiberius that Gaius had no more chance of becoming emperor than 'of riding a horse dryshod across the Gulf of Baiae'. The absurdity of this explanation – Gaius was after all already emperor so that the prophecy had been disproved – has not prevented solemn asses from repeating it. Yet a reasonable explanation may exist (though Gaius clearly failed to convince contemporaries of the fact): the building of the bridge could well have been a military exercise or experiment.

For Gaius was not only a playboy; he was still emperor too. He might fall short of the devoted concentration which both Augustus and Tiberius had shown; he might be easily distracted. He was nevertheless the supreme ruler, Princeps and commander-in-chief. Moreover, as the son of Germanicus, he inherited a certain position and a standing with the legions. This meant that he inherited a policy too. There were those who had never accepted the stabilization of the frontiers which Augustus had decreed after the Varian disaster, to which policy Tiberius had adhered. In particular Germanicus had entertained dreams of glory and imperial expansion in

Germany; he had resented Tiberius' order to withdraw, and his followers had seen evidence of the Emperor's jealousy in their hero's supersession. Gaius needed no prompting to revive the plan; it was in a sense a family duty. The huge engineering feat at Baiae may be seen as part of his preparation.

Problems of two kinds, both familiar, intervened to delay the enterprise. First he had to adjust his plans when he learned of a conspiracy on the northern frontier itself, the mainspring being the legate of Upper Germany, Gn. Cornelius Gaetulicus. Conspiracy at Rome was dangerous enough; disaffection among the legions even more alarming. Gaius acted at once, hastening north in September 39 to restore order with admirable speed. Not only was Gaetulicus executed. A fellow-conspirator proved to be Aemilius Lepidus, scion of a great consular family, widower of the beloved Drusilla, and now lover of Gaius' second sister, Agrippina. Neither rank nor connections could save him. He too was executed, and Agrippina and a third sister, Julia Livilla, having been compelled to accompany his corpse to Rome in ghastly parody of their mother's journey from Brindisi, were banished. The Senate, many of whose members had sympathized with the plot, despatched the Emperor's uncle Claudius to congratulate him. Incensed by their choice, for he had no better opinion of his uncle's wits than Augustus and Tiberius had had, Gaius had him ducked in the Rhine; to the huge amusement of the troops.

Meanwhile however Gaius had embarked on military manoeuvres which have easily been made to appear bizarre, and which have been described in such a way as to call the Emperor's sanity into question. Anxious to seem to be fighting but fearful of real war, so the approved version goes, he sent some of his German bodyguard across the Rhine with orders to hide among the trees; he then set off with the cavalry in pursuit. A few days later he did it again, this time awarding trophies. Gallic captives were ordered to dye their hair red and pretend to be Germans. The conquest of Britain was decreed, and the army drawn up on the Channel shore, ready to invade. Suddenly however the embarkation was cancelled, and the men were commanded to pick up sea-shells. This victory was commemorated by the erection of a *pharos*. Some of the stories – that he planned to execute the legionaries who, twenty-six years before, had besieged Germanicus in his headquarters – are just as incredible; most of them must have retired by this time. One can only reflect that, if these stories of his behaviour on the Rhine and in Gaul are true, then Gaius was indeed mad, and it is amazing that the legions tolerated such conduct.

What really happened in the north can however be discerned amidst the fog of enveloping rumour. Gaius arrived there to find not only conspiracy, but poorly trained and idle legions. That was not surprising, the northern frontier had known peace for years. Gaetulicus had latterly sought popularity at the expense of efficiency; there were too many soldiers, particularly among the senior centurions, who had outlived their usefulness; and some of these were no doubt implicated in the conspiracy. Gaius embarked on a policy that would restore discipline and military standards. His choice for the replacement of Gaetulicus was significant – Galba, the future Emperor, whose reputation for stern discipline was to endure all his life. The first task was to reorganize, and weed out the inefficient; the second was to give the troops some serious training – it was anyway too late in the year for a campaign, even if the army had been prepared for one. Hence the manoeuvres across the river, in which anyone not completely ignorant of military matters can see a stiff training programme, with field-days and prizes. As for the abortive invasion of Britain, explanations are possible that exclude insanity, though no certain one can be advanced. It may be that the troops were restless, still potentially mutinous, reluctant to embark on so dangerous an enterprise. Possibly they went so far as to refuse to obey an order to board ship, and Gaius, in a spasm of temper, gave them the deliberately insulting command to pick up sea-shells, which they sullenly obeyed, swallowing the insult, because they were ashamed of having gained their point. On the other hand, news from Rome may have caused him to cancel the expedition of his own accord; his order then being maliciously misinterpreted, for the word for sea-shells, *musculi*, is by a curious coincidence the same as the word for the engineers' huts, and a command to pick these up would make perfect sense.

At any rate the campaign was abandoned, with some loss of prestige, which Gaius, in the manner of politicians, attempted to obscure by making extravagant claims to have performed what he had no more than promised, and in the autumn of 40 he hurried back to Rome. Things were bad enough there, for at least three reasons. There was trouble in the provinces, which, long quiescent under the wise rule of his predecessors, were stirring, resentful of the Emperor's caprices; and this of course had repercussions in the capital. There was a financial crisis, caused by his own extravagance. Worst of all, relations between the Emperor and the Senate had deteriorated sharply. In fact, all might be considered different aspects of a central problem, which rested in Gaius' developing conception of the Empire: the Augustan dyarchy, that Republican façade of Empire, was on the point of collapse, and Gaius seemed about to convert the Principate into a thoroughly autocratic system.

He had departed from the wise policy of Tiberius, who had preferred to reduce the numbers of client-kingdoms and incorporate such territories in the Empire. Gaius, influenced by his friend Herod Agrippa and perhaps by his Antonian heredity, felt an affinity with royalty. The three Thracian princes, friends of his boyhood, were all found kingdoms – lesser Armenia, Pontus and part of Thrace. The effect of this was disturbing: client-kings could rarely satisfy both Rome and their subjects; they found intrigue irresistible, and always sought more power. So, while Gaius was establishing kingdoms in one part of the Empire, he sought to extirpate another elsewhere. Ptolemy of Mauretania, suspected of disloyalty, was called to Rome and ordered to kill himself. Meanwhile Gaius intended to annex his kingdom, but met resistance. None of this was likely to reassure the senators.

Even more unsettling, and quite unnecessary, was a dispute with the Jews that drove them to the brink of rebellion. The Jews were difficult; sullen and zealous monotheists, anomalous in the Ancient World, and far removed from the genial and flexible tolerance which characterized the best of Antiquity. This difficulty had not yet been felt by the emperors; Tiberius, sceptical and disdainful of notions of his own divinity, felt no animus against the Jews, so long as they obeyed the laws of Rome and did not trouble the public peace. But, at local level, they could easily be a cause of dissension.

It was particularly so in Alexandria. There a large Jewish community found itself recurrently at odds with the Greeks, who dominated that great city. Anti-semitic riots were frequent, for the Greeks considered that the Jews were unfairly favoured by Rome; they were permitted their own Senate and their own ethnarch. Trouble flared up in 38 when Herod Agrippa called at the city on his way to the East; he was hardly popular there, having urgently decamped a few years previously, leaving behind him a pile of unpaid debts. The Greeks sacked the Jewish quarter, and, in a move that must have seemed cunning, persuaded the Prefect, Flaccus, to order that statues of the Emperor should be placed in the synagogues. The Jews objected; the law of Moses forbade such idolatry. They sent a deputation to the Emperor, led by the philosopher and theologian, Philo.

They found Gaius' policy contradictory. On the one hand he had recalled Flaccus and put him to death. Yet, on the other hand and at the same time, he had ordered a statue of himself to be placed in the Temple at Jerusalem. What were they to make of such vagaries? Equally disconcerting was his treatment of the deputation, who had to chase him from room to room, eventually catching up with him in the palace garden. They found him whimsical, inattentive; his intellectual frivolity both puzzled and shocked. All the same he had a grasp of the point at issue: 'men who do not think me a god are worse than criminal,' he said. There was no escaping that. The idea might be blasphemous and absurd to the Jews, but it was a political reality. For a time, guided by Herod Agrippa and P. Petronius, Governor of Syria, Gaius seemed prepared to compromise. His mood changed again however. He could not compromise his divinity; did he not after all call on the Goddess Diana to share his bed when the moon was full, and had not Jupiter himself suggested that he lodge with him? Of course therefore the Jews also must acknowledge what he was. He revoked his revocation: the statue must be placed in the Temple. For good measure he ordered Petronius to kill himself. (By the time the order arrived Gaius was dead; Petronius was accordingly able to ignore it, and a Jewish revolt was averted.)

Gaius' extravagance had compelled him to impose new taxes. Worse, it had encouraged him to revive the practice of treason-trials. There was more behind this than shortage of money, however. Some time early in his reign, Gaius had had occasion to examine his predecessor's private papers, and had read the account of the evidence offered against his mother and brothers. The experience affected him profoundly, for he learned two things, knowledge which changed his way of looking at the world. First, he discovered that much of what he had been brought up to believe was false. Tiberius had been no monster; on the contrary he had indeed been surrounded by conspiracy and treason; that was the fate of emperors. Hence the bitterness of Gaius' remark that, on the evidence presented, Tiberius could not have failed to believe that Agrippina and her sons were guilty. Secondly, Gaius learned the names of their accusers, many of them senators who had played a double part and lived to offer him fulsome praise. His contempt sharpened; he came to see the Senate as a corrupt and faithless body. The Emperor could believe nothing; trust nobody. Early on, Gaius had begun to remove rivals, or men who might become a danger; neither Tiberius Gemellus nor Macro had lasted long; and later Lepidus' part in the northern conspiracy proved the point. Gaius therefore strove to separate himself from the Senate and to weaken and humiliate it: 'Let them hate, provided they fear'. So, for instance, he transferred elections back from Senate to the people; and he took away command of the legions in Africa from the senatorial proconsul and gave it to an imperial legate. Once, when two consuls offended him, he summarily deprived them of office and smashed their *fasces*. Nothing could have demonstrated more clearly that Gaius was no longer prepared to make even a pretence of respect for the Augustan compromise: he was headed for absolutism.

Inevitably fear and suspicion worked on each other. The Senate, offended by this emperor who sometimes dressed as a gladiator and consorted with dancers and actors, had quickly learned also to dread his caprice and cruelty. Now too he seemed to threaten the fabric of the State. He appeared determined to make them feel their impotence, 'Let him feel he is dying' was a sentiment that might indeed have a metaphorical significance. The Roman nobility found themselves at last unable to escape the fullest realization of what imperial power could mean. At the same time Gaius' contempt for the Senate, and his alienation from it, drove him into ever more extravagant conduct – there were rumours that he meant to shift the seat of government from Rome. No one could doubt even the most extraordinary story – his behaviour had become totally unpredictable and therefore frightening. Who knew what fantasies his febrile brain nourished in his sleepless nights? And he was still a young man, it was not this time a case of waiting for an aged recluse to die. Instead here was a prince, convinced that he was also a god, whose senses were disordered and whose judgement was impaired by alcohol and even perhaps by madness, who felt himself enmeshed in conspiracy and who knew no mercy. Naturally – inevitably – their response must be to plot his death. A mood hardened, like December frost after uncertain November fogs; enough of these emperors. A generation was there that knew nothing of Republican instability, but only of the fear and uncertainty of living in an atmosphere dominated by delation and infected by the diseased caprices of empire. Down with the Caesars; back to the Republic. . .

Yet, when it happened, the agent was no Brutus, fired by zeal for the Commonwealth. Instead a Praetorian tribune, Cassius Chaerea, resolved at last to avenge a long series of insults the Emperor had inflicted on him – for though Cassius was a hardened veteran, it had amused Gaius to twit him with effeminacy. Accordingly, whenever the tribune demanded the watchword from him, the Emperor would smile knowingly and choose something like 'Venus' or 'Priapus'; or when Cassius had occasion to approach him with some other request, Gaius would give him only his middle finger to kiss and would waggle it in an obscene gesture of invitation; to the delight, doubtless, of the troops. But Cassius was not alone in having a grievance, and there were many others prompted to act by fear. Other members of the Guard were involved, for it is the measure of Gaius' instability that he had also lost the support of his Praetorians. And behind them were the dissident senators, bent on the restoration of the Republic.

On 24 January 41, just after mid-day, Gaius was in the theatre. He could not decide whether to go to lunch – he still felt swimpish after a night's drinking. Some friends persuaded him to move, leading him to the spot appointed by the conspirators. He stopped there in a colonnade to watch some boys of an Asian noble family, rehearsing the Trojan war dance. He would have had them return to the theatre to perform at once; but their leader, well primed, complained of a cold. As he stood there chatting, the conspirators approached. Cassius struck the first blow, from behind, calling on him so that he turned his head to receive the upward thrust in his throat. The Emperor fell to the ground, twitching, his jaw-bone split. 'I am still alive,' he managed to say, no doubt hoping that his friends would come to his aid. But there were none there. The conspirators moved to finish him off, one thrusting his blade through the Emperor's genitals; perhaps that was Cassius too. Another centurion quickly murdered Caesonia, and a common soldier picked up their baby, little Julia Drusilla, and, with awful relish, dashed her brains out against the wall. When it was all over, Gaius' German bodyguard appeared on the scene, and killed one or two of the senators who were in the vicinity, in pointless barbarian revenge.

Gaius had reigned less than four years. His body was quickly disposed of, half-burnt on an improvised pile, and then shovelled into a shallow grave in the Lamian gardens. Later, when his sisters returned from the exile to which he had condemned them, they had it exhumed and offered the poor remains a proper burial: an act of exemplary family piety. It was thought to be just as well: everyone knew that his ghost had hitherto haunted the gardens. Yet such piety was not exorcism enough; Gaius' uneasy spirit could not be laid. He had taught subsequent emperors what licence was permitted to them – Nero was to be his disciple. But he had also shown that an emperor could be unmade by the sword, even gods could fall to the soldiers. It would not be long before the world learned, too, that emperors could be made somewhere other than at Rome.

Claudius as Jupiter. The eagle's expression, indicating surprise amounting to
scepticism, not necessarily intended, is yet a fair commentary on Claudius'
accession

CLAUDIUS

THE MURDER OF Gaius caused panic and confusion; for a few hours nobody knew what was happening. Such uncertainty is hardly surprising; it was not clear whether a coup d'état had taken place, or whether the murderers had simply neglected to consider the consequences of their action. The latter may indeed have been the case; the Roman world was yet unaware of the grammar of the coup d'état. Its bureaucratic structure still hardly formed, its centres of power still diffuse, it found it hard to recognize the influences that controlled the State. Thus the ignorance as to whether the conspirators were aiming at anything more than the removal of the tyrant. In the same way, their predecessors, the Liberators who had murdered Julius Caesar, had likewise lacked all understanding of how to proceed from their deed.

So, for a few hours, the Senate, their spirits lightened by the murder of their oppressor, played with the fancy of restoring the Republic – though none of them can have had any notion of how such a restored Republic would be governed. More realistic members considered which of their colleagues might be best suited to the purple; but, in Gibbon's words, 'while the Senate deliberated, the Praetorian Guards had resolved'.

A soldier of the Guard had found the dead Emperor's uncle, Tiberius Claudius Nero, sheltering behind a curtain in the imperial palace on the Palatine Hill. The elderly prince – he was fifty, but old for his years – had fallen in terror at the soldier's feet, clasping his hands round the man's knees, and begging him to spare his life. The soldier recognized whom he had at his mercy. He shouted to some of his comrades, and they hustled the stuttering Claudius, still fearful for his life, off to their camp. There he realized that they didn't know what to do either; he began to feel the strength of his position. The soldiers for their part, aware that they only desired a change of emperor, not a change of regime, showed themselves ready to be bought and still favourable to the Julio-Claudian house, of which their prisoner was the only surviving male adult. He offered them money – a hundred and fifty gold pieces for each man – they offered him the Empire. He then despatched his boyhood friend, the Jewish prince Herod Agrippa (who had characteristically appeared on the scene), to the Senate to plead his cause; and the senators, whose feeble resolution was easily unnerved by the spectacle of the decided Praetorians, acquiesced; Claudius became the fourth Princeps, in succession to his nephew.

So at least goes the traditional account; and specious though it may appear, there is no means of impugning it. No evidence exists of a plot to make Claudius Princeps on the one hand, while on the other his elevation dashed incipient but no more than half-formed hopes. Whatever the true circumstances of his rise to power, it yet revealed, starkly and unmistakably, the military nature of the State. Claudius was Princeps because the Praetorians, having removed one emperor, had chosen him, no other reason. He, now anxious to conceal the origins of his rise, commanded that the records of the two days' debate in the Senate should be expunged; and proclaimed a general amnesty which only excepted a few involved in the actual murder of Gaius. There was to be no investigation of the conspiracy; it might reveal too much.

That decision, and the all-important fact that the armies stationed on the frontiers accepted the new Princeps almost without demur, might suggest that there was something of deliberate farce in the comedy recounted; that Claudius had indeed been the intended successor, for whom the ground had already been prepared. Yet such speculation has nothing to rest on; the popular account must stand. If it does nothing else, it reveals the good-natured contempt with which the new master of the world had been regarded throughout his hitherto uneventful life.

Neither Augustus, his step-grandfather, nor Tiberius, his uncle, had considered Claudius fit for public life; modern historians, wiser than those who knew him, have reversed their judgement. Claudius has been judged one of the most capable and creative of emperors, even ranked with Augustus – and it is indeed the case that he was to be the first Princeps since Augustus to be posthumously deified by the Senate. (In contrast to Gaius, he showed the same good sense as Tiberius in his rejection of that honour in his lifetime, saying for instance to the Alexandrians who had offered to dedicate a temple to him, that 'he did not wish to be offensive to his contemporaries'.) Such a discrepancy of view is strange but not irreconcilable, power can change a man, or permit qualities, previously hidden and unsuspected, to develop. Historians have judged Claudius on his performance, while Augustus and Tiberius necessarily judged him by his manner and his apparent potential. Even so, the contradiction runs deeper still, since Claudius was a clown for Suetonius also, and a mere silly tool of his wives and freedmen for the deeply ironic Tacitus. The problem of his character and capacity can hardly be considered settled.

(*right*) Bas-relief showing Claudius receiving the symbols of power. The beard shows it not to be a contemporary work

He was born in Lyons in 10 BC. His father was Drusus, son of Livia by her first husband and brother of Tiberius; his mother Antonia, daughter of Mark Antony and Octavia; he was therefore the brother of the hero Germanicus. Such a birth promised him a distinguished if dangerous career; but Claudius suffered from physical and temperamental defects which made people think him an idiot. He was lame and awkward; he slobbered and stammered; not surprisingly he quite lacked self-possession. His own mother called him a monster; Livia detested him; and even Augustus' usual affection for the boys in the family could not overcome the horror he felt for dwarfs or people who were deformed, whom he regarded as freaks of nature and therefore bringers of bad luck. Moreover the imperial family lived publicly, always on display, at religious ceremonies, in the Senate, with the armies, in the theatre or arena; they could hardly be expected to relish the appearance of a member who was likely to attract the quick ridicule of the Roman; that would tarnish the whole family's reputation.

So the young Claudius became the subject of much anxious discussion. 'The question is,' Augustus wrote to Livia, 'whether he has full command of his five senses . . . should he turn out to be physically and mentally deficient, then we must not give the public (which is always amused by oddities) the chance of laughing at us . . . if only he would show greater powers of concentration and less capriciousness. . . I am sorry for the poor chap because in serious matters (when his wits are collected) he shows a good deal of high principle. . .' Yet, though he also said that he couldn't understand 'how anyone who talks so confusedly in private can nevertheless speak clearly and intelligibly in public', in the end he decided the risk was too great. Claudius simply couldn't be trusted to carry out a public career with the dignity and reliability that the imperial duty demanded. Tiberius concurred with this verdict. When the Senate wished to allow Claudius to address the House among men of consular rank, Tiberius rejected the proposal saying that Claudius' ill-health made it impossible for him to participate in debates.

That was that. Claudius was condemned to private life. True, the Equestrian Order honoured him, twice asking him to head a deputation to the consuls; and he was also granted a place in one of the priestly colleges. But this didn't amount to much of a career. While his brother Germanicus became the hero of the armies and the leader of the expansionist party in the State, Claudius languished at home, acquiring a reputation as glutton, drunkard and buffoon. The full measure of his insignificance may be gauged by the reflection that Sejanus had totally ignored him: the favourite's attacks on that branch of the family had never touched the wretched Claudius. Then his nephew Gaius had treated him almost as the Court Fool. Claudius had endured it; it was one way to survive.

Still, this was only one side of his character – the side admittedly which preserved him to inherit the Empire. Yet Claudius was not only this figure of fun, this drunken butt. All through his years of obscurity he was developing interests and qualities which fitted him, in some degree at least, for what he was to be. Deprived of the chance of an active career, he turned to the pursuit of scholarship. His principal interest was history, a fashionable concern in Augustan Rome. He became first a pupil of Livy, and then himself compiled a history of the Civil Wars. This was a risky theme, especially for Antony's grandson. He was persuaded to desist after he had written two books, and to resume his history at the year 27, when Augustus' victory had stilled controversy. It ran to forty-one books. He also wrote histories of the Carthaginians and the Etruscans, a defence of Cicero and a book on the Latin alphabet, as well as an autobiography in eight books; this last however can hardly have been crammed with incident.

At the very least this is a record of assiduous scholarship. It was not merely an act of flattery, an empty honorific, when the city of Alexandria acknowledged these works by adding a new wing to the public library and calling it 'the Claudian'. The contrast with the other side of Claudius' character is marked, but involves no necessary contradiction. No one acquainted with university life can fail to be aware of how fine scholarship may co-exist with drunkenness, boorish manners and a clownish obtuseness outside the field of study. Doubtless Claudius would have excited ridicule and remark wherever he found himself, but he would at least have been among his peers at the High Table of a university college.

All his works have disappeared, so that it is impossible to judge their quality. Some hint however is given by his surviving letters and edicts, all with a characteristic flavour which makes it probable that they were composed by him and not by his secretaries; and these show clear understanding though little elegance. What is certain is that his historical studies gave him a realization of how Rome had grown strong through the willingness of Romans to adapt to changing situations. He was to put forward this argument to the Senate in 48 when he defended his decision to strengthen that body by admitting members of the Gallic aristocracy: 'the experience of my ancestors,' he said, 'encourages me to employ the same policy in governing the State, that is, bringing men of outstanding merit to Rome, no matter where they come from . . . everything, members of the Senate, which is now held to be of the greatest antiquity was once new. First plebeians joined the patricians in office. Then Latins were added, then other Italians. The innovation which I now propose will establish itself. What I am defending by appeal to precedent will be cited as a precedent itself in its turn. . .'

His historical training therefore gave Claudius an organic conception of the State. He was able to regard himself as the heir of Augustus without necessarily feeling bound (as Tiberius had felt himself) to adhere in detail to the Augustan polity or policies. For he sensed that inasmuch as Augustus had been a conservative, he was one of the same stamp as himself. Both knew that things would have to change if stability was to be maintained.

As a result Claudius' reign saw developments in the Roman State which effectively destroyed the basis of the Augustan compromise, just as surely, though in a quite different manner, as Tiberius had made it temporarily unworkable by his withdrawal to Capri. The Augustan settlement was revealed to have been merely of and for its own time. Of course, like almost every Princeps, Claudius did pay lip-service to it; and he began by trying to co-operate with the Senate on Augustan lines, showing respect for its functions and attempting to persuade its members to do likewise. On one occasion for instance he urged the Senate; 'if you disapprove, say so now and offer another proposal. It is unworthy of the majesty of this assembly that one man and one man alone, the consul-designate, should repeat what the consuls have said, word for word, and give it as his opinion, and then that everybody else should nod their heads and say, "I agree" . . .' But it was useless. The advice might be sincere; it was also remote from reality. Neither Augustus nor Tiberius had been able to persuade the Senate to act with vigour and honesty; and there was no chance that Claudius' words could succeed where theirs had failed. Moreover, there was an essential element of falsity in these exhortations from successive Princeps. None of them could have lived with a sturdily independent Senate. On the contrary: the fundamental condition of empire was senatorial feebleness and corruption; anything else would have led to clashes which could not have been resolved.

The whole tendency indeed was in the other direction; away from senatorial co-operation, towards autocracy. As the Senate's responsibilities grew fewer, its capacity to exercise responsibility declined also. Inevitably, the emperors took more on themselves. So, during Claudius' reign, imperial officials took over from the Senate or from elected officials the care for the port of Ostia and the roads of Rome; and control of the Public Treasury (the *Aerarium*) at least for three years from 44; in 53, moreover, powers of jurisdiction concerning financial questions in senatorial provinces were transferred from the proconsuls to imperial agents called procurators.

Such developments might be considered reversible. What was less so was the development of a centralized bureaucracy with specialized departments, each controlled by one of the imperial freedmen; by representatives, that is, of the Princeps' own household. This was to form the basis of the imperial civil service, quite independent of older authorities such as the Senate or the equestrian Order. These freedmen were more likely to be Greek than Italian; they had no particular reverence for Roman traditions, but owed their place and therefore their loyalty directly to the Princeps. They were indeed his creatures; he had made them and could destroy them. Their power, though great, was in no way autonomous, depending as it did on their ability to retain the imperial favour. This, in turn, meant that they sought to control access to the Emperor, and so risked isolating him.

It was Claudius' achievement to regularize and make bureaucratic what had previously existed informally. The new ministers were his own freedmen: Narcissus, the chief secretary through whose office all official correspondence passed; Callistus, responsible for dealing with petitions to the Emperor and with judicial enquiries; Pallas, the financial secretary; and Polybius, librarian and researcher. They all used their position to acquire great wealth; it was their only security beyond what they could achieve by managing other potential influences on Claudius.

This reorganization of the government machine undoubtedly resulted in more efficient administration. But there was a corresponding loss. The gulf deepened between the Princeps and the old political class of the Roman aristocracy; and the balance of power, long favourable to the Princeps, shifted still more decisively as Claudius, whose upbringing and disabilities rendered him uneasy with his social equals, retreated behind the screen of his familiar servants. Accordingly, whatever formal obeisance was still paid to Republican traditions, the grip of monarchy tightened. Freedom became a mere memory, a word lacking precise definition, since none had experienced it. Consequently, whatever his pious intentions, Claudius quarrelled with the Senate. Its members distrusted him: in the thirteen years of his reign at least thirty-five senators and over three hundred equestrians were put to death on charges of treason and conspiracy.

That was the dark side of empire, the brooding suspicion, the fear and resentment, that Claudius could not escape. It was partly his heritage – the last twenty years had been a wasps' nest of conspiracy and terror; the changes of emperor do not conceal the continuity of mood. Ever since Sejanus had climbed to power the city of Rome had been a place where trust and loyalty had little meaning. It would have taken a far stronger character than Claudius to change that.

Despite this there were many areas where Claudius met with the sort of success that justifies the praise historians have given him. The administration, neglected and rendered capricious by Gaius, improved. These were early days of bureaucracy, its evils not yet apparent. First-century Rome benefited from its development just as Tudor England and seventeenth-century France did. The Princeps had a strong interest in legislation and the work of the law courts, frequently hearing cases himself. (Sometimes he was inconsistent; sometimes he fell asleep; but many of his judgements were shrewd and to the point.) He attempted to improve procedure and restrict the use of professional informers and accusers. He passed laws limiting usury and others enjoining humane treatment of sick slaves. He took new measures to ensure the supply of corn for Rome – this was of course prudent; nothing was so likely to lead to rioting, even insurrection, as a dearth of grain. Indeed Claudius himself was 'once stopped in the middle of the forum by a mob and so pelted with abuse and pieces of bread that he was hardly able to escape to the palace by a back-door'; thereafter he provided insurance for importers by guaranteeing them against any loss due to storms, and so encouraged them to risk transporting grain even in the winter. He also built a new harbour at the mouth of the Tiber to provide a safe winter landing-place; 'he excavated', according to Dio Cassius, 'a large area of shore, built walls on every side of it, and admitted the sea; then, beyond it in the sea itself, he constructed huge moles on either side of the entrance, and so enclosed a large body of water, in the middle of which he threw up an island on which he erected a lighthouse'.

Such care for the material well-being of the people was typical. He finished two aqueducts which Gaius had projected – stretches of the Aqua Claudia still stride across the Campagna – and he put 30,000 men to work draining the Fucine Lake in

Via Appia Antica, with remains of the Claudian aqueduct

the Abruzzi to reclaim a large area of land for agriculture. He also built many roads, both in Italy and the provinces. This enlightened government was the work of a man who had had the opportunity to think for a long time about the duties and responsibilities of his position and who, in contrast to his whimsical predecessor, was capable of managing a bureaucracy that could translate plans into action.

A similar thoughtfulness may be discerned in his provincial policy, where he showed himself the heir of Julius rather than of Augustus. Its animating force was that revealed in his Senate speech on the question of the admission of Gauls. Rome had brought the Mediterranean world the blessings of peace and order. But even that sort of satisfaction may pall; and Claudius sensed that the benefits of Roman citizenship must be spread to the municipal elites throughout the Empire. Seneca, the philosopher, dramatist and politician, whom he had sent into exile, might sneer that Claudius had decided that they should see all the provincials wearing togas; the Emperor's policy was nevertheless the one common sense dictated. He knew that the provincial elites could only be prevented from discontent that would eventually nibble away at the fabric of empire if they were allowed to share its rewards. They must learn to feel themselves Romans. He was in fact paving the way for an empire of all civilized men, which should draw its rulers from Spain (Trajan and Hadrian), Africa (Septimus Severus), Illyria (Diocletian) and Syria (Caracalla). In this respect he did more to render the Empire enduring than any other member of his house.

Care for the provinces, and the conviction that they must experience to the full the blessings of empire, were Claudius' constant concern. The trend was therefore towards uniformity, though in effect this was still far distant. Meanwhile foreign religions were tolerated, provided they seemed to offer no threat to Roman ideas and Roman rule: in Gaul, Druidism was suppressed; but Claudius reverted to the more liberal attitude towards the Jews that had been normal before Gaius. (All the same he took steps to check the spread of Judaism in Rome itself and accused the Jews of Alexandria of 'fomenting a universal plague'.) The worship of Attis, the fertility god of Asia Minor, was actually incorporated in the Roman calendar and therefore recognized as an official religion of the Empire; its chief priest henceforth was to be a Roman citizen, not an Eastern eunuch. This was Romanization indeed; it also meant of course that the devotees of Attis found nothing in their cult incompatible with Roman rule.

This conception of an organic Empire, one that could not be allowed to crystallize in a given shape, accounted, in part at least, for Claudius' decision to abandon Augustus' precept that the limits of empire should be regarded as fixed. Instead he pushed the frontier to the Black Sea, by annexing Thrace in 46; and he incorporated the client-states of Mauretania in North Africa and Lycia in south Turkey into the Empire proper. He also carried out Gaius' declared policy and in 43 embarked on the conquest of Britain. By the end of his reign southern England had been occupied, the frontier lying along a line formed by the extension of the Trent and Severn rivers. He thus inaugurated the last phase of Roman expansion, which was to come to fruition in the campaigns of Trajan and Hadrian.

But there was a more sinister reason at the root of this policy; and one which disclosed the rickety fabric of the State. Claudius was of course no soldier himself; his life had been passed in the study and at the dining-table, well away from the camp. But naturally too, as the son of Drusus and brother of Germanicus, he could hardly be without some sense of military glory, even ambition. And he also knew where ultimate power rested: with the armies. They had to be appeased, rendered content. Gaius had irritated them no less than the senators; Claudius must satisfy them. He showed skill and judgement in his choice of commanders two of whom, Galba and Vespasian, were to be future emperors. That helped to maintain discipline and morale, both damaged by Gaius' failures on the Rhine and the Channel coast; still it was not enough. It had been easy for Tiberius to follow peace; he had received triumphs and ovations, conquered Illyricum and Pannonia, subdued the Germans, led Roman soldiers in countless campaigns. His *dignitas* could not be questioned; his achievement shone. Not so with Claudius, bookish intellectual and stutterer. If he were to follow Tiberius' policy, it could not fail to be

Relief sculpture of gladiators and lions

interpreted as weakness. He had to satisfy the aspirations of the armies, certainly of his generals, or they might decide to dispense with him. For Claudius therefore war was a necessity as much as a choice. No wonder he sought the acclamation of the troops, visited Britain in time to participate in victory and justify the triumph which he granted himself, and had himself acclaimed *imperator* on no fewer than twenty-seven occasions. And no doubt it was psychologically satisfying for this child of Drusus, this brother of Germanicus, this shambling freak who had been denied the military career that should have been his due, now to receive the plaudits of marching troops and to hear himself acclaimed as a great conqueror. But it was more than that; it was also politic. If the Republic had collapsed because it had found no way within its traditional forms to satisfy the *dignitas* of the dynasts, so

142

the Empire's survival depended on the ability of the Princeps to feed the *dignitas* of the armies; only thus could he be granted their respect and obedience. Claudius, doubtless intuitively, was aware of this and acted accordingly; by contrast his stepson, Nero, was to be blithely oblivious of it, and perish.

For all his perceptiveness and good sense, Claudius could not escape the defects of his character and upbringing. He remained timid and awkward with his social equals. The timidity made him cruel. (In contrast to Tiberius, for instance, he took a greedy pleasure in gladiatorial contests; he ruled that all combatants who fell accidentally should have their throats cut, and took special delight in seeing this happen to net-fighters, because they wore no helmet which might conceal their death-agonies.) Hence, the plots, the executions, the conspiracies; hence also the elaborate precautions he took against assassination – he would never visit a sick-room without having it searched for any weapons that might be concealed; hence also the influence that the few freedmen he trusted were able to acquire over him.

For Claudius, unlike his predecessors, could be governed. All ancient testimony is agreed on this point, and it is not contradicted by the other evidence, which suggests that it is his will and his language that are expressed in official documents. Such contradiction is only superficial. Claudius was essentially an academic, a don with a taste for administration. In abstract or business matters his mind was clear and cogent, as Augustus had remarked in his youth. But he could not carry this capacity for discrimination over into personal affairs for which he was temperamentally ill equipped. This timid and self-centred man found it difficult to establish personal relations with the Roman nobility, whom, still, he suspected of contempt. It was natural that his freedmen were easily able to work on such resentment. They fed his fear and at the same time ministered to his lack of self-confidence in such matters; doing so, they came to exercise a measure of control over him.

This control was in general exercised in the interests of the State, which could indeed be identified with the Emperor's own. There was no discrepancy, no divergence, between the interests of these freedmen or of the public, though on at least two occasions their desire for influence or personal gratification did threaten the vital relationship between Claudius and the army: before the invasion of Britain he sent Narcissus to subdue a menacing mutiny, and at his British triumph he granted the eunuch Posides the honour of a headless spear along with soldiers who had actually fought in the field. There is also extant a letter of Pliny's in which he recounts with aristocratic distaste how a monument erected to the Financial Secretary Pallas testifies 'his insolence, Claudius' patient endurance and the Senate's servility'. This letter illustrates too the worst effect of this cabal of freedmen, with its reduction of the independence of the old governing class and the centralization of power in the imperial household.

Yet the freedmen were not the only, not even the most dangerous, influence. Claudius, unfavoured by nature as he was, was yet passionate and sensuous. At the time he became Princeps he was married to his third wife, Messalina. Neither of his previous marriages had been a success. His first wife, Plautia Urgulanilla, had been too much for him altogether, a formidable character of tempestuous passions; he had divorced her for adultery and on suspicion of murder. The second marriage, to Aelia Paetina, was no more successful, though it ended in less animosity – Claudius even considered re-marrying her at one point. The failure of these marriages did not deter him; he seems not to have reflected that a man who fails twice in such a relationship is unlikely ever to succeed. It was natural that he should try again; not only were his sexual desires strong, but, starved of affection in childhood and youth, he sought love. On the other hand he was as unattractive as he was ardent; the beautiful women to whom he was drawn were unlikely to be satisfied by his slobbering embraces.

Messalina had been only fifteen when they married. She bore him two children to add to the two or three he had by his previous wives, a boy later to be called Britannicus, in commemoration of his father's triumph, and a girl, Octavia, who was to be married to Nero. Messalina can only have married Claudius, who was her cousin, because she was told to. Now, surprisingly become Empress and therefore in full possession of power and luxury, with a husband thirty years older than herself, she found, like many who come to live only for pleasure, that she could in fact only derive satisfaction from new and sharper sensations. Like Augustus' daughter, Julia, her tastes coarsened and became ever more demanding. Like Julia she was accused of sinking to common prostitution; like Julia she became a by-word for vice. Who that has ever seen it can forget the Beardsley drawing of Messalina returning from the bath, her breasts exposed, a determined lasciviousness displayed by the droop of her full lips, and eager decision by her stride?

For a long time her infidelities and excesses were concealed from the doting Princeps, whom she could anyway always bend to her will; if not by bullying, then even more certainly by a flash of affection and the intimation of desire. And though she jealously attacked women like Poppaea Sabina, whose gardens she coveted and whose lover she destroyed, her adulteries were long tolerated by the Emperor's entourage; affairs with actors and ballet-dancers like Mnester, once the lover of Caligula, hardly threatened the State, hardly threatened what they might consider of more moment, their own power and position. But in 47 the position changed.

Messalina's gaze had now turned to a nobleman, Gaius Silius, described as the most beautiful man in Rome. Undoubtedly Messalina was thought to have made the running: Juvenal in his *Tenth Satire* cites the case of Silius as an example of the dangers of great beauty. Silius was already married, but quickly divorced his wife; it was said that he realized that the alternative was his own death – Messalina would have had no hesitation in trumping up a charge of treason, which would of course have been proved with equal ease. Perhaps such a motive is true; on the other hand Messalina was a great prize and one who offered more than her person.

This time she was not content with a simple affair. Tacitus says she was drifting, through boredom, into familiar vices. Danger lured her; and she and Silius now went through a form of marriage, 'for the purpose of rearing children'. An act of the

Messalina and her children

purest folly and utmost audacity, it amounted to a coup d'état, except for the single fact that they had neglected to strike. They had put themselves in a position which could only be protected by the murder of Claudius; but there is no sign that they had attempted this. While one may believe that Messalina was living in a state of disoriented unreality, it is hard to be convinced that this was true of her lover also. In short, the account so dramatically given by Tacitus is riddled with inconsistencies; the gaps are enormous; speculation inevitable.

However, it is clear that the association of the Emperor's wife with a rich, politically active nobleman (Silius was in fact consul-designate) put the regime in peril. Vice in imperial Rome could not escape punishment when such political elements were present; it was the case of Julia over again. The Emperor's freedmen, convinced of danger, knew that Messalina must be denounced, knew too that she must be prevented from meeting her husband. Nothing so clearly shows the contempt with which his uxorious warmth and pliability were regarded than this fear that Messalina would even now be able to turn his jealous anger away.

He was dumbfounded when told. For a few hours his nerve failed. 'Am I still Emperor? Am I still Emperor?' he kept asking anyone within earshot. His loyal freedmen, acting on an initiative he was incapable of providing, saw to it that he was. The conspiracy was crushed with ruthless decision. Silius and half-a-dozen

145

other noblemen, accused of having shared the Empress' bed, were summarily executed by the Praetorian Guard, who had been put under the temporary command of Narcissus, so grave and immediate seemed the danger, so uncertain the ramifications of the plot. Only the ballet-dancer Mnester almost escaped, for he complained that he had had no choice but to obey Messalina's summons to her couch.

Yet still the loyalists feared that the Emperor might soften towards his wife. At dinner that night when he was a little fuddled, his usual evening state, he was heard to mutter about 'the poor woman', and say that he would see her the next day.

That could not be permitted. The freedmen who had seen to the death of her lovers could not risk giving her the chance to regain control of her husband. Narcissus acted. He ordered an officer of the Guard to take a detachment to the Gardens of Lucullus on the Pincio, whither Messalina had fled that afternoon, terrified, in a dung-cart. Her mother, with whom she had quarrelled in her prosperity, was there with her; she urged the young Empress to meet death with dignity. This Messalina was unable to do, and died moaning. The news of her death was brought to Claudius while he was still at table. He heard without asking any questions, and then called for another flask of wine.

He was now fifty-eight, and probably failing. Nevertheless the immediate question was a new wife. Though Tiberius had never re-married after the divorce of Julia, nobody imagined that Claudius would remain single. The choice was therefore a question of some moment, for everyone believed that his new wife, too, would control him. In the end his niece Agrippina won the contest; she had made good use of her privileged position as niece, rousing his passions (never a difficult task) by kisses and caresses. Technically the marriage was incestuous; Claudius therefore introduced a decree legalizing marriage with a brother's daughter. He could hardly have chosen worse, but in effect he had hardly chosen at all; the wretched old man had simply been selected; picked off like a ripe pear from a tree.

This Agrippina was the daughter of the hero Germanicus and his virtuous and intolerable wife, the first Agrippina. She was therefore Caligula's sister and also sister to those two young princes, Nero and Drusus, who had fallen victim to Sejanus. With that background it is hardly surprising that she had grown up determined and unscrupulous (rumour had it of course that this marriage wasn't her first exercise in incest, since Caligula was reputed to have enjoyed all his sisters in turn). She knew all there was to know about failure and disaster; she knew too the limits of trust, and she had all her mother's strength of character without any of her obstinate and inconvenient virtue. From the moment of his marriage, Claudius was subject to what Tacitus calls 'a rigorous, almost a masculine, despotism'. Agrippina had waited a long time for power; she was determined to enjoy it.

This was in 48, when Agrippina was thirty-three. She had already been married once, to Cn. Domitius Ahenobarbus, himself a grandson of Mark Antony. They had had one son, Nero, born in 37. The boy was therefore directly descended from both Antony and Augustus, the wound of Actium being thus healed in his person.

Agrippina's intense ambition burned for her son as for herself; indeed she realized that her own power could not survive Claudius' death unless Nero were to succeed in the place of the Emperor's own son, Britannicus. It did not seem impossible to her that he should.

She now showed herself as greedy for power and intolerant of opposition as her brother Gaius Caligula had ever been; unlike him however she retained a cold balance. The exercise of terror again became public policy. Claudius was helpless in her hands, his mind in thrall to the plots against his life which she conjured up; and of course such imaginary plots spawned real ones. Agrippina acted with harsh logic. Everything was aimed at her own and Nero's elevation. She was proclaimed the Augusta; she persuaded Claudius to adopt Nero, ostensibly as a future guardian for Britannicus, who was however only five years younger. Then Nero was married to Claudius' daughter Octavia; the net was tightening. Agrippina had Seneca and other exiles recalled and placed in positions of power — Seneca became young Nero's tutor. These men owed gratitude to the Augusta, nothing but resentment to the Princeps. Soon the boy Britannicus found himself deprived of friends, tutors and adherents. Agrippina's henchman, Afranius Burrus, was appointed Praetorian Prefect, the key post which opened the doors to the succession. Nero was granted that title, *princeps iuventutis*, which Augustus had given to his adopted sons, Gaius and Lucius; the significance could not be missed. Meanwhile opposition was silenced. The treason trials which Agrippina encouraged were now heard in secret in the imperial palace; a sinister development. Agrippina, to advertise her power, entered the Capitol in a ceremonial carriage traditionally reserved for priests and sacred emblems. It was made apparent that the Roman world had fallen into the hands of a woman, for Claudius, descending rapidly into dotage, seemed quite helpless. Nothing showed that more clearly than his failure to defend Britannicus' position; that defence was left to the freedman Narcissus.

Narcissus had opposed the marriage to Agrippina. She could not forgive this, and he knew that Nero's succession would destroy him. She had already begun the work; he was accused of corruption and profiteering in his work as director of the Fucine Lake project. In return he accused Agrippina of aiming at dictatorship, but his attemps to open the Princeps' eyes were in vain. This time also, the freedmen who had collaborated to destroy Messalina were divided among themselves. It was said for instance that Pallas, the Financial Secretary, shared Agrippina's bed. (The same accusation was made against Seneca. Either accusation may be true; both indeed.)

All the same Claudius was not absolutely sunk in torpor; he had been heard to say, in a drunken mumble, that it was his fate first to suffer his wives' misdeeds and then to punish them. Such grumbles could hardly be ignored; Agrippina knew that the time had come to act. . .

For time was not necessarily on her side. True, her immediate power was enormous, but the terror she inspired bred enemies. Each nobleman she struck down had family who were ready to attach themselves to a rival cause; and

Britannicus was growing up. Moreover, Claudius' resentment, dull and sluggish though it was, might yet be stirred to action by those freedmen who had most reason to fear his death. And Claudius had been heard to say to Britannicus 'grow up, quickly, my boy'. Speaking of him to others he had declared that he would let Britannicus come of age early; it would 'provide Rome with a true-born Caesar'.

Yet, though now fearing and disliking Agrippina, he still did nothing. He had always relied on others to act for him in a crisis; now there was no one ready to do so, Britannicus being too young and Narcissus having been persuaded to retire on grounds of ill-health. Claudius was thrown back on the course of action which his early life had taught him was most expedient; he lay low and endured.

But Agrippina was made of different metal, a woman of action. She summoned a nurse called Locusta, described by Tacitus as 'a woman lately condemned as a poisoner, but with a long career of imperial service in front of her'. Locusta provided what was necessary, a poison that could be passed off as causing natural death. Her choice was a boletus, non-toxic, but cooked in a sauce made from a similar but poisonous variety. It didn't quite do the trick, perhaps because Claudius was drunk when he ate it. When he vomited it, however, a feather coated with the juice of the Palestinian colocynth, or bitter-apple, was thrust down his throat, ostensibly to encourage him to empty his stomach of whatever was distressing it. Even this device may not have been sufficient; it is said that he was finally smothered. The Senate was then summoned to offer prayers for the Emperor's recovery from his grave illness, for it was expedient to conceal knowledge of his death till Nero's succession had been assured.

The horror of court life and of Claudius' wretched last years should not be allowed completely to obscure what he had achieved. He was ridiculous certainly – his old enemy Seneca, who was probably privy to his murder, delighted the late Princeps' aristocratic enemies with a little piece of mockery – the pumpkinification (rather than deification) of Claudius. Nevertheless he was honoured in the provinces, where his personal oddities didn't hide the fact that he had worked honestly and intelligently for the welfare of his subjects. No doubt his drive for administrative efficiency had disturbed the precarious balance of the Augustan settlement; and no doubt his faults of character had prevented any alleviation of the rule of terror in Rome itself; yet the Augustan settlement could hardly have survived unaltered much longer, and the Empire's ability to withstand the reign of his frivolous stepson and to survive the convulsions that followed owed much to the administrative structures Claudius had devised. Similarly the extension of Roman citizenship in the provinces had given stability to Roman rule. It may be that the centralization of power and the creation of the imperial bureaucracy sowed the seeds of the Empire's corruption; but the first fruits were not rotten. From Claudius' work flowered the tranquil Empire of the second century. In this sense his true heirs were Trajan, Hadrian and the Antonines, monarchs of the veritable golden age of the Mediterranean world, of that time of which Gibbon wrote; 'if a man were called to fix the period in the history of the world, during which the condition of the human race was most happy and prosperous, he would, without hesitation, name that which elapsed from the death of Domitian to the accession of Commodus'. Yet Claudius' own life also revealed the truth of Gibbon's succeeding observation of 'the instability of a happiness which depended on the character of a single man'. The intelligence and public spirit of Claudius had enabled him to govern the wider concerns of the Empire with enlightened equity; the deficiencies of his character had ensured that vice and terror continued their sway in the imperial city itself.

Nero

NERO

AGRIPPINA HAD WON. Her control of the Guard, exercised through its Prefect, her protégé Burrus, ensured that she could determine the moment when Claudius' death should be announced. At that very instant the young Nero emerged from the palace with Burrus in attendance; the battalion on duty cheered him, placed a garland on his brow and raised him in a litter. They carried him, shoulder-high, to the Praetorians' camp, where he spoke, promising gifts as generous as those his step-father Claudius (whom he called simply 'father') had offered when Gaius died. They hailed him as emperor; and this time there was no debate in the Senate. What could they question or discuss? The act was accomplished; they could only acknowledge reality.

The black cloud of Claudius' death was soon dispelled. The despised old man became a god; meanwhile Nero's youth seemed to promise the sunshine of a spring morning. And certainly his first speech to the Senate reinforced this favourable impression. He paid tribute to the Senate's support and the army's backing; and spoke of the merits of his advisers, telling them that he brought with him no inheritance of resentment or vendetta. 'No civil wars or family disputes clouded my early years.' Who could doubt that the sun shone, that Apollo welcomed the young ruler? He promised open and impartial justice; the Senate would preserve its ancient functions; and there was to be honest administration and the separation of State affairs from his personal business.

Rome would have been at its most beautiful at that season, in October, the light still sharp but taking on a golden haze in the late afternoon. Such an air and such a light would likewise have been suited to the central theme of Nero's speech: *clementia*. That clemency which Julius had granted the defeated Pompeians, seeing it as the quality necessary to remove discord from the State, was now promised by the seventeen-year-old Emperor to a Senate still alarmed and disturbed by the secret treason-trials of the last years of Claudius and by their awareness of the grim shadow behind the throne, the Empress-Mother, the Augusta, Agrippina.

True, it was well known that the speech had been written by Seneca, and there were some who sneered that Nero was the first Princeps to have needed borrowed eloquence. But this was not necessarily cause for alarm; indeed it was rather a sign that Nero was willing to be guided by the wisdom and experience of such as Seneca and Burrus. The new Emperor seemed to deserve the popularity which young rulers are almost always granted. He was known to be a devoted son – his password for the Guard was 'the best of mothers'. For the first time since Augustus, Rome had a Princeps who both liked to be seen by the crowd and was pleasant to look at. He was not yet fat, and his light blond hair and pretty rather than handsome features, gave him a boyish charm which appealed to the mob. He was also affable and ingratiating, for he lacked the self-confidence that could tolerate unpopularity; the aristocratic disdain of Tiberius was quite foreign to his nature. So Nero's reign opened in an optimism as great as when Gaius had succeeded; it was moreover an optimism that seemed better founded.

Yet of all Roman emperors Nero's is the name that has become a byword for infamy and vice. The great Antonine emperor, the virtuous Marcus Aurelius who sits so serenely on his gilded horse on the Capitol, wrote in his *Meditations* 'to be violently drawn and moved by the lusts of the soul is proper to wild beasts and monsters such as Nero. . .' Hamlet advises himself: 'lose not thy nature. Let not ever/ The soul of Nero enter this firm bosom. . .' Voltaire shrank from the popular version of Nero's crimes: 'the interests of humanity require that such horrors must be exaggerated. They reflect too much shame on human nature. . .' Nero has entered proverbial speech as the man who fiddled while Rome burned; generations execrated him as the first emperor to persecute the Christians, the murderer of St Peter and St Paul. For the mediaeval world he was Antichrist, the Beast of the Revelation of St John. The modern tourist couples Nero with the Colosseum as the twin symbols of decadence and cruelty and pictures the depraved Emperor lounging with his favourites in the great amphitheatre, even though it never existed in his time and Nero detested the gladiators, instead engaging his energies in building a garden paradise where the Colosseum now stands.

After all this, therefore, it comes as a shock to recall the Emperor Trajan's observation that the 'quinquennium Neronis', the first 'five years of Nero', excelled the government of all other emperors. It is surprising too to learn that for years after his death a few friends would reverently place spring and summer flowers on his grave on the Pincio Hill, and that pretenders impersonating Nero received wide public support.

The paradox exists; yet Nero does not present a psychological puzzle, as Tiberius does. His journey from sun to shadow can be more certainly charted.

Ominous signs were not wanting even in the reign's morning sunshine. For those who believed in the power of heredity, optimism was not easy. His father, Gnaeus Domitius Ahenobarbus, had excelled even the members of his own violent and untrustworthy family. He had once killed a freedman for refusing to drink as much as he was commanded to. On another occasion he had turned on an equestrian who had criticized his behaviour, attacked him in the Forum and gouged his eyes out. He had quarrelled with his wife Agrippina, finding her temper equal to his own. When their son was born he remarked that any child of theirs was certain to be loathsome and a public danger; or so, with the advantage of hindsight, it was related.

As for Agrippina, her cruelty and appetite for power could be doubted by none. She had dominated Claudius; she now dominated Nero. Her face even appeared on the coinage, and, as an unprecedented revelation of her actual power, her image was on the obverse, Nero's being relegated to the lesser side.

Almost immediately, however, Agrippina went too far; it was as if the achievement of her ambition had totally destroyed that prudence which had previously taught her to veil her power. It was one thing to rule from the shadows behind the throne; quite another to seem to share it. Now, when an embassy arrived from Armenia, she had shown herself ready to mount the imperial dais and sit beside her son. 'Everyone,' reports Tacitus, 'was astounded. But Seneca saved the situation, murmuring to Nero that he should advance and greet his mother. So, with a display of filial decorum, scandal was averted.'

Scandal it would have been; Rome was not yet ready to be governed openly by a woman. Seneca and Burrus meanwhile, having risen to power as members of Agrippina's party and on her favour, were now eager to desert her. Their motives need not be impugned: Agrippina, capricious, violent, unscrupulous, could hardly give Rome the good government that was the sole acceptable compensation for the loss of Republican liberty.

First, though, it was necessary to detach Nero from her. His own feelings were confused. On the one hand he could always be bullied, and liked to be controlled; on the other he resented the person who thus made him realize his infirmity of will and the weakness of his character. His sentiments towards his mother were intense; scandalmongering Romans were quick to accuse them of incest. 'Whenever they rode in the same litter,' it was said, 'the condition of Nero's clothes afterwards showed only too clearly what they had been up to.' Even if this were true – and nothing in Nero's character makes it improbable – it would not make his feelings for Agrippina less complicated. Nero might be incapable of knowing shame; resentment however was an emotion that dominated him more readily.

He broke out, as might have been predicted, developing a fancy for another, an ex-slave called Acte. The choice indicates two aspects of his character; the attraction that the life of the common people held for him, one respectably manifested here, but also more disreputably and more frequently displayed in his liking for the life of the streets, taverns and brothels; second, it reveals Nero's lack of self-confidence. He had no difficulty in feeling himself superior to Acte; her humble position ensured it. The liaison also reveals something to Nero's credit; he aroused a deep and sincere love in this beautiful girl, and though he soon deserted her, she herself remained faithful to him.

Seneca and Burrus encouraged the affair, as a means of separating the Emperor from his mother; she of course was furious. It was outrageous that her son should consort with a former slave in preference to herself. In her anger she even took up the cause of Nero's wretched and always neglected wife, Octavia, Claudius' daughter. More recklessly still, she began to promote the interests of her stepson Britannicus. When her enemies further undermined her power by persuading Nero to dismiss the freedman Pallas, Agrippina's protégé and the Secretary of the Treasury, her rage waxed yet further. She allowed Nero to hear her say that Britannicus was now grown up and ready to take his father's position. 'I shall take him to the Guards' camp,' she cried in her rage. 'They will listen there to the daughter of Germanicus in her struggle against these upstarts and usurpers, the cripple Burrus and Seneca with his academic bleat.'

She exaggerated her strength however. Nero was quick to act. First he disposed of his stepbrother, poisoning the wretched boy at a State banquet and then hastening his burial in Augustus' mausoleum: that did open Agrippina's eyes to what she had brought into being. Nero on the other hand blandly assured questioners that poor Britannicus had long been subject to epileptic seizures; no one ventured further enquiries. Thus did Nero show Agrippina how well he had learned the lesson of power; he no longer required her to carry out murders on his behalf. Yet there was a difference between mother and son. Nero murdered only when he was afraid; if things were going well, his nature was still sunny. His harsher mother had murdered in order to arrive, as an act of policy.

Britannicus' death was shocking; yet many were relieved. Seneca and Burrus may or may not have been privy to it. The philosopher at any rate, strict exponent of Stoic virtue though he was, found no difficulty in excusing it. Britannicus alive could not fail to imperil the regime: his very existence represented an alternative. In the circumstances, considerations of *Realpolitik* easily justified the crime. Conspiracy was thus nipped in the bud; for it was not immediately easy to see where else it could flower, when no males of the Julio-Claudian family were left except the Emperor.

Agrippina was losing ground; but she was not yet defeated, and still constituted herself Octavia's champion. She cast around for a party to support herself and for a figurehead she could advance. She retained one great advantage: whenever she and Nero met, she could still overawe him. Aware of this, and ashamed, he never visited her without an escort of staff-officers; their encounters were formal and brief. But now Agrippina herself became the target of conspiracy, as old enemies sought to complete her disgrace. The matter remained in balance for months. She withstood one charge of plotting Nero's murder, defending herself so vigorously to Seneca and Burrus that they dared not take further action.

Her final fall was thus postponed – until the moment when Nero acquired a new mistress. This was Poppaea Sabina, possessed, in Tacitus' words 'of every asset

Nero and his mother Agrippina on a
gold coin minted in 54, with
Agrippina given precedence

Poppaea: a coin issued by Nero in
Greece. It hardly supports her
reputation for beauty

except virtue'. Beautiful, intelligent, rich, well-born, she was utterly careless of her
reputation. Sensuous, but indifferent to love – perhaps incapable of it – she set out
to capture the Emperor. The fact that she was married to his friend Marcus Salvius

Otho (who was briefly to be Emperor in 69) did not deter her; though she used Otho's love, and the trumpeting of her obligations to him, to fend off Nero till he was ready to agree to her terms. These were simple; she wanted marriage. In order to subjugate Nero she mocked him. She wasn't surprised, she said over and over again, that he had taken an ex-slave as his mistress; that was just what she would expect of a man who was afraid of his mother. Knowing that he would never dare divorce Octavia while Agrippina lived, she continued to spurn his advances and ridicule him to the point of desperation. She offered him everything desirable – beauty, luxury, infinite delight – wasn't she the first woman in Rome to bathe in asses' milk for the sake of her skin? – but first he must free himself from that terrible woman, his mother. She, Poppaea, could not be expected to marry a man who did not dare to be master of himself: 'I will go anywhere in the world,' she said at last, 'rather than see you so humiliated, and so in danger.' He would, she said, be neither truly emperor nor really safe while Agrippina lived.

Nero found himself between two terrible women and afraid of both of them. Since he now seldom saw his mother, while Poppaea was always to hand, it was Agrippina who lost. Rejecting the idea of exile to an island, whence she might after all return, Nero at last decided to murder her. The attempted assassination itself was both macabre and comic. First he designed a collapsible boat. He then invited Agrippina to dine with him on his galley in the Bay of Naples. After dinner he escorted her lovingly to the boat, which had been prepared for her. He embraced her fondly (Tacitus debates whether this was hypocrisy or whether 'even Nero's cruel heart was touched by this last sight of his mother going to her death'); she embarked, and the boat sailed off. Once it was out in the bay, on the way back to Anzio, its roof fell in. The mechanism, however, did not work as well as expected. Agrippina and her lady-in-waiting were indeed pitched into the sea, but there the waiting woman made the mistake of crying out that she was Agrippina, expecting that someone would hurry to save her. She had miscalculated: sailors beat her to death with oars and poles. The doughty and wiser Empress kept quiet and struck out for shore, and eventually a fishing-boat rescued the tough old thing.

Back at her villa she soon realized what had happened. Prudently, as it seemed, she decided to pretend ignorance, and merely sent a message to Nero telling him of the accident: by divine mercy and the Emperor's lucky star she had escaped.

Not surprisingly the news alarmed Nero. Seneca and Burrus, perhaps ignorant of the plot hitherto, were called from their beds. It was decided that things had gone so far their course could not be reversed. They could not believe that Agrippina did not realize what had happened – nor that she would long delay the revenge that would be her only security. The ex-slave Anicetus, once Nero's tutor, who had devised the collapsible boat, was commanded to retrieve his mistake. A sword was planted on Agrippina's messenger, and it was said that he had been sent to murder the Emperor. Anicetus meanwhile had led a gang of soldiers to Agrippina's villa, where, they battered her to death in her bed; it was subsequently rumoured that she told them to strike at her womb, whence Nero had sprung.

Nero hesitated before returning to Rome, unsure of how he would be received. But though privately men might look on him with horror, no one was yet ready to act. Few after all regretted Agrippina's murder; too many senators had had cause to hate her. Besides, this particular struggle for power had really been a contest for control of the Emperor's person, and one which impinged little on the Empire. The administration ran on smoothly, still guided by Seneca and Burrus, both of whom were unfailingly respectful to the Senate, putting honeyed words into their master's mouth and flattering and placating the commanders of the army.

Soon though there was occasion to test the quality of the government; trouble had broken out again in Armenia.

The eastern frontier of the Empire was the only one on which the Romans confronted an enemy whom they had to treat as an equal. The Parthian Empire, stretching from the sands of Arabia to the boundaries of India, was heir to the great empire of Persia. The desert acted as a buffer zone between the two empires, and the experience of Marcus Crassus had taught the Romans that the legions could not venture into that harsh open territory without grave danger; in such terrain the Parthian cavalry would always master the slower-moving Romans. In the north, however, Armenia comprised a disputed territory. Neither of the two empires could contemplate its domination by the other, for such domination would bring the potential enemy too close, would offer a base from which he might strike deep into their own territory. For the Romans, the conquest of Armenia was always a temptation. It would however have imposed a strategic imperative beyond their power, for in order to safeguard the southern frontier of Armenia it would have been necessary to advance their empire across the desert to the Euphrates.

Now however news had reached Rome that the Parthian emperor had established his brother Tiridates on the throne of Armenia. Nero accordingly dispatched Gn. Domitius Corbulo, who had proved his ability on the Lower Rhine frontier under Claudius, to restore the situation. After a harsh winter campaign, Corbulo captured the Armenian capital. He pursued Tiridates for three hundred miles, defeated him again, and drove him out of the country. Nero was hailed as *imperator*, and a Roman client, Tigranes, great-grandson of Herod the Great, was established on the throne. In the short term at least, it was a satisfactory victory.

Nero took credit for what had been achieved in Armenia; but in truth his political interventions as a rule were only spasmodic, and for most of his first five years he remained content to let his ministers rule. Part of the difficulty rested in the simple fact that he was still of course young. Like Gaius Caligula, he had received no training for empire. He had never had to work, had never commanded an army or held an administrative post, never previously felt responsibility, never enjoyed the discipline of limited or delegated power. In Nero's history in particular one can discern the outstanding weakness of the hereditary or quasi-hereditary system: that men with neither character nor experience to recommend them can come to positions of supreme power.

Politically, his actions were simply intuitive, and rarely thought out or based on anything substantial. So, for instance, he proposed a daring reform of Rome's taxation system. As it was, the State was responsible for the collection only of direct taxes – the poll and property taxes first levied by Augustus; indirect taxes, on the other hand, were still assigned to contractors as they had been in the days of the Republic. These sales taxes, levied on the movement of goods (internal customs duties in fact), were unpopular because of their mode of collection, and were an obstacle to commerce within the Empire. All the arguments that were to be directed against such internal tariffs by eighteenth- and nineteenth-century *laissez-faire* economists like Adam Smith and Ricardo doubtless applied in the Ancient World also. Now Nero, in 58, proposed the abolition of such taxes at a stroke. Commerce would be freed from parasitic duties; trade and wealth would increase accordingly; and the revenue lost to the State would be recouped from the greater return to be expected from direct taxes as a result of the increase in property values this new wealth would bring about. Moreover, the abolition of duties would shift the burden of paying for the cost of the administration and the armies from the poorer to the propertied classes.

As a scheme this was characteristic of Nero: imaginative, ambitious, impractical, blithely regardless of difficulties. In the same spirit he was to propose cutting a canal through the Isthmus of Corinth, and another, even more remarkable as an engineering project, to link Ostia with Lake Avernus and so improve access to Rome for sea-borne goods. It was the same spirit that, after the great fire of 64, was to lead him to lavish vast resources on his architectural extravaganza, the Golden House.

The truth was that Nero was not interested in governing the Empire. He never properly applied his intelligence to the task; and remained throughout his life the intuitive dilettante. In diplomacy this did bring him some success; his acute imagination gave him real sensitivity when it engaged itself in some forms of action. But the hard business of government, that devotion to duty which Tiberius had never abandoned even in his Capri retreat, was not for him.

In these early years this mattered less. Seneca and Burrus, and the freedmen who ran the State bureaux, were fully competent; and it might seem that Nero was content to live as a constitutional monarch. There was however no precedent for this, not even from the miserable years of Sejanus' ascendancy ; and indeed there was no constitution by which he could abide since the old Republican magistrates, though still elected annually, had effectively lost power. Instead, the Augustan division of responsibility had placed control of the army, the frontier provinces and a large part of the Revenue in the hands of the Princeps, who was, in reality, responsible to nobody.

Seneca, whose Stoic philosophy had not prevented him from acquiring vast wealth in his years of imperial service, was certainly aware that his own authority rested only on imperial favour. Though theoretically anxious to uphold the interests of the Senate, and giving lip-service to Republican ideas when it seemed desirable, he was fully conscious that his actions firstly had to satisfy the Emperor's vanity. Whether the Emperor directed the administration in person or not, the course of the last eighty years could not be reversed. Only the central administration vested in the imperial household, in the Emperor or his agents, grew ever stronger. It was the inevitable consequence of a system of government where the representative system never extended beyond a number of municipalities of which Rome was only the greatest. Though provincials might now be members of the Senate, nevertheless it remained true, for better or worse, that only the imperial government could transcend class interests and govern for the benefit of the whole Empire.

All reforms therefore tended to increase the power of the Emperor at the expense of the Senate. So, for example, in 56, two imperial prefects, men of proven ability, replaced the quaestors (the youngest and therefore least experienced of Republican magistrates) in charge of the Treasury (the Aerarium) which managed the revenues from the senatorial provinces. So, also, measures were taken to make the prosecution of extortionate governors easier – a blow at the remnants of senatorial privilege, for such accused tended to be the governors of senatorial provinces. In fact twelve Roman officials were prosecuted for provincial maladministration in the first seven years of Nero's reign, clear evidence of the imperial government's willingness to protect provincials against the rapacity of Roman aristocrats. It made for better government; but hardly enhanced Nero's popularity with the nobility.

Care was taken to keep the mob happy and well fed. The food supply was assured by the appointment of an efficient prefect, Faenius Rufus, and by completing Claudius' harbour works at Ostia. Nero claimed credit for this and stressed its significance by advertising it on the coinage, the easiest means of propaganda, telling people all over the Empire what the Princeps had achieved and how he wished to be regarded.

In the meantime, though Nero's lack of consistent application was harmful, neither Seneca nor Burrus attempted to correct it; on the contrary, they were only too willing to encourage his diversions. These were of three sorts: dissipation, sport and art.

The first does not require much attention. Nero was accused of indiscriminate sexual activity: incest with Agrippina; raping a Vestal Virgin; castrating his catamite Sporus and then going through a marriage ceremony with him, after which he carried the boy through the streets in his litter dressed as a bride, kissing him in public view. Men said it was a pity Nero's father hadn't married that sort of wife. (All the same, Sporus, like Acte, remained faithful to Nero and was with him right up to his death.) Nero also played a game in which he imitated a satyr, dressed in the skins of wild animals, and darting about making sexual attacks on men and women who were bound to stakes. Then he would allow himself to be taken, in his turn as it were, by his freedman Doryphorus, with whom also he went through a wedding ceremony; only this time it was Nero who played the bride and later imitated the screams of a virgin being deflowered.

More interesting than the details of these excesses, not after all very different from many other erotic fantasies, is Nero's conviction that chastity was impossible;

most people were hypocrites who concealed what they did. Hence he was always ready to forgive anyone who confessed to vice, for this proved him right. His Victorian biographer, B. W. Henderson, whose massively informed book *The Life and Principate of the Emperor Nero* remains the finest treatment of its subject and a store-house of information, believed Nero's sexual extravagance to be a mark of insanity. Possibly so; living however in an age that shares Nero's obsessions, we cannot be quite so assured. Nero, like a modern superstar, was able to translate fantasy into flesh. He did not fail to make use of his opportunities.

This sort of behaviour may have harmed his character more than his reputation. The Ancient World did not expect chastity or bourgeois morality from its rulers; many of its religions, such as the Eastern cults of Attis and Dionysus, recognized that the devotee might approach the god through sexual release. What the Romans required however was *dignitas*, a quality deserving of respect; and here Nero did fail.

Tacitus calls Nero's ambition to drive in chariot races 'deplorable'. A racecourse was built for him in the Vatican valley, and at first Seneca hoped that this private enclosure would satisfy him. Not for long however; soon the public were admitted to admire their Emperor's skill. Worse followed. He was addicted to athletics, introducing the Greek Games to Rome, and encouraging young aristocrats to participate. The military-minded Romans regarded this as too dishonourable. Hitherto, games in Rome had been the province of professionals, usually slaves; to perform in public was demeaning. The Youth Games which Nero instituted, also in the Greek style, included theatrical performances, also given by amateurs. 'Birth, age, official status,' Tacitus complains, 'did not prevent people from acting or from accompanying their performance with indecent and effeminate gestures and songs. Even distinguished women played indecent roles.' All this evidence of the effeminacy of taste that Nero encouraged amounted to the corruption of the social order; in like manner, the mediaeval baronage of England were to repudiate the unmilitary pursuits of an Edward II.

Worse still was Nero's own commitment to art. He fancied himself as poet, musician and – worst of all – performer. To be the first was no shame – Julius and Augustus had both written verses. But they had done so as a diversion; they never allowed scribbling to usurp the place of more dignified pursuits. Nero, seeing himself as an artist, went too far. Eventually he came to see the Empire as material for art; it has even been suggested that 'he intended to bring harmony to the world by giving aesthetics the place held by morality'. Such an intention was slow to develop (if indeed something may be said to have developed which he himself could never have formulated.) But from the first his devotion to poetry and music was offensive, because it excluded the proper business of a Roman aristocrat. His taste was lamentable, too: the hero of his poem on the Trojan War was neither Hector nor Aeneas but the cowardly effeminate Paris whose lust had precipitated disaster.

Soon Nero began to perform in public, appearing in competitions as an ordinary competitor, though one whom the judges were naturally inclined to favour. This behaviour was truly shameful. He even adopted an artistic hairstyle in 64, letting his hair grow long and loosely curling, a greenery-yallery style that disgusted the nobility.

Below the surface, discontent burgeoned even while Seneca and Burrus controlled Nero's wildest flights and governed well enough. An inadequate emperor, without *dignitas*, inevitably turned men's minds to thoughts of substitution. In 59 a comet appeared, token of a change of ruler. Men talked of one Rubellius Plautus who through his mother Livia Julia was descended from Tiberius and also from the union of Mark Antony and Octavia, Augustus' sister. Nero's reaction to the talk was restrained; he only requested Plautus to retire to his Asian estates.

Within two years the situation had deteriorated. The empire shuddered at its two extremities. In Britain Queen Boadicea led her tribe, the Iceni, in revolt; in Armenia, ever fertile of troubles, the Roman puppet Tigranes was expelled. Then Burrus died. Of course poison was suspected – such was the climate of opinion – but the cause may well have been a tumour or cancer of the throat. His death had two consequences: the elevation of one Gaius Ofonius Tigellinus 'because', in Tacitus' words, 'Nero was fascinated by his countless immoralities and his notoriety'; and the fall of Seneca.

This was the turning-point of the reign; like a chariot-driver in his beloved circus, Nero had rounded the *spina*. He was tired of his old tutor, who was still capable of abashing him. There were many jealous of the old man's wealth, and jealous also of his self-conscious virtue, who were eager to persuade Nero that an emperor of twenty-three should be free of his schoolmaster. The advice chimed in with Nero's desires. It was echoed too by Poppaea, still only his mistress – for Nero had not yet summoned up the resolution to divorce Octavia; when he had muttered of this intention, Burrus had said, 'in that case of course you must return her dowry'; and her dowry was the Empire.

Seneca, too prudent to resist the course of events, begged leave to be permitted to retire. Nero, protesting that he could never allow this, that it would inflict a wound from which he would hardly recover, tacitly permitted what he had volubly denied. They embraced, and Senaca departed from the palace.

The quinquennium was over; and Nero, having dropped the pilot, was bent on the course that would lead him to disaster. He felt free, free for the first time of disapproval and dominating elders, free to act as he pleased. Yet his freedom was illusory, for two reasons.

First, out of touch with the political world, he depended on Tigellinus and his spies for information. Naturally he believed what they told him; naturally they fanned his fears of conspiracy.

Second, these very fears restricted his freedom. He lacked the self-confidence to be master either of himself or of the Roman world. Such mastery as he felt – his sense of the unlimited power of his position – could only find expression in terror and fantasy.

Accordingly terror had to be provided. Tigellinus' position now resembled Sejanus'. His power rested on his control of the Emperor and of the Praetorians; he could only secure it by making himself the indispensable man. To do that he had to isolate the Emperor and feed his fears; plots must be encouraged or contrived, that they might be then suppressed.

In 62 he denounced two great aristocrats to Nero, Rubellius Plautus, still living in his Asiatic exile, and Faustus Cornelius Sulla Felix. Either, because of his great name, might become a focus for discontent. Both, banished to the provinces (Sulla was in Gaul), were said to be still more dangerous because of their distance from the Emperor's control. 'How,' Tigellinus asked, 'could sedition be dealt with so far away?' Their rebellion should therefore be anticipated. Murderers were despatched, and brought back their victims' heads. Nero commented derisively on Sulla's grey hairs and Plautus' long nose.

Emboldened by this success Nero at last divorced Octavia and married Poppaea. This was intensely unpopular. The Roman mob rioted, alarming its supposed master. For a moment he promised to reverse his decision; but Poppaea, herself frightened by his weakness rather than the mob's fury, regained control. There was only one thing to do: Octavia must be removed. Accordingly the wretched girl, still only nineteen, whose father, mother and brother had all been murdered, whose stepmother had been put to death just at the moment when she first took a friendly interest in her, whose husband had preferred one of her slave girls from the first and had never treated her with respect let alone affection, was confined on the island of Pandateria of melancholy memory, where the two Julias and the first Agrippina had dragged out exiles that had led only to murder. Octavia had not so long to wait. The loathsome Anicetus, murderer of Agrippina and now commander of the fleet at Micenum, was instructed to confess to adultery with the Empress. It was gently intimated that, in the unlikely event of his refusing to do so, the little matter of Agrippina's end might be exhumed. He did as he was bid and was permitted to retire to comfortable retreat in Sardinia while his alleged paramour, the innocent Octavia, was put to death. Her head was carried to Rome, that Poppaea, her rival, might delight in gloating over it.

For two years comparative calm followed while attention was focused on the Armenian campaign, and the Emperor wrote verses, sang, acted, feasted, performed and generally indulged himself. A daughter, Claudia, was born to him and Poppaea; his delight was unfairly described as immoderate, but she died within three months, provoking grief in like degree. She was declared a goddess. Later Poppaea herself was to die, reputedly kicked to death by Nero in a fit of drunken rage; her successor was of no importance.

In 62 Nero apparently embarked on a new policy in Armenia, one that would crown his reign with glory. Abandoning the attempt to establish a Roman protectorate with Tigranes as client-king, he sent one of the previous years' consuls, L. Caesanius Paetus, to drive out the Parthian prince Tiridates, and annex the country. It seems unlikely that the full implications of this new policy were realized; equally unlikely that the prudent and capable Corbulo, still Governor of Syria, approved of it. Paetus, of at best indifferent competence, soon ran into trouble. In the winter of 62–3 he found himself surrounded by the Parthians in his encampment at Rhandeia, and called on Corbulo for assistance. Then, with this only fifty miles off, Paetus surrendered. It was the most shameful disaster Roman arms had encountered in the East since Crassus' defeat at Carrhae a hundred years before; and the most complete anywhere since Varus lost his three legions in Germany. Since it was the result of cowardice as well as incompetence, the disgrace was unprecedented. Nero however, relying on Corbulo to redeem it, forgave Paetus with a sneer. He would pardon him at once, he said, because suspense might damage the health of such a timid person; it was characteristic of Nero to find it easier to forgive his subordinates' cowardice and failure than their courage or success.

Corbulo restored the military situation, but the attempt either to annex Armenia or to install a Roman puppet was abandoned. Instead it was agreed that the Parthian prince Tiridates should retain possession of the country, but should consent to receive it from Nero – in effect to do homage to him; henceforth there would be peace between Rome and Parthia. It was a solution of a sort, a symbolic victory which satisfied Nero's theatrical nature: the visit of Tiridates was to offer him the chance of an unparalleled display of splendour; also perhaps to imbibe Eastern ideas of divine monarchy.

By then however Rome had been devastated by the great fire of 64. This broke out in tinder-box July weather and raged for a week; two-thirds of the city was burnt, three of the fourteen Augustan municipal districts being totally gutted. Though Nero had returned from Antium on hearing of the fire, and had taken prompt and effective measures to relieve the homeless, it is a mark of his declining popularity that rumours soon accused him of responsibility. He had viewed the blaze from the Tower of Maecenas, it was said, singing his own epic poem 'The Sack of Troy' as he watched. So serious were these rumours that the Emperor urgently sought scapegoats. He turned on the little Christian sect, already unpopular and suspected of cannibalism. Of what atrocity might such dissidents not be thought capable? Some were thrown to the lions, others used as candles to light nocturnal games in the Palatine Gardens and the Vatican Circus. The cruelty showed the extent of Nero's fear.

Reason for such fear was growing. The year 65 saw a real and dangerous conspiracy, his murder actually being plotted, by a group of aristocrats, senators and equestrians. They were sufficiently close to Nero for the attempt to have a good prospect of success, and to make his escape a stroke of fortune. The conspiracy even included Faenius Rufus, who shared command of the Guard with Tigellinus. The nominal head of the conspiracy was G. Calpurnius Piso, head of one of the greatest noble houses, grandson of Tiberius' Governor of Syria who had so bitterly quarrelled with Germanicus. Seneca was probably involved; his nephew, the poet Lucan, was one of the leaders. Some of the conspirators still hoped to restore the Republic; others backed different candidates for the Principate; all were united in their wish to kill Nero. Still the diversity of purpose and the lack of coherence among the conspirators, allied to their wish to involve as many senators and equestrians as possible, led to delays and changes of plan. First Nero was to be invited to Piso's villa and murdered there; Piso himself vetoed this, saying that to stain his hospitality in this way would create a bad impression. Finally it was decided that Nero should be murdered at the Circus Games. One of the conspirators would fling himself at the imperial feet, as if craving a boon; then he would tackle him and hold him on the ground, while his comrades dashed in with their daggers. Consciously or unconsciously – and allowing for the departure from old Republican manners – the method resembled that by which the Liberators had despatched Julius.

It sounds amateurish; the whole enterprise was like that. Too many people's sympathies had been invited so that they knew of the plot's existence but were not fully committed to it. Probably few ever knew exactly who their fellow-conspirators were. Failure might have been predicted and the conspiracy was indeed betrayed. Flavius Scaevinus, who had been detailed to strike the first blow, could not even keep himself from dropping hints to his own household. One of his freedmen reported his suspicions to the palace. Investigations, accompanied of course by torture, were at once set going. The nebulous nature of the conspiracy is revealed by the fact that these were first prosecuted by Faenius Rufus himself, and by a Guards colonel, Subrius Flavus, who was another conspirator. These two had no hesitation in conniving at the torture and execution of their comrades. Even so the conspirators were only identified slowly. There was time for Piso's friends to urge him to make a public appeal, and mount an insurrection; he was assured of support. But his nerve failed, and he killed himself, leaving behind a letter of abject contrition.

It was some time too before the informers turned on the army conspirators. Only then perhaps did Nero fully realize his isolation. He had already ordered his old mentor, Seneca, to kill himself. Whom was there left to trust? He asked Subrius Flavus why he had forgotten his oath of loyalty. 'Because I hated you. I remained as loyal as anyone while you deserved my loyalty. But I changed when you murdered your mother and your wife and became charioteer, actor and fire-raiser'. The words may be apocryphal; they yet represent adequately enough the moral and social disgust Nero had aroused.

In the next eighteen months the trail of executions stretched beyond the conspiracy itself; Nero and his henchmen Tigellinus had gone down into a dark subway where their feet slipped on the bloody tiles. The plot revealed that no aristocrat could be trusted, for the connections of those who had been executed or driven to

Pompeii. Example of a Roman house with an impluvium

suicide extended all over the Roman official world. Distrust bred distrust; cruelty bred conspiracy; fear of conspiracy spawned more desperate and still more cruel preventive action.

Another plot was discovered at Beneventum in 66; it suggested that disloyalty had spread to the generals; and Corbulo and the army commanders in Upper and Lower Germany were summoned to meet Nero in Greece. They obeyed, and on arrival were ordered to kill themselves. Even Nero's former intimate, his arbiter of elegance, the great dandy Petronius, author of the *Satyricon*, did not avoid suspicion. He met death with notable indifference and, refusing to follow the fashion which decreed that the condemned man should try to protect his family by writing flatteringly of the Emperor in his will, he left behind him an annotated account of Nero's sexual escapades.

Pompeii: example of a Roman domestic interior showing frescoes

Alternating between bloody panic and blithe unconcern, Nero was fast losing his grip on reality, his ability (never perhaps of the greatest) to discern the temper of those about him. The Fire of Rome had offered him the opportunity to launch a great enterprise, the building of a palace that would do justice to his genius, and to the claim made at the very beginning of his reign that his too, like Augustus', was a golden age: 'aurea formoso descendunt saecula filo', as Seneca had put it.

Soon after his accession he had built himself a villa in the valley between the Palatine and the Esquiline, a magnificent house in the rural style, called a Casino, with a fanciful landscape garden, in the middle of the city. It was a fashion that would never quite die out in Italy, this taste for the *rus in urbe*; the finest surviving example being the Villa Borghese set in its gardens that extend from the top of the Via Veneto over to the Pincio, thence running round the line of the Aurelian wall. But the Fire, destroying the valley dwellings, gave Nero the chance to enlarge the grounds of his villa, to include all the low-lying ground around a lake where the Colosseum would be built by Vespasian. To the south, Nero's fantastic country seat in the city reached as far as the Temple of Claudius on the Caelian; to the east to the modern Via Merulana where the gardens of Maecenas then formed its boundary; the western limit was the Palatine; to the north this landscape garden extended to the Forum of Augustus. The whole area was about two hundred acres. No wonder a satirist complained 'all Rome is turned into a villa' and advised Romans to flee to Veii, 'if only the villa does not spread there also'.

Gold and jewels abounded in the decoration of this villa – the façade of the main palace was gilded, and everything was decorated with gems and mother-of-pearl. In the dining-rooms there were ceilings of ivory plaques through which flowers could be scattered; and some of them were also pierced with pipes for spraying perfumes. There was a domed dining-hall with a revolving roof which some scholars have seen as an imitation of the cosmic tents of the kings of Persia, wherein the Sun-God and Great King were made one. Nero's own recorded reaction was different: he said that now he could begin to live like a human being.

What Tacitus and Suetonius found amazing was not the luxury – first-century Romans were already acquainted with that – but the fact that in the centre of the city Nero's architects had created a landscape fantasy, with groves, pastures, herds, wild animals and artificial rural solitude. And what the people resented was not the luxury either, but the fact that Nero's egoism had deprived poor people of their homes. Nobody really resented Nero playing at divinity, if that is what he was doing; but it was intolerable that he should behave badly as a mere man.

One cannot resist the feeling that the Golden House offers the key to Nero's character. Yet a note of caution is necessary. Other rulers – Hadrian at Tivoli, Louis XIV at Versailles, to take only obvious examples – have built themselves palaces which expressed their ideal self-view without being accused of losing touch with reality. Yet the conviction that Nero's Golden House belongs with Ludwig II's Bavarian fantasy castles rather than with Tivoli or Versailles is well founded. Nero's paradise offered an escape from the world, rather than an extension or

Pompeii: a fresco depicting the Dionysiac Mysteries

deepening of experience. It was not a political statement like Versailles, nor a holiday retreat like Tivoli; it represented rather Nero's withdrawal into a dream world, his preference for fancy and make-believe to facts.

His megalomania increased. Coins depicted him wearing a god-like radiate crown. He treated the Parthian prince, Tiridates, who came to Rome in 66 to be crowned King of Armenia, with elaborate oriental ceremony; in turn Tiridates worshipped Nero as the god Mithras incarnate. All this was absurd and offensive to the Roman aristocracy who recalled the disdain Tiberius and Augustus had shown when orientals offered them worship. The month April was renamed Neroneus; rumour had it that Rome itself would soon be called Neropolis.

Discontent seethed. Nero, lost in his dreams of artistic glory, ignored it. He set off to Greece to compete in the Games as poet, musician and charioteer. The prudent judges awarded him one first prize after another, even at Olympia when he fell out of his chariot and had to be pushed back in again. His tour was a popular success; Nero for his part, elated by his reception, granted the Greeks immunity from taxation.

In Greece and in his building of the Golden House Nero was satisfying the deepest springs of his nature; but at the same time he was shutting himself away from the world of which he remained nominally master. He hardly seemed to care

Circus Maximus: view in 1933

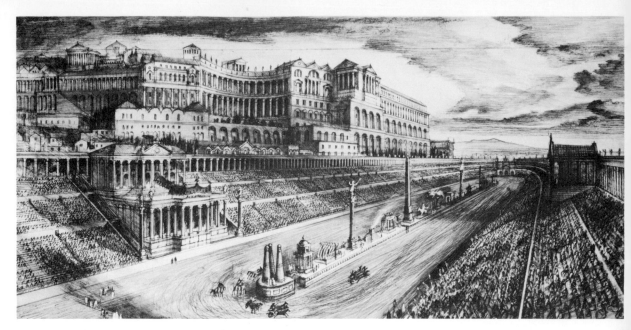

Circus Maximus: reconstruction

that Judaea was in revolt, that mutiny was simmering in the armies of the West, that the Roman nobility were united in their contempt, hatred and fear, and that even the mob no longer loved him but regarded him instead as the author of injustice.

He returned reluctantly to Rome in early 68, and hung up his 1,800 prizes for all to admire; corn-shortage made the populace unreceptive. In response to this uncongenial atmosphere, he retired to Naples, where, in March, he learned that G. Julius Vindex, the Governor of Gallia Lugdunensis, was in revolt. Nero delayed. The rebellion spread. Servius Sulpicius Galba, Governor of Hispania Tarraconensis, member of a great aristocratic family and a septuagenarian with a career of public service stretching back to Tiberius' reign, proclaimed himself 'legate of the Senate and the Roman People', an implicit denial of Nero's authority.

The Rhine legions hesitated. The Praetorians too did not desert Nero at once; resolution might yet have saved him. But he was incapable of it; he had been living too deeply in fantasy to confront this harsh revelation of reality. He made a gesture, naming himself sole consul, as if the illusion of power would be sufficient in itself. Tigellinus fled; and Nero found himself abandoned by all but his intimate household.

Irresolute in a villa near Rome, he learned that the Senate had declared him a public enemy, to be punished in 'ancient style'. He asked what this meant, and was told that the executioners stripped their victim naked, thrust his head into a wooden fork and then flogged him to death. Shaken, he picked up two daggers, but could not bring himself to use them. He begged Sporus, the catamite, who still had not deserted him, to mourn for him. 'How ugly and vulgar my life has become,' he said, achieving perhaps for the first time the detachment of the artist he had always sought to be. It was still as such that he saw himself: 'dead and so great an artist', he said, just before he managed to stab himself, with some help from his secretary, in the throat. He was dying when a troop of cavalry burst in.

Even his last words were a lie. He had not been a great artist, only artistic, his aestheticism not a deepening of experience but a substitute and escape from life. The work of art that he had tried to make of his life had turned out mere gimcrack and fancy. This, which would have been no more than a misfortune for a private citizen, had been disastrous for him as emperor. He had believed that everything was permitted to him, and had never realized that such liberty must first be achieved. He despised politics, though at the head of an intensely political system; and, as the chief of a great military Empire, revealed a timorous distaste for soldiers and for warfare. Thus, one mistake was piled on another, and little by little he deprived himself of the support and authority that alone gave reality to his power. Consequently – in that order – they fled from him: first support – and the Empire of Augustus had been built on the backing of a party in the State – then authority, the product of that respect which attaches good men to a party; and at last power itself. Without authority, power may become illicit and dependent on fear; but it trickles away once the man who held it is revealed to have forfeited its physical and moral props.

'The secret,' Tacitus says, 'was now revealed that an emperor could be made elsewhere than at Rome.' Perhaps so, but at the same time an older and more important lesson was written large again: the Empire could only be held by a man who had won the support of, and could control, the armies. Now the ignominious death of the last of the Julio-Claudians threw the trophy of government onto the battlefield. The next twelve months would show which of the generals possessed the character and ability first to win that prize and then to retain it.

Galba, with Medusa depicted on his breastplate

THE YEAR OF THE FOUR EMPERORS

THE JULIO-CLAUDIAN house was extinct. Nero had perished because he had disregarded his troops, scorned the art and practice of war, rejected the life of the camp and failed to understand the source of his power. Now it was revealed not only that an emperor could be created elsewhere than at Rome; but once again, just a hundred years after Actium, that supreme power belonged to the sword. The elegant screen with which Caesar Augustus had concealed the military nature of the Empire was torn down.

Yet there was no such thing, in one sense, as the Roman army. Though small in relation to the vast extent of the Empire, the army was divided and incoherent; if it could be described an organism, then it was an unwieldy one. There was no General Staff, no Ministry of War, no regular chain of command; the focus of unity remained simply the imperial household. Consequently, in the absence of an emperor, the armies did not know where to look. Moreover, except for the nine cohorts of the Praetorian Guard who were based in the city, a mere five thousand men at most, all the troops were normally strung out along the frontiers of the Empire, which now extended from Britain in the west to Armenia in the east, from the sands of Africa to the dark forests of Germany.

The military force of the Empire had changed little since Augustus' day. It still consisted of some thirty legions – about 150,000 men – and a like number of auxiliaries. In the year of crisis that followed the death of Nero it was the legions that counted, and their distribution that was vital. There were three legions in Britain, a province where the frontier had not yet been fixed and where the conquest was still proceeding. Three more were normally based in the Iberian peninsula, in Gaul one was sufficient. The Rhine frontier was guarded by seven, constituting the Army of Germany; the Danube by another seven. Eight were found in the East, command being shared by three governors who ruled the provinces of Syria (with responsibility for Armenia), Judaea (which was in revolt) and Egypt. There was one legion in Africa. There were therefore three great armies, the German, the Danube

Coin showing Galba seated

and the Eastern, and a number of smaller and scattered forces. Accordingly, in any contest, the issue of empire was likely to be settled by the decision of the three largest groupings.

Galba however had already been proclaimed, by the legions in Spain, where he was a governor. He had obtained the support of Marcus Salvius Otho, Governor of Lusitania; but the original impetus to revolt had been given by the rebellion in Gaul led by Julius Vindex, and this had been suppressed by the German legions, which had still remained loyal to Nero. Galba's problem after his proclamation was therefore to establish his authority over these German-based legions; who had, equally clearly, no reason to be well disposed to him.

This new Emperor, Servius Sulpicius Galba, was old, austere, high-minded, indulgent only to himself and a few intimates; chief among whom were Cornelius Laco, soon to be made Praetorian Prefect, and a freedman, Icelus, who was, according to Suetonius, the aged Emperor's bedfellow. Galba came from an ancient aristocratic family – on his father's side he traced his ancestry back to Jupiter. Both sides of his family tree could boast consuls. His own experience of public life stretched back to the reign of Tiberius – he had been a protégé of the Augusta Livia herself; indeed, now that he had been elevated to the purple, a prophecy of future greatness made by Tiberius was conveniently recalled or appositely invented. He had succeeded the traitor Gaeticulus as Caligula's commander in Germany; had even been urged in 41 to assert a claim to the throne in place of Claudius. The fact that he had served four emperors might be taken by his admirers as evidence of his merit, by detractors of his mediocrity. He has gone down to history damned by

Tacitus' icy verdict: 'capax imperii nisi imperasset': 'worthy of empire if he had never ruled'. Perhaps; howbeit, at the age of seventy-three, he was too stiff, prejudiced and stupid to succeed.

The inheritance was difficult, for not all recognized his claim to empire, and few who did so were unconditional in their acceptance. Spain was his. Gaul, mindful of Vindex, was bound to him by the promises of citizenship and the remission of taxes which he had made. The Danube legions acquiesced. In the East Licinius Mucianus, Governor of Syria, 'a man' (in Tacitus' words) 'who would find it easier to transfer the imperial power to another than hold it himself', made no hostile move, while the Governor of Judaea, Flavius Vespasianus, himself fully occupied in the suppression of the Jewish revolt, acknowledged Galba, and sent his son Titus to bear witness to his loyalty. (Subsequent events suggested that he hoped the childless Galba might adopt the handsome young man.)

But in Africa, the Governor, Clodius Macer, rebelled; unsuccessfully and fatally. More important, the German legions were turbulent. Then, on arrival in Italy itself, Galba foolishly alienated the Praetorians and also a legion which Nero had hurriedly recruited from the fleet, by denying them the donative which his own emissaries had promised. The promise had been necessary because Nero's prefect, Nymphidius Sabinus, having betrayed his master, had himself aimed at the throne. Now the soldiers were angry that their refusal to follow him was denied its reward. Galba's statement that 'I choose my soldiers, I do not buy them', however redolent of Republican virtue, did not reconcile these troops to his rule. It was indeed an expression better suited to the theatre than to the world of real politics.

Galba's entry to the capital was therefore bloodily opposed and the opposition still more bloodily suppressed. Rome was indeed unusually full of troops, for besides the new Emperor's Spanish legions, the Guards and Nero's recruits, there were also various detachments the late Emperor had collected in his last endangered months. Rome simmered, ready for another revolution. Galba's actions had neither been sufficient to overawe nor of a nature to conciliate.

The real danger to his power seemed however to rest in the German legions. These had no reason to be well disposed. Galba had come to power on the shoulders of the Gallic rebellion which they had themselves put down; he had then recalled their popular commander Verginius Rufus and put him on trial. The first replacement sent was hopelessly incompetent, the next treacherous. This was Aulus Vitellius, a man who had won the favour of Nero by his shameless addiction to vice, who had so run through fortunes that to finance his journey to the province he had needed to pawn his mother's earrings, and had even then left his family in a rented garret. But this Vitellius had a name of sorts, and was considered genial and generous. The young legates who dominated the legions, Fabius Valens and Alienus Caecinus, both popular with the troops, and hostile to Galba, saw that he would make a figurehead. They spread disinformation, and dissension grew. By the end of the year 68 sedition had been prepared on the Rhine frontier.

On 1 January the soldiers of the Fourth Legion, stationed in Upper Germany, tore down statues of Galba. They were quickly joined by others in abjuring their allegiance, substituting instead a protestation of loyalty to the Senate and the Roman people. 'Such a form of oath seemed meaningless' to Tacitus; everyone knew that the Senate was incapable of governing an empire where ultimate power rested with an army it could hardly control. On the third of the month all the legions of Upper Germany saluted Vitellius as emperor. Those based in Lower Germany soon followed suit; likewise those in Britain. In a matter of days all the legions spread along the north-western frontier of the Empire were in rebellion. It could only be weeks before an invasion of Italy was mounted and war, absent since Octavian cleared the Antonian army from Perugia, returned to the peninsula.

Meanwhile in Rome the news of what was happening in Germany momentarily disturbed the aged Emperor's equanimity. His immediate resources were few, for his initial popularity had ebbed away. The soldiers resented his refusal to pamper them, and all who had benefited from Nero's extravagance were angered by his attempts to restore the finances of the State.

Accordingly Galba decided to broaden his support and secure his power by associating a younger man with himself in the government of the Empire. The decision, which had its precedent in Augustus' actions, was wise; its implementation however proved lamentable, and fatal to its author. With Galba in Rome was that Marcus Salvius Otho who, as Governor of Lusitania, had been one of his first adherents. Otho was not perhaps the best choice as associate Emperor. His reputation at Rome was that of a playboy, the friend of Nero and former lover of Poppaea. He was known to be a dandy (he shaved all his body-hair) and a spendthrift (he moved through the Forum among a cloud of creditors). But he had been a good governor of his province, he was popular with the soldiers and the mob, his help had been valuable to Galba, and he was ambitious for empire as the reward for that support.

Galba, self-consciously virtuous, thought nothing of his claims. (He disregarded young Titus also – that young man's father, Vespasian, though a provincial governor in command of a fighting army, was too meanly born.) Equally important was the fact that neither Laco nor Icelus supported Otho. What was to be done? Where could they find a candidate whose claims overpowered Otho's and who lacked his defects? Galba himself had little doubt. As one who could claim birth superior to the Julians, it was natural that he should turn to a member of the old aristocracy. His choice fell upon the young Gn. Licianus Piso, 'in appearance and manner a man of the old school'. It was however a wretched choice, for Piso had spent most of his life in exile, and had neither experience, reputation nor manner to endear him to the armies.

Undeterred, Galba, announcing his regret that he could not restore the Republic – 'an action of which I would have been worthy if the vast frame of empire could have stood and preserved its balance without a directing spirit', took young Piso by the hand and told him 'not to be alarmed if after a movement which has shaken the world, a couple of legions are not yet appeased. When men shall learn of your adoption,' he continued with a stronger optimism than sense of reality, 'I shall no longer be thought old, and this is the only objection now brought against me. . .'

So, self-deluded, he spoke; or so Tacitus relates, marking down the aged Emperor as a man infatuated with his sublime vision of his own state, a vision that accorded ill with the turbulence that seethed around him. On a wet, windy and gloomy day, he took Piso to the Guards' camp to announce the adoption. He told them of the German revolt but discounted its seriousness. The officers responded encouragingly, but the mass of the soldiers looked on as dark and gloomy as the skies above; Galba had said nothing about money to them, and they were already considering that they could sell their favour elsewhere, secure in the belief that no emperor could survive without it. Apparently blind to this mood, Galba and his new son proceeded to the Senate, where they were received with the respect due to their birth and manner; however the approval of the Senate was irrelevant to the issue of power.

Otho was disappointed and increasingly desperate. He required the Empire, for he was being pressed by his creditors, with whom he had no means to settle. He reacted like the gambler he had always been: 'I might as well fall to an enemy in battle as to my creditors in the Forum.' Fortunately he had just been paid a bribe of 10,000 gold pieces – the price of a recommendation to a stewardship in the imperial household – and with this he financed his coup.

Success depended on the disaffection of the Guards, many of whom were already sighing for the licence of Nero's time. Otho's agents had been distributing money for several days; the rumours from Germany encouraged a mood of apprehension. The Empire had become a casino table; the croupier of Fortune was calling on men to lay their bets.

On 15 January Otho slipped away from a sacrifice Galba was conducting in the Temple of Apollo; a messenger had just told him 'that the architect and contractors were waiting for him', and he gave out the excuse that he had to inspect some property he was thinking of buying. Instead he proceeded through Tiberius' palace and on to an appointed meeting-place by the Temple of Saturn where a couple of dozen guardsmen were expecting him. These hailed him as emperor, raised him high on a chair and carried him off to the camp. There uncertainty reigned, for few were emotionally committed either to Otho or to Galba, while all wished to back the side that seemed likely to win. The momentum was with Otho and he, unlike his rival, knew how to play the part of demagogue; in Tacitus words, 'he acted the part of slave in order to make himself the master'.

He told the troops that they had bound themselves to him in a common danger. As they were partners in that, so they would also be partners in success. He rehearsed the story of Galba's harshness, parsimony and bloodthirstiness, and told them that Galba's household had seized treasures which could have been theirs. Having thus aroused their hatred and their greed, he allayed their fears: Galba, he said, was already all but deserted. It therefore remained only to finish the job; and he ordered the armoury to be opened.

All day the mob had swirled round the imperial palaces and the Forum in a state

Otho

of excitement, aware that a coup d'ètat was underway, ignorant of its progress. They had begun by calling for the death of Otho and the conspirators 'just as if they had been demanding some spectacle in the circus or amphitheatre'. They would soon be affected by the zeal of the troops and the obvious indecision of Galba's supporters, some of whom urged him to remain in the palace, others to march out and crush the rebellion before it acquired momentum.

A rumour was brought that Otho had been killed. Immediately senators and equestrians fell over themselves in protestations of loyalty to Galba. Meanwhile Piso had been despatched to rally the soldiers of the duty cohort, and others to summon other troops. Yet while this was happening power was already falling away from Galba's hands. As the afternoon wore on, the mood of the city sensibly changed; the mob fell silent. In its place the roar of the soldiers acclaiming Otho could be heard across the city. It came to Galba and Piso, now descending from the palace to the Forum, and brought new hesitation to the party surrounding the old man. Hesitation bred dissension. Galba was hurried now this way, now that, the crowds still thronging him, jostling his attendants, blocking the path of his litter. Nothing like this had been seen in Rome since the days of the Republic; the murder of Gaius had been a short, sharp, private affair.

Otho ordered his troops to hurry, fearing another rumour that Galba was ready to arm the mob. The soldiers entered the Forum at a run. All who stood their ground were regarded as enemies; even the standard-bearer of the cohort that surrounded Galba threw down the Emperor's effigy. Galba himself was killed in his litter. As usual there were contradictory stories of how he died, as a brave man or a coward. Tacitus' habitual ironic tone does not desert him in recounting the death: 'to those who killed him it mattered not what he said'. Piso, who had slept a mere five nights as Caesar, was dragged from the Temple of the Vestal Virgins, whither he had fled in hope of sanctuary, and murdered on its steps. In the evening one of the praetors summoned the Senate. The magistrates were profuse in flattery; Otho was granted the tribunician power and named Augustus. Thence he was carried across the Forum and up the steep hill to the Palatine; the soldiers' sandals may have slipped on the blood that still gleamed in the torches' light on the Sacred Way.

A day of drama, important as symptom rather than achievement. It had done little to settle the fate of empire, for it had been a struggle merely within a party, brought on by Galba's foolish decision to prefer Piso to Otho. Galba and his immediate associates had been liquidated – for Laco, Icelus and the consul Titus Vinius all followed their patron to the tomb; Otho had become Princeps; the Praetorians rejoiced in having found a more genial and open-handed master; the mob an emperor who would flatter them. But that was all, and the legions of Germany were already on the march.

The prospect for Italy was fearsome. The Principate had originally rescued the Empire from civil war that seemed endemic; now it was itself to be the prize of such a war, one in which no principle was at stake, nothing but the desire for power and the fear of danger. Moreover, whereas Caesar and Pompey, Antony and Octavian

Otho. The coin has a
personality not found in
the bust on p. 178

had been leaders of stature, men of achievement and proven merit, the new
contenders for empire, Otho and Vitellius, had been distinguished for nothing but
their vices, and could be described as 'among the most contemptible of men'. The
grand-historical drama was being replayed as bitter burlesque.

Yet it was an indictment of the rule Augustus had established and his successors
developed, that events could hardly have turned out otherwise. Public life in the
Empire had become a charade, as ghostly consul succeeded ghostly consul and real
power was concentrated in the hands of the Emperor's household freedmen. There
was consequently nothing to test a man of character in civil life, only in the army –
and there in recent times, character and ability had become dangerous possessions.
The last three emperors had none of them been soldiers, though Gaius and Claudius
had been careful to establish a close connection with the armies. In these circumstances merit became something the ruler feared: Nero had found it easier to forgive
Paetus his disgrace in Parthia than Corbulo his victories. The army was the only
school where merit might flourish; yet the fate of Corbulo taught generals that a
suspicious monarch made a bad master. Accordingly it was scarcely surprising that
three of the four emperors of this terrible year should have been mediocrities; what
was strange was the emergence of a man as honest and capable as Vespasian. Yet he
had only survived because his humble birth had served to cloud his merit and make
him appear insignificantly dangerous. It was a symptom of the Empire's reduction
to an extreme of degeneracy and prospective disintegration that the rule of one so
lowly born should become acceptable.

Yet in fact in the character of Otho and Vitellius and in the war's unprincipled
nature lay the best hope that the conflict would be short and its effects limited. No

violent attachment drew the soldiers to their leaders; no cause inflamed their minds. As they were fighting simply for supremacy and material gain, the defeated might more easily accept the decision of the battlefield. The fact that it was a purely military struggle, a war contained within the army, gave hope that its effects might be similarly confined. Moreover, no one was questioning the structure of the State; the object of each contestant was merely to capture it. That too held out the prospect that the Empire might survive this dislocation without lasting damage.

The war between Otho and Vitellius can only be of interest to the military historian. Its appeal is purely intellectual and rests in the study of strategy and tactics. Superficially it might seem that Otho was in the position of Pompey, and Vitellius – or rather his legates Caecina and Valens, for Vitellius himself played no part in the direction of the campaign – was in Caesar's. Certainly Otho, like Pompey, held Rome and Italy, and could look for support to the East; while the Vitellians advanced, like Caesar, from the north; but, whereas Pompey had withdrawn across the Adriatic, surrendering his first base to Caesar, Otho determined to stand and fight. Furthermore the position differed in that Italy had been enlarged, and now included what had formerly been Cisalpine Gaul, one of Caesar's provinces. This pushed the frontier to the north and meant that Otho could choose between trying to hold the Alpine passes or establishing a battle-line further south. He decided on the latter course, partly because of the greater ease of supplying his army and the advantage of using a ready-made line of defence on the River Po. Cremona, just on the north side of the upper reaches of the river, became the focal point of the campaign.

Otho's title had been recognized by the legions on the Danube frontier and those in the East, and there were many who advised a defensive campaign, which would postpone a decisive battle till reinforcements arrived. Such reinforcements would moreover bear in on the flank of the Vitellian army and render its position untenable; it would itself be thrown on the defensive, compelled to fall back to protect its line of communications and supply. Yet, in Otho's mind, a stronger argument prevailed and led him to a bolder course. In a war of this sort inaction was likely to breed uncertainty in the minds of the soldiers; and being without a strong motivation of party or attachment, no troops could be considered wholly reliable. One feature of these wars was to be the readiness with which generals and soldiers changed sides: Otho himself led an army which only a few months back had acclaimed Galba. And why not? As professional soldiers the legions and their commanders were principally interested in finishing on the winning side; in this respect the civil wars of 69 far more closely resembled, say, the English Wars of the Roses than a struggle like the American Civil War, where deep-rooted loyalties and principles were involved.

Otho therefore determined to defeat the Vitellians without waiting for the Danube detachments to arrive. He sent a small force to Fréjus in an attempt to distract the second Vitellian army, which was marching down the Rhône valley, and himself embarked on a hazardous encircling movement at Cremona. Viewed in the abstract the conception was sound; though condemned by Tacitus (who may not have understood what Otho was trying to do) it has been admired by modern historians like Henderson, who described it as 'a masterstroke'. Yet, uncomprehending or not, in the end Tacitus may have been wiser in his condemnation. Campaigns are not after all fought as abstract exercises where the prize goes to the most ingenious construction on the drawing-board, but are decided on the physical plane with fallible material.

Otho's plan would have been demanding for an experienced army which trusted its commander and was capable of carrying out manoeuvres that called for exact coordination. But the Othonian army was hardly that, though its spirits were raised by initial successes in three skirmishes. It was actually made up of a number of detachments from different legions: some cohorts had arrived from the Danube ahead of the main body of the army; there was an inexperienced legion recruited by Nero from the fleet; there were Galba's Spanish legions, whose loyalty might be considered doubtful; and the Praetorian Guard, whose great reputation was not supported by recent battle honours. Moreover the soldiers distrusted many of their officers (often hardly known to the troops they commanded): and Otho's decision – strategically desirable – to supervise the campaign from the rear rather than lead the attempted encirclement in person, depressed the soldiers, who then as always liked to be made aware of the presence of their commander.

Whatever the exact combination of reasons – and Henderson is quite right in asserting that Tacitus' description of the campaign suggests little understanding and can only be followed by hazardous guesswork – the Othonians, in circumstances of extreme confusion, were heavily defeated, at Bedriacum just outside Cremona. Their position was by no means irrecoverable; the Danube reinforcements were coming up fast, the Guard was unbroken, and they still held the line of the Po. They had failed to break the Vitellians; nevertheless their defeat had hardly damaged their own defensive position; and certainly a resolute commander would not have despaired – Octavian had suffered as severe disasters, on his route to empire.

Otho, however, the Princeps of three months who had staked his life and fortune on the throw of the dice, reacted differently. He decided to kill himself. He did so calmly and deliberately, taking formal leave of his friends, smoothing arrangements for those who wished to depart from the army and return home, even quelling some mutinous soldiers who tried to prevent desertions; and then going through his correspondence in order to destroy any letters which might compromise their authors with Vitellius. Towards evening he drank a glass of water, and then tested the edge of two daggers. He lay down to sleep. In the morning he stabbed himself, so coolly that one thrust was sufficient. By the manner of his death he won a reputation he had never enjoyed in life.

Yet this death suggests a curious failure of nerve, an especial lack of resolution. Otho had embarked on a great adventure that could not be anything but a gamble;

whoever aspired to the purple, that year particularly, abandoned certainty. And now he threw in his hand when the first trick went against him. The humanitarian reasons he gave for his suicide do him private credit; yet they reveal him as a man unworthy of the prize he was seeking. Again, one cannot imagine the young Octavian contemplating so feeble a surrender. But one must always reckon with the Roman propensity for suicide, something that sits oddly with the robust common sense generally demonstrated. Such fatalistic reluctance to combat ill-fortune, such failure of intellect and will, was alike the case with his predecessor Nero as with Otho himself.

Vitellius was now master of Italy and the West; but not yet of the Empire. The Danube legions, which had committed themselves to Otho, were not ready to accept his conqueror; and in the East other ambitions were burgeoning. Rumours of troop transfers, which would take the legions there from the comforts of Asia to the inhospitable regions of Germany and Britain, fed discontent and resistance to Vitellius' rule. Later propaganda was to represent the challenge from the East as impelled by the troops; certainly they were reluctant to accept Vitellius as emperor.

All the same the organization of the opposition to Vitellius and the network of Flavian supporters established in different parts of the Empire suggests that the

Vitellius: a late
seventeeth-century
portrait

emergence of Flavius Vespasianus (Vespasian) as a candidate for empire did not come in response to the will of the common soldiers; nor even the centurions. The fact that he was neither to relax military discipline nor lavishly to reward his soldiers indicates either that the movement started at a high level, or that he betrayed them. Bearing in mind Titus' embassy to Galba and the hopes placed in that, it seems most probable that from the moment of Otho's death Vespasian was cast by his own will and by his party as the future emperor.

Meanwhile Vitellius neglected to consolidate his position. True, he made gestures towards the Senate, whose members having hailed first Galba and then Otho within the space of a few months saw no reason not to accept Vitellius as their new master; could the degradation of that body be more clearly exposed? Vitellius did make a bid for popularity, however. Though, unlike his immediate predecessors, he honoured Nero's memory – the German legions had never abandoned Nero – he was willing to suggest that he would a pursue a different track from the Julio-Claudians; he declined the title of Caesar, for instance. It may even be that he toyed with the notion of a senatorial monarchy, which was perhaps the closest that the Romans could now come to a Republic. If so, this never developed beyond an idle fancy, a little exercise in propaganda. He had not the time to discover if such an empire was possible; very likely he did not have the character to bring it off in any case.

He soon displayed his fundamental irresponsibility; he behaved as if the civil war was won and surviving opposition could simply be allowed to wither away. The Borgia Pope Alexander VI greeted his own election with the words: 'God has given us the Papacy; let us enjoy it'; such sentiments might have been Vitellius' own. He embarked on a long round of dinner-parties and orgies of eating and drinking. There was no dignity in his behaviour; already he had disgusted men of sensibility and honour by the remarks ascribed to him on surveying the battlefield of Bedriacum: 'only one thing smells sweeter to me than a dead enemy, and that is a dead fellow-citizen': clearly there was no message of hope or moral renewal there.

No one should have known the hazards of empire better than Vitellius. He had been the favourite successively of Caligula, Claudius and Nero. Caligula had admired his skill in chariot-driving, Claudius enjoyed playing dice with him, Nero delighted in his extravagant immorality. They had patronized him, given him office, made him rich. But his riches had survived no better than his patrons; they had been so dissipated that he had become importuned by crowds of creditors. As for the emperors who had nourished him, two had been murdered, one driven to suicide. If anyone was alive to the mutability of fortune, it should have been Vitellius.

Not so however. True, his suspicions might have been allayed by the co-operation he at first received from Vespasian's brother, Flavius Sabinus, the City Prefect, who persuaded all the troops in Rome to swear an oath of loyalty to the new emperor. Yet Vitellius, one would think, could hardly fail to be aware that such oaths were of little value; he had sworn oaths himself, to Galba for instance.

The measures he took to secure his position were all half-hearted. A few leading Othonians were exiled or imprisoned; and some centurions were put to death, a mean and petty action which confirmed the dislike the Danube legions already felt for Vitellius. Such conduct was at once excessive and insufficient; it inspired resentment but not fear. A victor in civil war can successfully pursue one of two opposite courses: conciliation of the defeated or their ruthless suppression. Vitellius feebly pursued a middle path which neither won his old enemies' hearts nor established his authority.

Debauchery was more to his taste than government. He banqueted three or four times a day, generally going to bed drunk. Leading citizens were commanded to provide marvellous feasts for him – his journey through Italy had left a trail of bankrupted hosts. On his entry to the city his brother had prepared a meal at which two thousand fish and seven thousand game-birds had been served. Vitellius himself devised a dish to which he gave the absurd name the 'Shield of Minerva' (he had taken the Goddess of Wisdom as his protectress). The recipe called for pike-livers, pheasant brains, peacock brains, flamingo tongues and lamprey milt. It must have been perfectly disgusting.

Though it was not the conduct of a leader in what was still a civil war, such behaviour is not quite inexplicable. Vitellius had never sought empire; it had been thrust on him by his lieutenants and legions. He could not cope with its demands – he may never have believed his luck would hold anyway – and instead he retreated into the fantasy world of alcohol, where disasters may be laughed away, and despair cheated by a new bottle of wine. He was the Emperor of make-believe.

He could, in the grey moments of hangover, see clouds piling up on the eastern horizon. Vespasian had repudiated his authority; the Danube legions had followed suit; war was on the march again. Meanwhile his own forces had deteriorated; their self-indulgence had resembled their master's with the added disadvantage that they had been housed not on the airy Palatine but in the insalubrious plain of the Vatican across the river. Mixing Tiber-water with their wine brought on dysentery; summer encouraged malaria. Discipline vanished as disease and debauchery infected them. The army, accustomed to the bracing severities of the Rhine frontier, disintegrated in the city. When in the autumn the Vitellian generals, Caecina and Valens, led their legions out of Rome to repel Vespasian's advance on the same line of the Po which they had themselves crossed a few months before, the force at their command was a mere shadow of the one which had conquered Otho.

Caecina realized this. He had also resented the greater favour which he thought Vitellius had shown Valens and others who had merited it less. He opened negotiations with the enemy. These were discovered and he was put to death; but his treachery and attempted defection showed the direction of the wind. The party of the unwarlike Vitellius was breaking up as certainly as the discipline of his legions.

Valens was defeated in the north. The news was brought to Vitellius, whose connection to reality was slackening daily. It was suggested that he might save his life and protect his family by resigning the Empire to Vespasian. Negotiations were conducted by Vespasian's elder brother, Flavius Sabinus, who during these difficult months had maintained his place as Prefect of the City, a fact which reveals more clearly than anything else how authority had decayed, how uneasily all in Rome regarded the future. An agreement was made between them in the Temple of Apollo. Vitellius and his family would be spared; he would be compensated for the loss of empire with great wealth – a million gold pieces, it was rumoured – and an estate in Campania.

Vitellius, who had stumbled into empire because he was too flabby to resist the offer, and who had failed to maintain it for the same reason, was now only too happy to be relieved of the dangerous honour. He proclaimed of course that he was moved by public duty; he resigned his position for his country's sake. But Vitellius, pawn and figurehead that he was, could not be permitted to abdicate, and so easily evade the consequences of his actions. His supporters, rightly fearing that they would lose possessions, even life, thoroughly sceptical of any proclaimed amnesty, refused to permit him to surrender the emblems of imperial power; they declined to allow him to retire to a private house and compelled him back to the imperial palace.

While this was happening, Sabinus, with his troops and many of the senators anxiously awaiting the fulfilment of the agreement, occupied the Capitol. The city was still full of soldiers loyal to Vitellius; and suddenly Sabinus, who had that morning thought that he had engineered a peaceful settlement, found himself endangered, and then besieged. One messenger was sent to the Flavian generals outside the city to inform them of his peril, which was now so acute that he had thought it safer to bring his own children and his nephew, Vespasian's younger son, the future Emperor Domitian, with him into the Capitol fortress. At dawn another messenger, a centurion called Cornelius Martialis, was despatched to Vitellius to enquire why he delayed to carry out the terms of the surrender. Martialis reminded the declining Emperor that though he might still be master in Rome, Italy itself was in the hands of Vespasian. Accordingly, if Vitellius now repented of the agreement, he should march out of the city at the head of his remaining troops, and dispute the Empire with the Flavian legions.

The wretched Vitellius understood the strength of this argument, but he could not dispute the power of the soldiers who refused to accept his abdication. He himself had lost all freedom to act. In Tacitus' words: 'he was no longer Emperor; he was merely the cause of war'. In fact he was less than that, being merely the excuse.

His soldiers, fearing that they were about to be betrayed, now assaulted the Capitol. The first attack, up the rock from the Forum, was repelled, tiles and stones being hurled down on the Vitellians. They then skirted the hill to the flank of the Tarpeian Rock and the grove of the Asylum. Preparations against an attack from that quarter had been inadequate, and resistance was soon overcome. In the course of the fighting lighted brands had been thrown. The Capitol was soon in flames. The Flavian supporters tried to break out; few managed to do so (though Domitian was one who succeeded); Sabinus and the consul Quinctius Atticus were among those captured. They were led before Vitellius whose abdication they had negotiated a few hours previously. He may have wished to save them – if he retained a glimmer of realism he must have realized that such clemency offered the sole chance of his own safety. He was unable to do so: both were murdered on the spot, and their bodies dragged to the Gemonian Steps. Such was Vitellius' authority in his last hours of empire.

This skirmish at the Capitol was the dying flicker of resistance from the Vitellians. Two Flavian armies were already advancing on the city; one down the Via Salaria from the Sabine country, the other by the Via Flaminia. The vanguard, briefly was checked in a cavalry skirmish, and it was rumoured that Vitellius was arming the mob. Amid universal uncertainty, a delegation of priestesses, the Vestal Virgins, guardians of Rome's sanctity, approached the Flavian camp with a letter from Vitellius proposing a day's truce and new negotiations.

It was too late for that. The treachery shown to Sabinus had sealed Vitellius' fate. The Flavian army pressed on, entering the city in three detachments, by the Via Flaminia and down what is now the Corso; by the Via Salaria and the flank of the Pincio Hill; and along the bank of the Tiber. The Vitellians offered the resistance of the doomed, and the citizens, devotees of gladiator shows, found a chance to take part in their favourite sport, as Rome was given up to the horror of street-fighting and private revenge.

Vitellius himself, desperate, tried to flee. He had himself carried in a litter by his pastry-cook and another slave to his wife's house on the Aventine, whence he might escape south. There, however, either his nerve or the opportunity failed him. He crept back to the palace and found it deserted. All the slaves had fled in terror, the enemy had not yet arrived. It was late afternoon and December; cold, with the wind blowing across the mountains from the north. He hid in a janitor's room, tethering a guard dog outside and jamming a bed against the door. But he had not found himself a refuge; and perhaps he no longer believed in the possibility. Soon he heard the sound of running feet and the cries of soldiers. They broke into the room and asked him where the Emperor had gone. He said he didn't know, but, even in the dark, one of the men recognized him. Amused by his degradation, which aroused their contempt and therefore their brutality, they tied a noose round his neck and dragged him down to the Forum. One soldier grabbed him by the hair, another held the point of a sword under his chin so that he was forced to keep his head up. He was half-naked. Other soldiers, or perhaps the mob, who had yesterday cheered him in the streets and the Circus, now flung dung and insults at him. 'Yet I was your Emperor,' he cried, salvaging an instant of dignity from the accumulating horror. They paraded him along the Sacred Way and put him through the torture of the little cuts before despatching him. His body was impaled on a hook and consigned to the Tiber.

He had been Emperor for eight months. It was less than a year and a half since Nero's death. That time had consumed three other emperors, and no one could look with confidence to the future.

Vespasian. A portrait bust which could be that of an Italian farmer

VESPASIAN

THE YEAR THAT had begun with Galba's murder in the Forum ended in the nightmare theatre of Vitellius' death and the confused slaughter and acts of private revenge of the Flavian victory. That year had threatened destruction, to tear up the fabric of the State and plunge Italy and Empire back into the chaos of the late Republic. Yet somehow the balance of government restored itself. Though in Gaul and on the northern frontier resistance to the Flavians continued well into the year 70, the paradoxical result of this year of imminent disintegration was the strengthening of imperial authority. This outcome may be ascribed partly to the inexorable logic of circumstances, partly to the character of the new Princeps and of his elder son.

Power in the Ancient World still centred on the city of Rome. But for what reason? The Senate might have been reduced to a shadow; the Assembly of the People was moribund; the metropolis itself produced nothing and only consumed; it was not a key military point, for the armies were habitually distant, strung out along the frontiers of the known world. The city's continuing importance was maintained by custom, by the influence of settled ideas over men's minds, rather than by arms; on the other hand there was nothing to disturb that custom.

The legions hardly identified their interests with those of the regions where they were stationed; no local autonomous structures retained more than municipal importance. The governors of provinces and the generals of armies kept their gaze fixed on the city whence power was still seen to emanate, whither ambition was directed. Since the legions and provincials could find no common cause, separatist movements, such as those of the sixties in Gaul and Judaea, found only local response and were invariably suppressed. Throughout the five hundred years of the Roman Empire in the west, and the millennium and more in the East, fragmentation of the structure from within was never likely. When the Empire eventually collapsed it did so in response to pressure from beyond its frontiers.

But if Rome retained this authority, it was in a sense hardly Roman by now. It could only be exercised through the government of a single person; and the secret had been revealed that he could rise to power in the provinces. It could hardly be otherwise. The old nobility of birth had been destroyed; the new was incoherent, its members being drawn from any source, creatures of the Emperor's pleasure. Since the old Republican constitution had failed to adapt itself to the growth of empire so as to provide stable and effective government; since representative institutions, such as might possess authority, had not been conceived in the Ancient World, there was now no alternative to monarchy. It is a curiosity of history that before the advent of mass democracy, which is dependent on technical advance in the means of communication, Republican institutions have flourished only in small states.

In these circumstances – highlighted by the events of 69 – the nature of the Empire could not be in question. What was disputed that year was the person, not the institution. From it emerged one clear, if tacit, conclusion: henceforth the Emperor must either be a soldier himself, or must associate a soldier with him in government. This had indeed been implicit in the days of the dying Republic; Julius and Octavian had been carried to power on the triumphant shoulders of their army. But the civil cloth Augustus had cast over the imperial structure which he had created, had concealed this reality. His personal authority had allowed him to wear the citizen's toga, not the soldier's breastplate. He had treated the Senate with deference, acting the old Republican part. During his long supremacy the imperial family had crept into being, disguised as the greatest of aristocratic clans. In the city itself, the old nobility, hardly yet diluted by non-Italian blood, had been permitted to enjoy their consulships and pretend that their servitude did not really exist. The military nature of the Empire, resting securely on the Princeps' command of the armies, was kept at a distance. Few were completely deceived by the charade, although Nero, least military of emperors, allowed the theatrical show inherent in his position to warp his sense of reality. His transient successors of 68–9 could not share his illusion. They knew how they had come to power; they knew what they would have to do to retain it. Henceforth, with one brief exception, soldier emperors were the rule.

That exception indeed emphasized the rule's logical force. The murder of Domitian in 96 gave birth to a last flicker of Republican enthusiasm, and the modest Nerva, a man of peace and law, became emperor. But within months a threatened coup persuaded him to associate Trajan, greatest of contemporary generals, with him in the management of the Empire, and to nominate him as his successor. The sword could no longer be ignored.

The victor of 69, the new Emperor Vespasian, was not a man for illusion or self-deception. Far from it; his most clearly marked characteristic was his capacity for just discernment and appropriate action. His background hardly resembled his predecessors', though comparison may be made with Augustus' paternal line; but this in itself made him a significant phenomenon representing in his own comparatively low-born person the degradation of the Republican nobility.

Titus Flavius Vespasianus was now just over sixty, having been born in the year

9, at Reiti in the Sabine Hills. He was brought up in the country, partly by his grandmother who had a farm or small estate at Cosa. He retained his affection for her and happy memories of his childhood, often revisiting her house where he allowed nothing to be changed, a touching and sympathetic trait, and drinking her health on feast days from a little silver cup she had once owned. He felt a continuing piety for his native district; at Roccagiovine a Roman inscription records that Vespasian 'restored the Temple of Victory' – Horace's 'crumbling temple of Vacuna' (for Vacuna was the Sabine Goddess of Victory). He kept his rural accent too, saying 'plostra' for 'plaustra', for instance. (This pronunciation was also a mark of class: 'Clodius' was the plebeian form of the aristocratic 'Claudius'.)

The family however had been rising on both Flavian and Vespasian sides for a couple of generations: centurions became tax-collectors, tax-collectors became bankers. Their history offers a good example of how the imperial military-administrative machine gave opportunities for advancement to the more able and

Maiden Castle, Dorset. A British fort reduced by Vespasian. Aerofilm
reveals lines of later, Roman, ramparts

diligent members of inferior classes. Vespasian himself, though, didn't rise simply by personal merit; indeed until the late sixties it was his elder brother Flavius Sabinus who had the more distinguished career. Pushed on by his family, Vespasian had joined the army and served as a young man in the Balkans. In Gaius' reign he first became quaestor, then aedile, in which post he attracted sharp criticism from the Emperor himself for the condition of the streets. Subsequent advance was the result of favouritism or of establishing good connections; no man could rise in Rome by personal merit alone. Vespasian found a patron in Narcissus, Claudius' freedman and minister, thus gaining the entrée to court circles – something from which his son Titus was to benefit enormously.

It also advanced his military career. Narcissus soon procured his command of a legion; and Vespasian served in Germany and in the conquest of Britain, taking part in over thirty battles and subduing the Isle of Wight. The extent of this was exaggerated back in Rome; it was reported that he conquered 'the whole island', as though Wight had been on the scale of Sicily. He was rewarded with triumphal decorations and a substitute consulship.

Then, due a proconsular appointment as governor of a province, he was threatened with a setback in his career, as Nero's accession saw the downfall of his patron Narcissus. He obtained a place eventually, however, becoming Governor of Africa. The post was evidence in a way of the low regard in which he was held; a useful man who could never be dangerous. His rule there was competent, but lacking in dignity; once he was pelted with turnips in an urban riot. On his return, his career foundered, he was no courtier and had no means of recommending himself to Nero; once indeed he fell asleep at a recital given by the Emperor. Impecunious, in fact deeply in debt, he was forced to mortgage his estates to his brother. In his mid-fifties he seemed to have arrived at his limit.

Nevertheless he retained his reputation as a competent fighting soldier, and this stood him in good stead. In 66 he was suddenly recalled from retirement and given command of three legions to suppress the Jewish revolt, an invitation which rescued him from obscurity as certainly as the outbreak of the American Civil War saved Ulysses S. Grant from the leather store in Galena, Illinois. The reasons for his selection are clear enough. The job required a fighting soldier, preferably one with experience of small-scale actions in difficult terrain. At the same time Nero's distrust of the aristocracy and of the glamour of successful generals precluded anyone of higher rank or more distinguished record than Vespasian. He was chosen because he could win the war without threatening to become a rival to the Emperor.

Yet his success in Judaea established him as a man of substance; nothing after all can equal real achievement. When the crisis of 68–9 broke out, Vespasian, as an army commander, could not fail to be a key figure. The fact that he had a son, Titus, who had been associated with him in the Jewish War, was also important. Suddenly the Flavians were a family with dynastic possibilities.

Vespasian's first move to power may have been the attempt to force Titus on Galba. It failed; but events followed so quickly that this failure lost any importance

Coin of Vespasian, showing his sons
Titus and Domitian; 'Non olet'

it might have had. The armies in the East had adhered to Galba; they likewise
adhered, a little more doubtfully, to his successor Otho. But Otho once dead, they
felt their power, and with it their opportunity.

In the East likewise, there did exist a possible rival to Vespasian. This was L.
Mucianus, Governor of Syria, a man with the advantage of noble birth and who had
previously been on poor terms with Vespasian. Titus is said to have brought them
together; not the least of his services to his father. Mucianus remains a mysterious
figure. Tacitus calls him 'fitter to make an emperor than to be one', but gives no
adequate reason for this judgement. It seems likely though that he lacked the
popular touch. He was shrewd, luxurious and depraved, followed everywhere by a
train of catamites; not necessarily a disrecommendation, as the careers of numerous
generals testify. But more important, he lacked both charm and nerve – ambition
too, probably, for he never made a real bid for the highest place, preferring to
exercise influence rather than power.

At any rate he was involved early in the Flavian conspiracy; and without him and
his Syrian legions it could not have succeeded. The origins of Vespasian's bid for
empire are necessarily obscure, hidden by the successful party's historiography.
This presents Vespasian's emergence as a response to the will of the soldiers; a
quasi-democratic form of acclamation. Contradictory evidence is strong; the
Flavian coordination of support throughout the western half of the Empire as well
as the East was too efficient to be the result of chance or improvisation.

On 1 July 69 Vespasian was hailed *imperator* in Alexandria; on the third of the
same month, in Judaea. Of course it was well arranged; the comedy had to be
played out with due thoroughness. On the appointed morning 'as Vespasian

193

emerged from his bedchamber, a few soldiers, standing by in the usual formation for saluting a legate, hailed him as *imperator*; then others ran up calling him Caesar and Augustus and heaping on him all the titles of the Princeps'. The cooperation of the Danube legions, some of which had served under Vespasian, had been achieved; his brother, Flavius Sabinus, was recruiting a party secretly in Rome; agents worked among the fleet; the whole movement, in other words, was orchestrated. No wonder Vespasian 'showed no elation, arrogance or change at the turn of events'; they hadn't caught him by surprise; besides which his conscious role was that of the plain man set to restore order and dignity to the State.

He took no part himself in the Italian campaign which destroyed Vitellius. Instead, his care was to secure his base in Egypt, making Alexandria his head-quarters. That showed strategic sense; a check in Italy would not reduce the campaign or end the war. Moreover, Alexandria, through its command of the corn trade and the decline of Italian agriculture, exercised a stranglehold over the Roman economy.

Vespasian was still in Alexandria when on 22 December 69 the Senate, acknow-ledging reality, recognized him as emperor with the same rights as Augustus, Tiberius and Claudius. This decree of the Senate's was to be confirmed by the moribund Assembly, convened for the purpose, early in January. Vespasian however, more of a realist still, always dated his reign from 1 July, the day the legions had acclaimed him *imperator*. He knew whence this power derived; he knew what the Senate's decree was worth. The Senate could no longer will the distribution of power – perhaps it had never been able to do so – but it was no longer even worth the Emperor's while to go through the charade of pretending it could. A comparison of the debate in the Senate after Augustus' death, which had preceded the elevation of Tiberius, with Vespasian's attitude now, shows how the thin disguise which had once been cast over the nature of empire had been discarded. Though disaffection lingered in some parts of the Empire, notably on the Rhine frontier, and though Titus was still engaged in the suppression of the Jews, Vespasian was in a position to proceed straightaway to the restoration of the State. The Senate's decree of *imperium* had granted him the right to recommend candi-dates for all magistracies, which ensured his control of public appointments; and it was symptomatic of his new attitude to the Principate that his right of *commendatio* had none of the limitations which his predecessors had accepted. Henceforth the imperial dominance of public affairs was not to be obscured by any decent civil pretence. Accordingly, even before he arrived in Rome, where his second son Domitian was acting as his deputy, Vespasian was ready to embark on the most thorough programme of renewal since Octavian had made himself into Augustus. It was exactly a hundred years since Actium.

Vespasian faced problems of finance and organization; the gravest challenge however was that which had been posed to the concept of authority. The treasury was empty, the frontiers endangered; but, worst of all, the habit of obedience had been lost. Emperors had been resisted, conspired against, insulted, and murdered before the eyes of the mob. Vespasian perceived that the true problems of empire lay in men's minds; and all his first actions were calculated to change the way people were thinking.

His coins bore the legend *Roma Resurgens*. As a practical demonstration of this idea his first act was to command the rebuilding of the burnt Capitol and of the Temple of Jupiter which had for so long dominated the hill. The ruins were carried off to the marshes of the Campagna, and the new buildings constructed on the original site to the original plan; a symbol of continuity and renewal. The work was inaugurated on 21 June, the longest day of the year, in a solemn religious ceremony. In this way Vespasian allied his regime to the venerated past and held out the promise of a secure and splendid future. By the time he reached Rome that October he had already demonstrated that he stood for order and peace; it was well known also that he had cured the blind in Alexandria, a rumour sedulously spread to impress the vulgar.

Vespasian was not deceived by his own propaganda. He had too much experience of life to lose the habit of irony. The stories told about great men, even when apocryphal, illustrate at least how they are perceived by contemporaries, and this gives them figurative truth. The two best-known anecdotes of Vespasian illustrate his ironic humanity and common sense. When he imposed a tax on the use of public urinals, his elegant son Titus protested that the association was undignified and distasteful. Vespasian held up a coin and remarked 'this doesn't stink, does it?' Finally, on the point of death, he first turned to his companions and said, 'good heavens, I seem to be turning into a god'. (He was.) But after that he insisted on being helped to his feet: 'an emperor should die standing'.

His sturdy sense of reality, so rare in rulers, told him well enough that propaganda requires substance; it must be backed by achievement or it soon withers. He saw too that the emperor must exercise total control over the structure of the State. The Flavians were to monopolise the consulship, still important because of the ceremonial duties that devolved on the office, in a way not seen since Augustus had done so in the years immediately after the ending of the triumvirate. With Titus as colleague, Vespasian held consulships in 70, 72, 74, 75, 76, 77 and 79. Everything indeed was done to associate Titus with his father. On his return from the East in the spring of 71 he received the proconsular *imperium* and was made a partner in Vespasian's tribunician power, which offices together gave him formal control over the machinery of State. He was also named Caesar; and he and his brother Domitian were appointed *principes iuventutis*, that title Augustus had bestowed on his beloved grandsons. Crucially, too, in view of memories of Sejanus, of Gaius' murder and Nero's accession, Titus himself took command of the Praetorian Guard. Thus were the Flavians' dynastic intentions made clear; not for nothing had Vespasian said, 'my sons shall succeed me or no one shall'.

But first the victorious party must impress the world with the majesty of their achievement. The civil war itself could not of course be celebrated, since the old maxim that victories over fellow-citizens must not be honoured still endured. The

Colosseum; a Flavian amphitheatre

ruthless suppression of the Jews was another matter, fit material for a triumph and the demonstration of Flavian greatness. Wrote the Jewish renegade and historian Josephus:

Not a soul among the countless multitudes of the city remained at home. The troops while it was still dark had all marched out in centuries and cohorts. . . At dawn Vespasian and Titus emerged, crowned with laurel and wearing the traditional purple, and proceeded to the portico of Octavia, where the Senate and chief magistrates and a contingent of equestrians were waiting for them. The princes were unarmed, wearing silk robes. Vespasian gave the signal for silence. Then, in deep and universal stillness, he rose. Covering his head with his cloak, he recited the age-old prayers. Titus followed suit. Then, having put on their triumphal robes and offered sacrifice to the gods they set the procession in motion, themselves driving through the theatres that they might be better seen by the crowds. . .

The religious ceremony was followed by spectacle. The war was shown in numerous representations . . . here was to be seen a prosperous country being

196

laid waste, there whole battalions of the enemy were slaughtered, here they were shown in flight, there being led into captivity. Cities and garrisons were shown overcome with an army pouring across the ramparts. A quarter was all deluged with blood, the hands of those who could no longer resist being raised in supplication. Temples were set on fire, houses pulled down over their owners' heads; and after general desolation and woe, rivers were displayed flowing, not over a cultivated land nor supplying drink to man and beast, but across a country still burning on every side. . .

Marvellous theatre, its implications clear; this was the full majesty of the Roman Empire. Here too were the horrors of war from which Vespasian had rescued Italy.

Conspicuous above the other spoils rose those captured in the Temple at Jerusalem: a golden table, many talents in weight; a golden candelabrum; tablets displaying the laws of the Jews. Then followed a large party carrying images to victory, all made of ivory and gold. Behind these drove Vespasian, followed by Titus, while Domitian rode by their side, magnificently dressed and mounted on a marvellous horse. . .

The triumphal procession ended at the Temple of Jupiter Capitolinus, where they halted, for it was a time-honoured custom to wait there until the execution of the enemy's general was announced. . .

Vespasian showed all the contempt of the impresario for the spectacle he had devised to impress the people. 'What an old fool I was to demand a triumph'. He was heard to mutter, as he squirmed with boredom. But it was a far cry from being pelted with turnips in Africa.

He was of course not ignorant of the value of spectacle; he knew too the insidious force of public opinion even in a despotism. He appreciated how disaffection could spread; had he not exploited it himself? Such knowledge found expression in his most permanent monument: the Colosseum. This massive amphitheatre, capable of holding 87,000 spectators, was built in that territory which Nero had appropriated after the Great Fire of his Golden House. The choice of site not only expressed an old ambition credited to Augustus; it satisfied the enduring resentment the Golden House had fostered; while the magnificence of the new building delighted the mob for whose benefit and pleasure it was raised. The reproach that the Roman people were bought off with bread and circuses as a substitute for their lost liberty dates properly from Flavian times – the first such gibes came from their contemporary, the satirical poet Juvenal. The need to satisfy the plebs in this way had long been a fact of imperial politics; the Colosseum merely realized the policy in marble. Though Vespasian was aware of the debilitating effect of idleness – Suetonius relates how he declined an offer from an engineer to haul huge stones up the Capitol at moderate expense by the use of a simple machine with the words 'I must always ensure that the working classes earn enough to buy bread' – this was little more than sentiment. There was not, and could never be, work enough to occupy the Roman mob – nor were many of them fit for it in any case. Bread and circuses: these constituted the dole of empire.

To appease the plebs was easy enough; all it required was the provision of food and entertainment. To ensure control of the State was another, and more difficult, matter. Republican sentiment, though weakened by the dreadful events of 69 as well as by the enduring establishment of empire, still lingered, and, in doing so, fomented disaffection and provided a rallying-point for the disgruntled. One senator, Helvidius Priscus, the son-in-law of Nero's old enemy the high-minded Thrasea Paetus, persistently insulted Vespasian in word and deed, attacking the monarchical system and praising Republican institutions, and, in addressing the people, openly preaching revolution. It was too much even for Vespasian; Priscus was exiled and then put to death.

Less dangerous opponents were treated with more leniency and greater contempt. Philosophical sects, Stoics and Cynics, both deplored the Empire. Their theories, though irreconcilable, both chipped at its foundations. At last Mucianus persuaded the Emperor to banish all Cynic teachers. One of them, a certain Demetrius, continued his sniping from exile. Vespasian merely responded, 'you are trying hard to get me to kill you, but I don't kill dogs for barking'.

Nevertheless disaffection of any kind was disturbing for an emperor whose authority, not being inherited, was so purely personal. It was necessary for Vespasian to exercise a closer and more rigorous control over the instrument of State than the Julio-Claudians had been accustomed to do. Accordingly in 73 he revived the censorship, sharing the office with Titus. This old Republican magistracy allowed him to act the moral reformer; more important was the opportunity it gave to revise membership of the Senate and magistracy. Gibbon was acutely to see how important the censorship was in the establishment of the imperial despotism: 'the principles of a free constitution are irrevocably lost when the legislative power is nominated by the executive'. Titus and Domitian were to follow their father in using the censorship to suppress any opposition from the nobility; the beauty of the weapon lay in its irreproachably Republican origins. At the same time Vespasian set out to win the support of the equestrian order by associating them more closely with government. Whereas the Julio-Claudians had increasingly relied on their freedmen to administer the departments of State, thus incurring unpopularity and separating the upper reaches of the bureacracy from the opinion of the wealthy and well born, Vespasian encouraged the equestrians to take up posts in the imperial service.

So, at Rome, he flattered the people by the magnificence of the entertainments he provided for their pleasure, controlled the nobility through his monopoly of the consulship and through the traditional office of censor, and offered opportunities of service and wealth to the bourgeoisie.

All this was important, but imperial authority depended finally on the Princeps' relations with the army. Fortunately Vespasian, unlike any emperor since Tiberius, was a soldier of reputation. He was also sufficiently tough and self-confident to decline to truckle to the soldiers. The Flavian pretence that Vespasian had been spontaneously elected by the legions collapses before the control which he exercised over them; far from ushering in a period of licence and reward he dealt with them as sternly as Galba had promised to do. Many of the legions which had supported Vitellius were disbanded; individual soldiers often being transferred to other units. Nor was their pay increased; there was not enough money in the treasury to permit it. He estimated publicly that 400 million gold pieces were needed to restore the State's finances. The legions had to content themselves with the assurance that pay and pensions would not be in arrears.

There were however other means of engaging the soldiers' affections, and these Vespasian did not neglect. Their self-esteem was flattered by an emperor and his heir who had themselves endured the hardships of campaign; their morale was improved by success. Certainly there was a limit to what Vespasian might achieve; the Empire's resources were so stretched that an advance in Britain meant a halt in Germany, and vice versa. Still, on the northern frontier Vespasian annexed the Agri Decumantes and penetrated up the Lower Neckar. And in the Balkans the Dacians

Colosseum: interior

and Sarmatians, who had taken advantage of the troubles of 69 to invade the Empire, were thrown back across the Danube.

The great work of Vespasian and his sons lay however in Anatolia, where the long troublesome Armenian frontier was at last to be given the security it had lacked. Three great camps were built guarding the mountain passes to the east, and communications were established by a network of highways, one stretching right across the country from Trebizond. The frontier, formerly running from Syria to the centre of Anatolia, was now pushed eastward to the line of the Euphrates. In the north, where the river narrowed, the boundary of empire now became the rampart of snow-covered mountains that extended to the limits of Pontus. This was work worthy of the greatest periods of Roman history; Vespasian in short achieved in Armenia what had been beyond the power of either the Republic or the Julio-Claudians. No wonder that after such efforts he felt able to dedicate the Temple of Peace and issue coins calling himself 'conqueror, peace-bringer, restorer of the State. . .'

Conqueror, peace-bringer, restorer of the State: this was the image Vespasian sought, deliberately and with success, to attain in history. He attracted admiration in his lifetime, even more thereafter, because he presented himself as the embodiment of that civic virtue which had been the distinguishing feature of Republican Rome. His personal simplicity recalled earlier times; he could have walked out of the *Georgics* or, better, the first heroic chapters of Livy. He had married only once, and on the death of his wife, Flavia Domatilla, herself of humble birth but the mother of his three children Titus, Domitian and Domatilla, he had taken up with a freed slave called Caenis and lived contentedly with her even after becoming emperor. He was a man's man, a soldier, and his amours were casual; women were kept in their place at his court; the petticoat government so resented in the days of Claudius and Nero had vanished. Vespasian lived simply, rising early, dealing with correspondence and documents before daylight, and eating modestly. He even restored something of Republican freedom and dignity in personal matters; he was always affable and accessible. Best of all, he discontinued the practice, begun by Claudius, of having visitors to his morning audiences searched.

All the anecdotes emphasized his earthy humanity. Even his stinginess became a subject for affectionate gossip – it was not only appropriate to an emperor of small farmer stock; it was absolutely in character. It was said that he cornered commodities and then put them on the market at inflated prices; that he demanded fees from candidates for public office, and sold pardons to innocent and guilty alike. The Alexandrians had named him 'Cybiosactes' – 'a dealer in small cubes of fish'; when he died the actor Favor, who wore his funeral mask in the procession and imitated his gestures and words, called out 'how much will this funeral cost me?' 'A hundred thousand,' was the reply. 'In that case,' he exclaimed, 'give me a thousand down and pitch the body into the Tiber.'

This miserliness was no doubt natural, but it was also part of his public *persona*, like Abraham Lincoln's homespun proverbs. It pleased the Roman people and soldiers to think that after the madman Gaius, the old pedant Claudius, the aesthete Nero, and the fleeting pretenders of 69 – unbending Galba, dissolute Otho and gluttonous Vitellius – they were now ruled by this humorous, close-fisted Italian, who could take a joke against himself and had no illusions. Where it mattered however, or appeared seemly, he could be generous enough. There was nothing parsimonious about his rebuilding of Rome: apart from the Colisseum he started work on a Temple of Peace near the Forum and a temple to Claudius the god on the Caelian, and he also ordered many cities throughout the Empire to be rebuilt. He granted pensions to senators whose own income did not allow them to maintain a state suitable to their rank, and an annual pension of five thousand gold pieces to ex-consuls. Regular salaries were also paid to teachers of Latin and Greek rhetoric. He built a new stage for the Theatre of Marcellus and distributed prizes and grants to the actors. Poets and artists were similarly rewarded; he paid lavishly for the restoration of the Venus of Cos, a copy of a statue by Praxiteles, which was installed in the Temple of Peace, and for the Colossus, a huge statue of Nero (whose head was now tactfully replaced by Apollo's). The Emperor indeed was an Arts Council in himself, the careful financier becoming a munificent patron as public policy demanded.

Vespasian's achievement is manifest. He found the State in ruins, the armies contending for the right to appoint an emperor, the frontiers neglected and open to barbarian invasion, the treasury empty. When he died of fever nine years later, all had been repaired. His boast had been made good; the State was restored, Rome indeed resurgent, the army disciplined again. He had secured the eastern frontier, settling the long-vexing problem of Armenia. The advance in Britain continued. If he couldn't claim, like Augustus, that he had found the city of brick and left it of marble, he had rebuilt its temples, built a new Forum and Baths, and, most significant of all, embarked on the construction of the Colosseum, which his son would complete.

The Colosseum is his true monument. It has been for almost two thousand years the symbol of imperial Rome; but it was at the time a symbol also of the new relationship between the Emperor and the people. Of course previous emperors had troubled themselves to flatter the people and secure their submissive content – Tiberius indeed had been the sole exception. But there was an unprecedented blatancy about the Colosseum. It was the statement, perhaps unconscious, of a creed. Augustus had solemnized his *imperium* in the Secular Games; he had encouraged Livy and Virgil to elaborate a myth of Rome; he had called for moral renewal. Vespasian instead built an amphitheatre where the people might merely be drugged by spectacle. He had secured the empire, but he could not regenerate society; and he did not really do more than pretend that he could.

It may be said that because everything about Vespasian is consistent, it is for that reason suspected. All rulers are to some extent fabrications; they create conscious *personae* for themselves, presenting a mask to their own public and to posterity. In its turn posterity selects from the available evidence, and models only the figure it chooses to recognize. Accordingly Vespasian is 'the good Emperor', a man free from excess, ruled by common sense; the restorer of balance. And up to a point this is true – history seldom lies outright.

The conventional picture was there by design. It was subsequently fleshed out by those who cast themselves as Vespasian's heirs, who wished to acknowledge him and Titus, while disowning Domitian. Succeeding emperors thus had the problem of building on the Flavian achievement while repudiating the most forceful, and in certain respects, most successful, of the three Flavian emperors. One way of doing so was to elevate Vespasian and Titus at Domitian's expense; to grant the two former all praise due to the Flavians, Domitian all obloquy.

But the historians who praised Vespasian failed to ask the first question prompted by his astonishing career. How did the dogged plodder, whose career once seemed to have been smothered in the hail of turnips in Africa, come to flower as emperor? In a sense this is a modern question, for the Ancient World provided an answer that satisfied itself. The goddess Fortuna and the omens that were there for men to read provided sufficient explanation of any man's fate. Suetonius collected no fewer than eleven examples of how the Fates foretold Vespasian's glorious future, the first very properly dating from the moment of his birth. At the very least this industry on the historian's part may be taken as evidence of how urgent it seemed to establish Vespasian's claim to be a rightful Princeps. Only Fortuna could justify so extraordinary a transformation; and to be persuasive she had to multiply the clues.

Some of the indications were fanciful enough. For instance 'a stray dog picked up a human hand at the cross-roads, which it brought into the room where Vespasian was breakfasting and dropped under the table; a hand being the symbol of power. . .' On another occasion 'an ox shook off the yoke of its plough and charged into Vespasian's dining-room, scattering the servants before falling at his feet, where it lowered its neck as though suddenly overcome by exhaustion. . .' Or this one, 'while Galba was on his way to be elected consul for the second time, a statue of Julius Caesar turned of its own accord to face East' where Vespasian was of course to be found. There were dreams and oracles which had told Vespasian himself of his change of fortune. And so on: such pointers to imperial destiny may seem childish and unconvincing to the modern reader. But a Roman would have read them differently; else none would have bothered to collect the stories or invent them.

Yet, in a sense, the Roman historian may have been right. Fortune, as much as character and capacity, brought Vespasian to the fore. The opportunity was provided after all, by others; in the first place by Nero's folly, in the second by Galba's lack of judgement or pliability. And Vespasian's success was not just personal; the Flavians were a party, representing interests and family groupings, who saw him as the means by which they might themselves attain power and wealth. Even his success as emperor may be attributed to something other than his own ability; or even to his son Titus' qualities. The welter of 68–9 had been exceptional; the circumstances necessarily pulled the Empire back to balance.

Vespasian himself was no innovator, hardly a reformer; he was competent and he applied the existing machine – even his great work in Anatolia built directly on Corbulo's previous achievement. Certainly, he was more than a figurehead; he was indeed a tough and prudent ruler. But the real triumph of his reign was not a personal one. On the contrary what it most clearly revealed was the efficiency and adaptability of the system, however flawed in spirit, that had been created in the years after Actium. To work, however, it required a firm hand on the tiller; and it was Vespasian's ability to provide this that ensured its success.

Titus

TITUS

AT THE END of the Sacred Way, on a rise below the Palatine and overlooking the valley of the Colosseum and the Circus Maximus away to the right, stands the finest of triumphal arches to be found in Rome. Placed under it, with your back to the Forum and the Capitol above, you look eastward to the billowing blue line of the Alban Hills; the mind's eye may be carried beyond them, across Italy and the Eastern Mediterranean, to Palestine, and the imagination will be aided by the bas-reliefs on Titus' Arch, which depict the suppression of the Jewish Revolt, the sack of Jerusalem, and the triumph of Vespasian and Titus. Another relief in the vault of the arch shows the dead Titus being carried by an eagle to meet the gods, one of whom he has just become. The whole history of Titus is revealed here in this celebration of his greatest military feat, revealed as it was designed for public consumption: this is the great, the good, the noble, the beloved Emperor, carried off in his prime. He was aged only forty.

Titus had been born in a slum tenement in the year of Gaius' murder. Vespasian was still only a junior officer. Thanks to the patronage of Narcissus the boy was introduced to court life as a child – the gentle and elegant manners that characterized him were due to this early experience. Indeed he was brought up as a companion of Claudius' son Britannicus. There was just ten months between them. They did their lessons and played games together, and they became close friends. (Later, when Titus had become Caesar and his playmate was long dead, a story was told of how a physiognomist, called in by Narcissus, had prophesied that Britannicus would never succeed his father, while Titus would follow his.) Titus was present at the banquet at which Nero murdered his half-brother; his devotion to his friend was reported to have been so great that he had drunk from the same cup and been dangerously ill himself. Whatever the truth of this tale, Titus did not forget Britannicus, and was to set up two statues of his boyhood friend; like his father, Titus was master of the popular gesture.

No doubt he had difficulties after the murder; it could have been neither safe nor

Arch of Titus. Bas-relief on interior of the arch showing the spoils from
Jerusalem being carried in Titus' triumph

easy to be marked as the confidant of the dead prince. However, not being an
aristocrat, he was able to slip back into obscurity. He served in Germany as a young
man; great merit was subsequently to be discovered in his conduct there. Eventually
it was to be his father's unexpected appointment to the command in Judaea in 66
that gave him his chance.

He had grown up handsome and talented. One attribute was as important as the
other. Later he grew fat – coin portraits show a head that speaks of good living, like
a Renaissance Pope's – Alexander VI perhaps. But he looked well on parade; the
military and populace alike responded to his splendid appearance, which gave him
what so many of the emperors had lacked: charisma. He was intelligent as well,
reputed to possess a phenomenal memory. That at least testifies to his capacity, for,
if it wasn't true, it shows he took care to be well briefed. He was at ease in his body,

Arch of Titus, with the Colosseum beyond

rode and handled weapons skilfully and distinguished himself in battle. He spoke Greek as well as Latin and was capable of making a good speech off the cuff in either language. He claimed to be able to imitate any hand-writing; Suetonius says he could have been the most celebrated forger of all time.

Accordingly his reputation was destined to flower, bolstered by the Jewish success – however his role in that was stage-managed by his father and his father's advisers. Yet in fact Titus did not become popular till he was emperor; in Vespasian's lifetime he was distrusted and even feared. Report said that he was debauched and cruel. Ruthless too; hadn't he murdered an ex-consul, Aulus Caecina, at his own dinner-table? (Caecina had prepared a seditious speech to be delivered to the soldiers, or so it was claimed.) He was also said to be immoral, owning a troop of catamites (dancing boys), and nursing a passion for the Eastern queen, Berenice.

She was the daughter of Herod Agrippa, King of the Jews, a woman of scandalous reputation, who had deserted two husbands and lived incestuously with her brother, King Agrippa II. She had dabbled dangerously in politics, only adhering to the Roman cause just before the Jewish Revolt. Over forty when Titus fell in love with her, she revived all the old Roman fear of the sinful allure of the East, as invoked by the spectre of Mark Antony's entanglement with Cleopatra.

In addition to all this, Titus was corrupt and greedy – as greedy as his father and far more corrupt. He would accept bribes and use his influence, to settle cases in his father's courts in favour of the highest bidder. It was muttered that he would prove a second Nero.

Such conduct – apart from the murder of Caecina – was little worse than the behaviour of most Roman nobles; but in Titus it was frightening in that he was a man of power. Certainly it points to a darker side of the Flavian absolutism, that was hidden by Vespasian's success and geniality, and that would be likewise concealed under a mask of benevolence by Titus when he became emperor himself.

For Titus was associated with his father in government more closely than any heir had been since the last days of Augustus; and, as often happens in such circumstances, all the animus aroused by the government was directed not at its titular head, but at the associate who was believed to exercise the real power. Titus not only shared the consulship, the tribunician power and the censor's office with his father; he commanded the Praetorians. This post had hitherto generally been entrusted to a soldier of equestrian family, and Titus' decision to retain the command himself displayed his political acuity; it showed also how uncertain the Flavians were of the stability of their recently established regime. Titus used the Guard, in effect, to establish a police state in Rome. Detachments of soldiers habitually arrested those suspected of disloyalty; did so moreover in public places, the theatre or the camp; and carried out summary executions. Thus in these early years did Titus put into practice the old Roman maxims: 'let them hate provided they fear' and 'to spare the subject and subdue the proud'.

His accession was therefore greeted with some trepidation; this was soon dispelled however. And why not? The task of establishing the Flavian dynasty had been accomplished; the government of the Empire was securely in his hands. He could now afford to play the benevolent father of his country. Indeed he was soon given the opportunity to display the depth of his care for his subjects. The summer of 79 saw the eruption of Vesuvius which destroyed Pompeii and Herculaneum, a great fire in Rome and an outburst of virulent plague. The Princeps' response was prompt. He set up a government board, staffed by ex-consuls, to organize relief in Rome, ostentatiously stripping his own palace of decorations to provide for restoration, and he resorted to all sorts of remedies – medical and sacrificial – in an attempt to alleviate the effects of the plague. Public disaster enhanced the Emperor's reputation; he was now compared favourably with Nero. His military reputation meanwhile ensured an absence of trouble with the legions in his brief reign; the achievement in Judaea was still fresh in men's minds. Anyway the influence he had exercised over the government in his father's lifetime meant that positions of power and responsibility were everywhere held by his supporters.

To what extent Titus' reputation was posthumous, to what extent contemporary, is hard to say. The subsequent unpopularity of his brother naturally caused men to look back with regret on the promise he had shown, to paint his time in golden colours. He had a winning personality such as was denied Domitian: Gibbon observed that 'the beloved memory of Titus served to protect above fifteen years the vices of his brother'. Certainly he possessed a mastery of public relations: the dedication of the Colosseum offered a spectacle of unprecedented splendour, the spectators being delighted with the slaughter of five thousand wild animals in a single day.

More humanely he let it be known that he would never dismiss a petitioner without leaving him some hope that his request would be favourably considered, a piece of propaganda that could hardly be carried out in practice. He maintained that no one should go away disappointed from an interview with the Emperor, and the story was circulated that, realizing one evening that he had done no one a favour since the night before, he lamented that he had wasted a day. It was the same understanding of the importance of his public image that led him to use the new public baths as a means of keeping in touch with the opinions of the people.

In the same way he sought popularity by making an attack on the informers who still disgraced Roman life and occupied the law-courts. He had them arrested, whipped, clubbed, and paraded in the Colosseum before being sold into slavery. But this too was a gesture; informers did not disappear as a breed. Only a thorough reform of the legal system, abolishing private prosecutions, could have achieved that. A few years later, we are told, Domitian also observed that a Princeps who did not punish informers encouraged them to breed. The probability is that Titus, like other emperors, used informers when they seemed useful, and at other times punished them in his search for popularity.

He had taken the office of *pontifex maximus*, and, stressing his magnanimity, assured people that this would be a safeguard against his committing a crime.

Coin of Titus commemorating the
conquest of Judaea

Perhaps. It helped anyway to emphasize the distance between himself and ordinary
men. When two patricians were accused of aspiring to the Empire, he told them that
they should abandon their hopes as it was 'a gift of Destiny'. The implication was
clear. What was in the gift of the gods would only be granted to a god-like man.
Augustus and Tiberius had disliked the term *dominus* – 'lord'. In Flavian times the
imperial palace became the *domus divina* – 'the divine house'. The Emperor himself
was called *dominus et deus* – 'lord and god'. On this occasion Titus went to great
lengths to reassure the guilty pair of nobles and their families. 'Finally,' Suetonius
relates, 'after having them as his guests at dinner and the Games, he consulted their
horoscopes and warned them that danger threatened from unexpected quarters –
quite correctly as it turned out.' The meiosis of the last phrase is masterly in its grisly
suggestiveness.

Titus was struck by fever in August 81 after reigning a mere two years. On his
deathbed he complained bitterly of the injustice of fate (that Fortune he had always
honoured) and said that only a single sin lay on his conscience. Some took this to be
a reference to alleged acts of incest with his sister-in-law, Domitia. (She denied the
allegation, and Suetonius says that she would have boasted of it if it had been true,
as she did of all her other misdeeds.) Others believed that he repented his impious
invasion of the Holy of Holies in the Temple at Jerusalem. (Queen Berenice may
have told him with what loathing this was regarded by the Jews; certainly they
ascribed his early death to God's displeasure with this act.) The Emperor Hadrian,
on the other hand, believed that Titus had murdered his father Vespasian.

This last accusation illustrates how little Titus' great reputation may have owed to fact, and how much it may have been merely created by propaganda. A century which has seen monstrous dictators flattered and revered cannot doubt that it is possible to manufacture a quite synthetic great man. Whatever the truth, Titus' death provoked an orgy of official, and even unofficial, lamentation. Yet even here Suetonius' native scepticism does not desert him. The senators, he says, at once started to speak about him 'with greater gratitude and praise than they had ever displayed when he was alive. . .'

None of the emperors described in this book died so greatly regretted as Titus, cut off in his flower. None did so little to merit the praise showered on him. . .

Domitian

DOMITIAN

DOMITIAN WAS READY for Titus' death. He had been waiting for years. Once indeed he had even asserted that Titus had altered their father's will, and that this had originally assigned him a half-share in the Empire. The claim was ridiculous; all Vespasian's actions had indicated that Titus, and Titus alone, should succeed him. Domitian had been kept in the background. Nevertheless Domitian, throughout his brother's reign, was reported as brooding on conspiracies. Probably his plans never got further than idle dreams, Titus always treated him with the respect due to a brother who was his heir. Possibly indeed the conspiracies never existed, even in Domitian's imagination; but his later unpopularity made everyone ready to believe in them. Certainly he was prompt to act on Titus' death to secure the Empire; it was the only prudent thing to do, of course – though the rumour went that his death had been presumed before he actually expired.

In his upbringing, Domitian had been almost as unfortunate as Gaius Caligula and was as likely to be as little fitted for the responsibilities of empire. It had made him reserved, even secretive, which was the first reason why unfriendly rumours were so easily believed. He quite lacked Titus' ability to charm; it was easy moreover to suggest that Vespasian too had not trusted his younger son. Domitian, though he had been granted honours, though he had held a consulship and been named *princeps iuventutis*, had always been condemned to a role subsidiary to the glittering Titus.

It was of course partly a question of age. Domitian was born in 51, the year in which Vespasian, as Narcissus' client, was first a consul. But Claudius had died, and Narcissus had fallen foul of Agrippina, when Domitian was only three; and he had accordingly passed his boyhood in the year of his father's obscurity before the Jewish Revolt gave Vespasian the chance to establish his reputation. Domitian had therefore known genteel poverty – often there was no silver on the family dining-table – and he had not experienced the upbringing at court which had fallen to Titus as the playmate and schoolfriend of Britannicus. Instead of these advan-

213

tages he had first known a narrow garret in the Street of the Pomegranates in the Sixth Region of Rome, hardly a fashionable quarter; then he had been left behind in Rome when his father and brother set off for the East. In place of court or camp, he had been brought up by an aunt, almost as an only child. It was a childhood and adolescence which had left him deficient in social ease, reticent, even misanthropic. He grew up solitary, unsure of his talents or his future. Suetonius records that a certain senator, one Claudius Pollio, an ex-praetor, used to be happy to produce a letter from the young Domitian promising that he would go to bed with him. If true, the story reflects worse on the man who retailed it than on the lonely boy who wrote the letter.

He was in Rome in the desperate year of 69, where the Flavians' fortunes were guided by his uncle Sabinus. Domitian escaped from the Capitol when it was captured by the Vitellians, and took refuge in the Temple of Isis, disguised as a neophyte in that disreputable order. Thence he managed to escape across the river to Trastevere, where the mother of one of his fellow-students was persuaded to hide him in her house. He was therefore on hand when his father's supporters took the city and was at once hailed as Caesar and appointed city praetor with consular powers. His uncle being dead, he was nominally head of the Flavian party in Rome; but as he was still only eighteen and entirely without experience, his power remained largely formal. He did however take the opportunity to distribute patronage (rather lavishly) and thus take the first steps towards the establishment of a personal clientele; and he persuaded a woman who took his fancy, Domitia Longina, to divorce her husband and marry him instead.

Vespasian kept him in the background. It was natural that on the occasion of the Emperor's Jewish triumph, Titus should travel with his father in a chariot, while Domitian rode behind on a white horse (the conventional mount for young princes on such ceremonial occasions), for Domitian had after all taken no part in the war and Titus was the hero of its successful conclusion. But it was another matter that he should always be treated as of inferior status, be denied military experience despite his repeated requests to be sent to the armies, and receive only one full consulship in the reign. Such neglect might be sound policy on Vespasian's part; he had no wish to imperil the dynasty by suggesting that the succession was anything but clear cut; but it did nothing for Domitian's self-esteem.

A political cipher, Domitian cultivated sport and the arts. He was a fine archer and killed hundreds of wild animals on his estates in the Alban Hills, his skill being reputedly such that he could shoot an arrow between the outstretched fingers of an obedient (if trembling) slave. Things Greek were his passion. He had a devotion for Minerva, Goddess of Wisdom and patroness of poets, and, like most educated Romans, wrote poetry himself; one poem to celebrate Titus' conquest of Jerusalem, another didactic piece on 'The Care of the Hair'. Neither has survived, and neither may have had much merit; but the former at least testifies a willingness to please his brother, while the latter was as vain as most instructional verse, for Domitian himself became bald early. Though he stopped writing verses after he became

Temple of Minerva, Rome, showing a part used as a bakery

emperor – perhaps because he had the same realistic appreciation of his literary work as Augustus had had of his, more probably because he found in empire a more satisfying means of self-expression – his devotion to Minerva and his zeal for literature persisted. He founded a College of Priests in Minerva's honour; one of their duties was to sponsor competitions in rhetoric and poetry. More importantly perhaps, he went to great trouble and expense re-stocking the libraries, many of which had been sacked in the civil wars or burned in subsequent fires; he organized a search for lost volumes and sent to Alexandria for copies, ordering transcriptions to be made if none were available. He was described as 'a veritable Maecenas to the libraries'.

As emperor, however, Domitian suffered from three things: his own temperament; his inexperience; and the reviving hostility of the senators. They were all of course connected; the first and third destroyed him in the end.

No one, except possibly his wife Domitia, ever came close to him. Vespasian and Titus had been genial and companionable, gregarious Italians; café men, always ready with a joking familiarity. Domitian, more complicated, unsure of himself, sat in the palace alone. What was he doing? Catching flies and stabbing them with a pen that was as sharp as a needle. Asked one day whether anyone was with the Emperor, the senator Vivius Crispus wittily answered: 'No one. Not even a fly.' It was an image worthy to describe Tiberius; and Domitian not only recalled the old and legendary Emperor, it was soon known that he spent his leisure moments reading Tiberius' memoirs. The sinister import was evident. The picture of Domitian closeted in silent communion with his imagined Tiberius seized the imagination. The Romans, always unable to understand a taste for solitude, invented appropriate stories. The tale of the flies was one such, eagerly repeated by gossip-historians, a picture so dramatically pleasing that none questioned its provenance – though if Domitian was alone, who could know what he was doing? Enough, though, it was a suitable occupation for one surrounded by 'an atmosphere of mourning and gloom'.

Domitian would have experienced difficulties even if he had possessed Titus' geniality. Unlike him his father and brother had benefited from a reaction to the horrible events and still more horrible implications of the year 69. The threat of social disintegration, the revealed terrors of civil war, had encouraged a state of mind in which the senatorial class was ready to forget Vespasian's humble birth, and submit to despotism for the sake of the order it ensured. That reaction had now spent itself. Once more the remnants of the Roman nobility chafed against the restraints imposed by empire; once more the seductive word 'Republic' breathed its old attraction.

Another factor disturbed relations between Emperor and Senate. Originally it had been the personal *auctoritas* of Augustus which had exalted the office of Princeps; now the office itself must exalt an emperor who, unlike all his predecessors, had neither birth nor achievement to commend him. Little wonder therefore that Domitian should seek to enhance his position, should mark out what separated him from the general run of the nobility, the generals and adminstrators. Such a widening of the gulf between them accorded well enough with his personal inclinations; it accorded also with his understanding of political necessity.

So from the start the inexperienced Princeps revealed a determination to concentrate power in his own hands and elevate himself above those who might regard themselves as his social superiors and superiors in achievement. Even more than his father had done, he monopolized the consulship, holding the office every year from 82 to 88, and again in 90, 92 and 95. Like his father and brother he appreciated the power offered by the office of censor, assuming the *censoria potestas* in 85, and then naming himself perpetual Censor. It suited his temperament to exercise the control over morals that the post traditionally afforded; more important, his political acumen seized on the opportunity it gave him to control the membership, and hence ultimately the conduct, of the Senate; indeed it held out the eventual prospect of permanent and undisguised mastery. Moreover, this was a logical development, for the growth of the imperial bureaucracy was gradually changing the Senate from an aristocracy of birth and family to an aristocracy of office. Yet for all that, Domitian's award to himself of the censorship was deeply resented.

So too was the whole tenor of his behaviour. Soon he was expecting to be addressed as 'master and god' (*dominus et deus*). After his first German campaigns he assumed the cognomen Germanicus, rightly seen as an attempt to associate himself with the glories of the Julio-Claudian dynasty. The months September and October were renamed Germanicus and Domitianus, though one month each had been thought sufficient for Julius and Augustus. In everything he did Domitian emphasized that he belonged to a superior order of being; the palace became known as the 'divine house' (*domus divina*); he even spoke of taking his wife 'to my divine bed'.

This was at first policy, not megalomania. Domitian, accepting the logic of the proposition advanced by Seneca forty years earlier, that 'Caesar owns the world, Caesar may do all things', yet realized the fragility of his personal position. How could he fail to? He had grown up in a dangerous and insecure world; before he was twenty he had seen Nero and Otho driven to suicide, Galba and Vitellius murdered; he knew that emperors were not protected by the purple.

Mindful of Nero's fate and the reasons for it, he set out to ingratiate himself with the armies. He paid careful attention to their welfare and raised their pay by a third. Moreover no reigning emperor since Augustus spent a greater portion of his reign with the troops than Domitian did. It partly satisfied the youthful ambitions for military glory which Vespasian had denied him; more important however for the practical Domitian it represented an attempt to provide against disaffection. This emperor would be known to his troops; and sure enough within a few months of his accession he was on the German frontier: it was a pattern which would be followed by the great emperors of the second century, Trajan, Hadrian and Marcus Aurelius.

One effect of Domitian's shy egotism was that it made him nervous of others' renown. He remembered too that his own father's act of usurpation had been made possible by the success he had achieved, and the authority he had established, in Judaea. It was partly for this reason that Agricola was recalled from the conquest of Britain in 84–5; in part too the recall indicated a change of emphasis. The resources of empire were limited; and for a long time it had been clear that advance in Britain precluded anything more than a defensive policy in Northern Europe. Now Britain was to become a sleeping frontier; more urgent military requirements dictated that the Rhine-Danube gap and the Danube itself should be attended to. This was understandable; correct policy indeed. But what was also significant was the failure to employ Agricola again. Like his father, Domitian insisted on having efficient and experienced commanders, but they had to be secondary figures, incapable of winning such a reputation that they could be seen as rivals for empire. In Tacitus' words: 'other forms of genius would somehow or other be kept in the background, but military distinction was a kingly quality.'

Domitian's first campaign was against the Chatti, a warlike tribe based on the northern side of the upper Rhine. It was not a glamorous undertaking and its strategic imperative was not clear in Rome. It was easy therefore for the Emperor's enemies to put it about that it had been launched merely to win cheap glory for Domitian or to give him the chance to ingratiate himself with the troops. Rumours of the war's course were soon rife, and spiteful. It was said that the captives he paraded had been bought in the slave market and 'tricked out with costumes and wigs'. Exactly the same stories had been told of Caligula's campaigns across the Rhine; and in both cases the remoteness of the action and the Emperor's unpopularity had made the stories credible, at least to those willing to believe anything unfavourable to the Emperor.

In fact there is little mystery attached to the significance and purpose of Domitian's war against the Chatti. It followed logically from the policy Vespasian himself had pursued; one that took note of the changing realities of Rome's geopolitical position. Rome had long been pushing out against corrupt states or into territories inhabited by weak or fragmented tribes. Now, in the deep forests of remoter Germany, and beyond on the plains of Eastern Europe and the still more distant steppes of Russia, great forces were gathering which were to put a stop to Rome's expansion and indeed test the security of her frontiers. For this reason a preoccupation of all three Flavian emperors (and of their successors) was the establishment of a more secure defence line. With this went the improvement of communications and the disciplining of the legions under experienced commanders.

Domitian's own campaign, against the Chatti, drove back from the Rhine the only formidable tribe still to be found near the frontier. This done, he was able to establish a larger fortified zone on the north-east side of the river. It provided for the security of the whole frontier to the south; the logical next step being a Roman advance in that region to control the valley of the Neckar. In this way the line of communication between the armies of the Rhine and the Danube, hitherto the weak link of Rome's European frontier chain, was shortened, the new line running roughly Mainz-Heidelberg-Stuttgart-Ulm.

To have perceived the importance of this territory and given precedence to the establishment of this secure frontier over the more glorious, but far less important, conquest of northern Britain, is evidence of Domitian's strategic sense. It was his misfortune that Agricola, the displaced commander in Britain, should have been the father-in-law of Tacitus who wrote unforgettable prose but had so little understanding of military strategy that he has not left an easily comprehensible account of any campaign.

Domitian's attention to the northern frontier was paid none too soon. The dangers lurking beyond it manifested themselves in 84 when the Sarmatians crossed the Danube, destroyed a legion and killed its commander. The following year the Dacians raided deep into Moesia, killing the governor, Oppius Sabinus. His successor, Cornelius Fuscus, did not survive long enough to restore the situation, and Domitian had to attend to the Danube frontier himself. He led two punitive expeditions across the river to quell the tribes, after one of which he reported 'I have ended the existence of the Nasomenes'. That might be so; however it made less impression on Rome than the earlier disasters had done.

Nevertheless these campaigns showed that Domitian had military skill, strategic sense and an understanding of where his responsibility to the Empire was best discharged. They showed too that he had learned the importance of the legions: a Princeps' authority, as well as the survival of his power, derived from his control of the armies. Failure to give them a lead endangered the regime; Nero had fallen for no other reason.

But if his authority derived from this source, and therefore drew its life-force from the frontiers, it was at Rome that it was best displayed: in public works, in the construction of roads, temples, aqueducts, theatres and arenas. Augustus' boast that he had found Rome of brick and left it of marble expressed something more than pride in that which he had done for his fellow-citizens; the words revealed that his authority was manifest in the beauty and grandeur of his city. It was a precedent that duly impressed later emperors, none of whom followed it more assiduously than Domitian.

He restored the Capitol, which had been burned down again in 80. All glory for this re-building was to be reserved to him alone; even the original builders' names disappeared from the inscriptions. He built a new temple to Jupiter on the Capitol, and a temple to glorify his own family. Of more immediate value to the citizens was his construction of a new Forum (now called the Forum of Nerva), which would relieve the congestion of the city's business quarter and provide a site for new libraries, law courts and shops; it was an enterprise that was to be imitated, more splendidly still, by Trajan. This creation of a new market may also be seen as an attempt at social control: Domitian had already tried, ineffectually, to prevent shopkeepers from cluttering the streets with the wares they were accustomed to display outside their shops. He also built a new stadium, the shape of which is preserved in the Piazza Navona, loveliest of Rome's public places; and he con-

Domitian and his wife Domitia Longina

structed an artificial lake for sea battles and a new concert hall on the Palatine Hill.

Unlike that other great builder, Nero, Domitian was active in administration; unlike Claudius, he had judgement and energy. He was conscientious in the administration of justice; Suetonius says that 'he exercised such close control over city magistrates and provincial governors that the general standard of justice rose to unprecedentedly high levels'. He was a passionate legislator, too. Like many rulers autocratic by nature but lacking experience of life, he was convinced that morals themselves could be corrected by legislation. Some of his decrees aimed to eradicate specific abuses: the castration of boys and young men was forbidden, and the price of eunuchs who remained in the hands of slave owners was strictly controlled. But in other respects he revealed the despot's itch to reform morality in general: he instigated prosecutions under the Scantinian Law, which forbade unnatural sexual practices; he expelled an ex-quaestor from the Senate for being too fond of acting and dancing; forbade women of notoriously lax morals to use litters in public places or to receive legacies; struck one knight from the jury roll because he had divorced his wife and then taken her back; and took a far more severe view than either Vespasian or Titus had done of unchastity among the Vestal Virgins.

All his social legislation and adminstrative and judicial activity indicate a strong vein of puritanism in Domitian. Though not as abstemious as Augustus had been, Domitian lived simply enough. He generally ate a large luncheon and then contented himself with an apple and small carafe of wine in the evening. He didn't indulge in prolonged drinking bouts, preferring to spend part of the day alone, strolling in the palace gardens.

Yet there were plenty ready to claim that he enjoyed those practices which he publicly prosecuted. (Certainly he took back Domitia, after he had divorced her because of her adultery with an actor called Paris.) In fact, though described by Suetonius as extremely lustful and given to what he himself called 'bed-wrestling', Domitian was probably the sort of intensely private man whose life attracts rumours only when he finds himself in a position of power. He was not given to public show: when his father's former mistress Caenis offered him her cheek to kiss, he preferred to shake her by the hand. His treatment of Domitia suggests he needed her even if he didn't love her. All the same for a time she had to share him with his niece Julia, Titus' daughter, whom he had refused to marry but who later took his fancy. Nobody came really close to Domitian; relations between him and Domitia were always a matter for speculation; people were ready to believe, that she was eventually an accessory to his murder. Still, compared with some of his predecessors, Domitian's life was chaste and seemly; most of the accusations are unspecific.

Domitian might control the offices of State, exercise a close supervision over the composition of the Senate and the conduct of the upper classes through the censorial power, win the allegiance of the armies, and show himself, in Mommsen's phrase 'one of the most careful administrators who held the imperial office'. None of it was enough to secure his position.

First, whatever his achievement on the frontiers – and it was real enough – it yet made less impression than the disasters which had preceded it. The success against the Chatti was laughed away; the disaster of the Dacian incursion shook the regime. The late eighties were years of tension and danger for Domitian. To offset the effect of distant calamities, at Rome he offered splendour and pageantry. In 86 he inaugurated the Capitoline Games, a festival of music, horsemanship and gymnastics, to be held every fifth year. Two years later he imitated Augustus by holding the Secular Games, ignoring Claudius' more recent celebration of them.

All this was more than an entertaining distraction; Domitian was proclaiming his fellowship with Augustus, and with the historic genius of the Roman people.

Though it might delight the public, it wasn't enough to make him safe. Disaffection among the nobles was growing; there were army commanders too who felt slighted or endangered. Though Agricola himself remained ostentatiously loyal, his fate might be read as a warning by other successful generals. Apart from such fears, simple ambition encouraged treason; there were generals and nobles who could not forget the humble soil from which the Flavian dynasty had sprung, nor the manner in which it had come to power. The atmosphere of Rome was again infected with uncertainty. In 87 the priests of the Arval Brethren were sacrificing 'ob detecta scelera nefariorum': 'that the conspiracies of evil-doers may be detected.' Domitian himself, who had once said that 'the Emperor who does not persecute informers, encourages them', now found that he himself was relying on these unsavoury but necessary tools.

In 89 came the reign's most serious crisis to date. L. Antonius Saturninus, Governor of Upper Germany, rebelled and was hailed as emperor by his troops. It was an act all too reminiscent of the year 69 and of Vitellius' repudiation of Galba. Worse till, Antonius had entered into an alliance with some of the German tribes, and it was only a sudden thaw of the Rhine which prevented the barbarians from crossing the river and bringing him their active support. Domitian hurried north on hearing of the rebellion – a prompt reaction that compared favourably with Nero's supine behaviour in a similar crisis; this though it was the middle of January and the Alpine passes were dangerous. In fact his speed was superfluous; the care he had taken to secure the loyalty of at least some of the legions proved sufficient; and before he had struggled across the Alps, word came that L. Appius Maximus Norbanus, army commander in Lower Germany, had suppressed the rebellion. Though Norbanus attempted to limit the extent of the Emperor's revenge by burning Antonius Saturninus' correspondence, Domitian, thoroughly alarmed by the rebellion, was ruthless. He tortured prisoners to make them reveal the whereabouts of any rebels who had escaped (a new torture, it was said; scorching the genitals); and Antonius' head was sent back to Rome to be displayed on the Rostrum as a warning of the fate of traitors.

It is impossible to know the ramifications of the revolt; even whether it was limited to the army of Upper Germany or whether Antonius had sympathizers or fellow-conspirators elsewhere. Certainly Domitian's actions show him convinced that Antonius was merely one of a number of disaffected. From this time he relied heavily on informers, who came to extend from senators to professional dancers, and philosophers; and he embarked on a policy of deliberate terror: G. Vettelenus Civica Cerialis, proconsul of Asia, was executed in 90; the Governor of Britain, Sallustius Lucullus, followed suit. In Tacitus' words, 'Domitian, no longer at intervals, but by a continuous and, as it were, single blow, put our country to the sword. . . His fierce ruddy countenance was capable of noting down the pallid faces of so many men.'

Domitian found himself, whether he wished it or not, locked in a duel with the senatorial class which could only end either in his death or in the reduction of that body to a state of absolute subservience. In his renewed determination to assert himself, his aim appeared to be the exaltation of the Princeps as a ruler supreme over Senate, people and army alike and the consequent lowering of all to the rank of ministers and servants. The Augustan dyarchy, which some may have hoped would be restored by the Flavians, was dead. Whether this had been Domitian's original intention does not matter; what is clear is that a combination of character and circumstances drove him to try to establish this permanent absolute and undisguised control over the Senate. In making this bid he went further than any emperor save Gaius Caligula; it would take skill, luck and judicious management of opinion if he was to avoid Gaius' fate.

His cruelty might be fuelled by fear, most dangerous of emotions; it was none the less real for being so explicable. 'I like not so many Caesars,' he sombrely remarked, gazing at the Senate. He proceeded to thin its ranks. Two methods were at hand: treason-trials and simple confiscations. His rapacity, says Sir Ronald Syme, coincided 'with the climax of his struggle with the Senate, 93–6, which Gsell calls the Reign of Terror'. As usual the pretexts were flimsy: Aelius Lamia is said to have lost his life because of some feeble witticisms at the Emperor's expense; Salvius Cocceianus because he continued to celebrate the birthday of the Emperor Otho, who happened to have been his uncle; Metteius Pompusianus because his birth was said to have been attended by imperial portents; Junius Rusticus because he had praised long-dead Republicans; even Domitian's own cousin had been killed in 84 (before the Terror was properly launched), because he had mistakenly been announced by a herald as emperor-elect, not consul-elect.

What is one to make of such trivialities? They appear to have satisfied contemporaries; and, even if they are ridiculous as reasons, they cannot be called absurd as excuses. Similar petty explanations have accounted for the despatch of countless victims of tyranny this century, to Gulags or execution squads. Domitian's contempt for his enemies may be deduced from the flimsy reasons given for their deaths. And the triviality had another justification too; it made the terror sharper. Nothing after all works so effectively in a terror as the incalculable. No one, under Domitian, could relax, conscious of innocence, for the most harmless action might prove offensive to the Princeps. Finally, such explanations as were given, feeble as they may sound, may yet have been evidence of the Emperor's prudence. It would not do to advertise the extent of conspiracy, for that might encourage his enemies. Far better to despatch them on whimsical grounds.

The Terror was accompanied by a financial squeeze. Domitian was engaged in expensive building projects – all despots like to build; nothing so clearly expresses their greatness. At the same time he had raised the pay of the army; all despots, likewise, cherish their armed forces. Finally he had offered lavish entertainments to the people and on three occasions had distributed bounty of three crowns a head to the Roman mob. It all had to be paid for, of course; yet there was more to it than that. Financial pressure was a means of cowing the opposition. So, although he had previously been lenient and undemanding, even going so far as to refuse bequests from married men with children, and decreeing that suits against debtors to the Public Treasury should lapse after five years, he now showed himself greedy for cash and estates. Charges of treason were employed to justify large-scale confiscations. He prosecuted strict financial measures against the Jews, forcing even non-practising Jews to pay the Jewish Sanctuary Tax. (This, originally levied to pay for Temple expenses, was now imposed by the Romans, who had destroyed the Temple.) Pliny, complaining that Domitian was the 'despoiler and murderer of the best classes', also stated that Domitian laid 'unsparing hands on the property of senators'.

So terror raged at Rome and discontent festered. But meanwhile this Princeps who was concentrating unprecedented power in his own hands, continued, beyond the confines of the city, to pursue a policy that was both responsible and enlightened. Mommsen speaks of his 'sombre but intelligent despotism'. Concluding that Italy's deepening agricultural problems stemmed from the substitution of vineyards for cornfields, he issued an edict forbidding any more vines to be planted in Italy, and ordering the acreage in the provinces to be reduced by half. Like most such efforts in Antiquity to direct the economy, this showed an appreciation of a problem rather than an understanding of how to solve it; but it also revealed an emperor who cared for the welfare of his subjects.

Of longer lasting and more certain benefit was an edict reserving half of the more important court appointments (previously held by freedmen) for members of the equestrian order. This was an important step for two reasons. First, it ensured that the most productive and creative class in the Empire should continue to be involved in its administration. Second, it was every bit as significant as Claudius' development of the imperial household into an embryonic civil service. By opening the service to equestrians, Domitian in fact reduced the personal element in it. Civil servants henceforth would not be ex-slaves and intimates of the household; they would be members of a class with a stake in the economy. It was a piece of intelligent despotism analogous to that performed at the instigation of Thomas Cromwell in the reign of Henry VIII or by the cardinals Richelieu and Mazarin in seventeenth-century France. It gave a substance to the administration which had previously been lacking.

Finally Domitian exercised the same sort of close control over the work of the law courts and the administration of provinces which had characterized at least the first part of Tiberius' reign. Easy to detect here the beneficial influence derived from his long reading of the old Emperor's memoirs. Suetonius, a gossip unfavourable to Domitian, with no reason to flatter his memory, observes that 'he exercised such control over city magistrates and provincial governors that the general standard of justice rose to a high level never before achieved – you need only note how many people have been charged with corruption in later reigns'.

But good government for the provinces could not allay the fears of the thwarted and anxious senatorial class. For them Domitian had become by the early nineties that most terrible of beings: the irresponsible tyrant. Everything he did, from his assumption of divinity downwards, angered them. He terrified, yet he did not win respect. Because his achievements, military and civil, were not glittering, they were able to ignore the solidity of these and to regard him nonetheless with contempt; they despised even while they trembled. Pliny, giving expression to their resentment, called him 'insidiosissimus princeps' ('the most encroaching emperor'). He told of one Cornelius Rufus, a sufferer from the agonies of gout, who asked 'why do you suppose I endure life under these cruel tortures? It is in the hope that I may outlive that villain if only by a single day.' When Agricola, to protect his family in some degree, named the Emperor as joint heir with his wife and daughter, Tacitus found Domitian 'overjoyed by the supposed honour and appreciation'. 'So blind and demoralized by unending flattery was his mind that he did not realize that only a bad emperor is made his heir by a good father.'

And terror stretched its icy fingers even into the recesses of the imperial household itself. Domitian had a cousin, Flavius Clemens, a man, it was said, of the utmost stupidity; one from whom the Princeps had nothing to fear. Indeed he had just allotted him a consulship, and he had named Flavius' small sons as his heirs, changing their names to Vespasian and Domitian. Yet now, suspecting that Flavius had been converted to Judaism, and was practising that faith, which he himself persecuted and which alone among the innumerable religions of the empire, denied divinity to any man born of woman, he ordered his cousin's execution. Not long before, as if blindly destroying the security of slaves and freedmen as well as family, he had had his secretary Epaphroditus put to death. This time the reason given was that the wretched man had reputedly helped Nero kill himself — a quarter of a century back — after the rest of his entourage had deserted him. Suetonius says that this execution was intended 'to remind his staff that not even the best of intentions could justify a freedman's complicity in a master's murder'; but it can hardly have had that effect. More likely it convinced them that no one was safe from their lord god's capricious wrath.

At any rate conspiracy was now hatched in the palace itself; his much-loved, yet long-suffering wife Domitia was herself said to have connived at the plot. As for Domitian, he had, as a reluctant but compulsive student of astrology, long feared assassination; for he knew his death had been foretold; he even knew the date and hour at which it was due. True, for his own peace of mind, he took measures to disprove the accuracy of astrological prediction. Hearing, for instance, that a certain astrologer called Ascletarion had laid claim to a mastery of the science, Domitian asked the unfortunate man whether he could predict the manner of his own death. 'Of course,' Ascletarion replied, 'I shall very soon be torn to pieces by stray dogs.' Domitian's response was quick; he ordered the astrologer to be executed at once, and commanded that his funeral be conducted with the greatest care and expedition. But not even the lord god Domitian could thus cheat what Fate had decreed. A sudden gale scattered the funeral pyre, and in the ensuing confusion a pack of scavenging pariahs tore and gnawed at the astrologer's half-burned body. Or so it was said. (A comic actor, Latinus, claiming to have been a witness of this extraordinary event, recounted it to the Emperor at the dinner table as a choice item of city gossip. If so, he must have been a man of singular rashness and aberrant judgement; he could hardly have imagined that his anecdote would entertain Domitian.)

Immured in the palace, Domitian took such action as might cheat Fortune. He had the walls lined with shiny moonstone, so that no one could surprise him from behind. No imperial audiences were granted to prisoners except when the Emperor was alone with them and they were tightly fettered. He vetoed a senatorial decree that, whenever he held a consulship, a group of equestrians, dressed in purple-striped robes and armed with lances, should walk among the lictors and attendants: opportunities for a treasonable attack were too obvious.

Meanwhile bad omens accumulated, either at the time or in the memory of those who survived the reign. Lightning struck the Temple of Capitoline Jupiter, and the Temple of the Flavians; it struck even Domitian's bedroom in the palace. A hurricane (or perhaps the hand of a disaffected man) tore the inscription plate from the base of a statue of Domitian and hurled it into a tomb which stood conveniently close. A celebrated cypress tree, which had once blown down but then rooted itself anew when Vespasian himself was still a private citizen and indeed one in disgrace, now crashed to the ground again. Even Minerva was reported to have deserted Domitian, telling him in a dream that she had been disarmed by Jupiter and could no longer protect the Emperor who revered her.

How could Domitian fail to be apprehensive? Yet he retained a grim gallows-humour. On the day before the one named by his horoscope as his last, someone brought him a gift of apples. 'Give them to me tomorrow,' he told his slaves, 'if tomorrow ever comes. . .' He went on to predict blood on the moon, and the performance of a deed about which everyone would talk.

Midnight arrived and he could not keep to his bed. At dawn he condemned a German soothsayer to death; the wretched man had opined that the lightning foretold a change of government. The Emperor then scratched nervously at a spot on his forehead. Observing the blood, he murmured, 'I hope this is all the blood required.' He asked for the time. His freedmen told him that it was the sixth hour, knowing that it was the fifth he feared. This lie, prompted perhaps by their apprehension of what he might do to them in the most perilous hour – or perhaps by the historian's wish to sharpen the story's dramatic edge – is said to have convinced him that the danger has passed and that he could now relax.

At any rate he went off to take a bath. His chief valet, Parthenius, informed him that someone had called on urgent and secret business and was waiting in the imperial bedroom. Apparently unsuspecting, despite his previous fears, Domitian dismissed his attendants and hurried thither.

226

He found there a steward from his niece Domatilla's household. This man, Stephanus by name, had recently been accused of embezzlement. Presumably in an attempt to cheat the law courts, he had somehow attached himself to a group already plotting Domitian's murder, and offered his services. Then, to divert suspicion (says Suetonius), he had pretended to have an injured arm and for some days had gone about the palace with this swathed in bandages. Suetonius also says that he had concealed a dagger in these bandages for several days, which sounds absurd. One would think that in the mood of heightened tension in which Domitian passed his last days, anyone wearing such a bandage would become an object of suspicion. Yet apparently it didn't work out like that; this morning he was able to force himself on the Emperor without being searched; an omission that indicates complicity amongst those responsible for the Emperor's security.

Stephanus used the murderer's time-honoured excuse, announcing that he himself had uncovered a plot against Domitian, and refusing to divulge details to anyone but the Emperor himself. Closeted with Domitian he produced a list of names; then, while Domitian was perusing it, stabbed him in the groin.

Domitian grappled with him, fighting for his dagger and calling on a page to bring him the one which he kept under his pillow. But someone – Parthenius the valet? – had removed its blade; and the page found the door to the servants' quarter locked. . .

Struggling on the floor with Stephanus, Domitian tried to gouge his eyes out: but Stephanus' cries brought other conspirators at the double. Seven more wounds finished the Emperor off. His murderers included an officer of the Guard, Parthenius' freedman, a head-chamberlain and one of the imperial gladiators. It was a very domestic murder.

The date was 18 September 96, and Domitian had reigned fourteen years; the dynasty itself had lasted just over a quarter of a century. Domitian had once claimed that all Emperors are necessarily wretched, since only their murder could convince the public that conspiracies against their life really existed. Now, the point proved, his body was hustled away on a litter by the public undertakers. His old nurse Phyllis took charge of it and had it cremated in her garden on the Via Latina. She took his ashes by night to the Flavian Temple and mingled them with the remains of his niece Julia. Perhaps she hoped this would ensure that they were respected.

The mob, having been unaffected by Domitian's tyranny, was indifferent to what had happened. Besides, they could not doubt that whoever succeeded him would continue to provide lavish entertainments; there was therefore no cause for rejoicing or dismay. Detached as they now were from the political process, they would find their life continued unchanged no matter who wore the purple. Their indifference was a measure of how the Roman polity had been demoralised in the hundred and fifty years since Julius Caesar had been murdered. Then, there had been riots, and bloodthirsty calls for the death of the self-styled Liberators; now, there was indifference, and the scrutiny of the next race-card or Colosseum programme.

Ruins of imperial palaces, Palatine, Rome

The legions' reaction was different. They had fully accepted Domitian and benefited from his care for their interests. Now they began to speak of him as a god. They muttered of revenge and looked only for a lead from their commanders which did not come; but they passed resolutions in camp that his assassins should be brought to justice.

In one quarter, delight at the murder was unrestrained. The senators crowded eagerly into the Senate House to denounce the Emperor at whose nod they had yesterday trembled. They quickly elevated one of their members, the aged and decorous Nerva, to the purple; they sent for ladders that men might mount the walls of public buildings and smash Domitian's images and any inscriptions that commemorated his greatness; and they ordered all records of the late Emperor's reign to be obliterated.

The raven, bird of ill-omen to later ages, had a different reputation among Romans, for they interpreted his cry as 'cras, cras' – 'tomorrow, tomorrow'. A few months before, one had perched on the Capitol and croaked out words of hope. As Philemon Holland, Suetonius' Elizabethan translator, put it,

228

The crow which lately sate on top of Tarpeia newes to tell,
'Tis well, whenas she could not say, said yet 'it will be well. . .'

The raven's cry might be considered justified. The years that followed attracted from the greatest of all historians of the Roman world an encomium that surpasses the commendation offered to any other period of history. Edward Gibbon wrote:

> If a man were called to fix the period in the history of the world during which the condition of the human race was most happy and prosperous, he would, without hesitation, name that which elapsed from the death of Domitian to the accession of Commodus. The vast extent of the Roman empire was governed by absolute power, under the guidance of virtue and wisdom. The armies were restrained by the firm but gentle hand of four successive emperors, whose characters and authority commanded involuntary respect. The forms of the civil administration were carefully preserved by Nerva, Trajan, Hadrian and the Antonines, who delighted in the image of liberty, and were pleased with considering themselves as the accountable ministers of the laws. Such princes deserved the honour of restoring the republic had the Romans of their day been capable of enjoying a rational freedom.

Yet even this praise cannot escape Gibbon's sombre irony, and perhaps the capacity for rational freedom had never existed since Rome acquired its Empire. Certainly it was long dead by the end of the first century AD, and the sage and benevolent administration of the good emperors of the second century rested instead on the achievement of Augustus, Tiberius and the Flavians, who had transformed the chaotic Roman Republic into a military monarchy exercising its power behind the authoritative façade of 'the forms of the civil administration'. Trajan, Hadrian and Marcus Aurelius had learned the lessons of their predecessors. They were all to be seen more frequently on the camps of the frontier than on the Palatine; and to subdue Rome itself they divorced themselves from the city that had spawned their Empire. Like them, the detested Domitian had understood well enough how the imperial role should be developed; and though he himself had been undone by faults by character and accidents of fortune, such could not destroy his work.

ACKNOWLEDGEMENTS

Aerofilms: 191
British Museum, London: 32, 36, 111, 123, 124, 155 (below), 174, 180, 193, 210
Giraudon: 80, 86, 145; Lauros-Giraudon: 22
Mansell Collection: 4, 38, 55, 70, 84, 87, 100, 140, 183, 199; Mansell-Alinari: 14, 39, 42, 43 (below), 59, 81, 121, 132, 135, 142, 166, 168, 169, 178, 188, 206, 212, 215; Mansell-Anderson: 17, 40, 43 (above), 52, 75, 85, 88, 91, 118, 150, 165, 172, 196, 204, 207, 220, 228
Werner Forman Archive: 155 (above)
On p. 170 the drawing by the late Alan Sorrell is reproduced by courtesy of Mrs Alan Sorrell.

All coins are shown approximately 1½ times their original size.

INDEX